THE PICTORIAL LUCKNOW

D1860196

THE PICTORIAL LUCKNOW

P. C. MOOKHERJI

WITH PLATES

GYAN

Published by

GYAN

Gyan Publishing House
5, Ansari Road
Daryaganj, New Delhi-110002
Phone: 011-47034999, 9811692060
E-mail: books@gyanbooks.com

Distribution Network
gyanbooks.com
India, USA, Canada, UK, Australia, France

© Publisher

All rights reserved. No part of this work may be reproduced, stored, adapted, or transmitted in any form or by any means, electronic, mechanical, photocopying, micro-filming, recording or otherwise, or translated in any language, without the prior written permission of the copyright owner and the publisher.

ISBN : 978-81-212-3891-5 (PB)
First Published, Lucknow, 1883

2nd Impression 2020

Printed at: Gyan Press, Delhi.

The book is sold subject to the condition that it shall not, by way of trade or otherwise, be lent, resold, hired out, or otherwise circulated without the prior publisher's written consent.

The Pictorial Lucknow
Author: P. C. Mookherji

PREFACE.

—o—

Lucknow has lost much of its former splendour and glory; yet it is still a very interesting city to visitors from distant countries, not only for its palaces and magnificent ruins, and its picturesque people, but for the notoriety it acquired during the terrible days of 1857 and 1858. But as there are many, who cannot afford to come here, the want of an illustrated work on the subject, is a much-felt desideratum; and of those, who do visit it, only a few can with difficulty get any idea of the inner and historical life of the capital Lucknow was, a few years ago, the Paris of India—"the City of Roses."

Moreover, as the spirit of vandalism is not yet extinct, the edifices, which have historical association or otherwise any architectural pretension, are gradually transformed into debris and ruins; while none yet takes the trouble to prepare a pictorial record of what Lucknow was,—so as to snatch whatever he can from the inevitable oblivion that follows. It is a matter of deep regret to see how the city is throwing off its skin; and its arts and manufactures, its old picturesqueness, and its peculiar civilization, for which Lucknow was famous, are dying an unnatural death. The citizens look on, shed tears like women; and there their business is ended. They do nothing more; for deterioration, the daughter of idleness, is taking place in their physical and mental formations, as in all things else.

The time is now come to raise the question, which naturally springs from a thinking mind,—is there nothing in the native civilization worth preservation? Has the European civilization become so indispensable to us, that we should at once throw away what is national, and adopt the other without pausing to consider where are we drifting to? Is the past history of Oudh so despicable an affair, that no lessons can we derive therefrom for our future guidance? Is there nothing in the dying local arts, especially architecture, which requires enquiring into, and which deserves encouragement?

These are the reasons, which incited me to the difficult undertaking of writing a pictorial work. For this purpose, I made a good collection of old sketches by native artists, availed myself of all sources of original and recorded information I could get; and personally I mixed among the citizens, studied their inner life, and took notes and sketches of what struck my attention. The result of these investigations is the illustrated work I now offer to the public.

It is natural to expect great defects in an attempt at a work of this kind, especially from the pen of a Hindu, who has had no training for it; for irrespective of my disqualification, I laboured under great disadvantages. I could not, to the fullest extent, carry out my original intentions; nor can I publish all that I have collected; for then the work will be too bulky. While I could get but very little time from an humble, though laborious, official life, my limited means did not allow me to command all the materials I could have got. The Chapter III. of Part I., Chapters I. and VI. of Part III. have been written in the hurry of a camp life. The sketches and copies of pictures I could not, for want of time, finish into drawings. No good printer could I find for printing even my rough lithographs. And to crown my ill-luck, the book itself has been very badly got up and printed, being full of typical mistakes.

I must express my gratitude to the several officers, whom I showed my book, and who encouraged me by their kind advice.

An indulgent public will therefore, I hope, judge leniently of the work of an earnest mind. I do not lay claim to artistic skill or command of the English language. My aim is to give a general idea of facts, simply and concisely.

26th May, 1883. } P. C. MOOKHERJI.
Golagunge, Lucknow }

CONTENTS

Preface I

Introduction, Physical and Architectural features, growth and decline of the city, a sketch of political history. 1

PART I. HISTORY POLITICAL.

CHAPTER I.—MOHAMEDAN PERIOD.

Saadut Khan Subedar, *Sufdar Jung* Nawab-Vezeir; *Shujah-ud-dowlah*, his war and connection with the English; *Asuf-ud-dowlah*, bad condition of Oudh. *Vezeir Ali* deposed, *Saadut Ali Khan*, persecution and extortion of money and territory; *Gazee-ud-deen Hyder*, King, loans and non-intervention; *Nasir-ud-deen Hyder*, British assumption mooted and then abandoned, *Moonna Jan* imprisoned, *Mohamed Ali Shah* under a new treaty; *Umjad Ali Shah*, the orthodox; *Wajid Ali Shah*, persecution and deposition of 7

CHAPTER II.—ENGLISH PERIOD.

Annexation and introduction of the Company's rule, universal discontents, outbreak of the rebellion, battles and siege of Baillie Guard, British reinforcement and blockade, Relief, Alumbagh, final siege and capture of the city, the rebels fly to Mohumdee, Boondee and Nepal, Pacification of the province... 43

CHAPTER III.—ENGLISH PERIOD, AFTER EVENTS.

Chief Commissioners of Oudh, confiscation of the proprietory right in land in the province, Talukdari policy, Summary Settlement, form of administration as compared with that of the late kingdom, Revenue and taxation, Permanent Settlement, Survey work and registers, revision of assessment, different land tenures, Cession of Terai to Nepal, Reforms in the Judicial Department, Municipalities and Honorary native officers, Finance, Education, Public Works, State-visits, Amalgamation. Self-government Policy, Agriculture and Exhibition, a review of the past, forecast of a happy future. 57

PART II. ETHNOLOGY.

CHAPTER I.

A brief history of the people, their caste, religion, character and condition. 95

CHAPTER II.—CITIZENS OF LUCKNOW.

SECTION I.—Hindus, their physical and mental features, Brahman, Kashmiri Pundits, Chhatri, Kaith-Lalas, Marhwari, Beniah, Bengali, an anecdote of Gazee-ud-din Hyder.... 105

SECTION II.—Mohamedans, their physical and mental features, high class, middle, low, Syuds, and Shodahs.... 112

CHAPTER III.—SOCIETY.

SECTION I—General sketch of society, relation to neighbours, mediation, mode of living 116

SECTION II.—Mardana or male Society, dress, master of the house, etiquette, astrology 119

SECTION III.—Female dress, a Queen of *Nasir-ud-din Hyder*. 124

SECTION VI.—Inner life and society, *Musnud, Purdah-nasheens*, eating, procession, conversation, Begum, Bahu, village girl 126

CHAPTER IV.—SOME SKETCHES OF LOCAL LIFE.

General sketch of a life, Hindu or Mohamedan, Punditji, a Sudra, Nawab-Saheb, General Claude Martin, Lieutenant-Colonel John Mordaunt. 131

CHAPTER V.—EDUCATION.

SECTION I.—Mohamedan education, Zenana influence, Moulvi, defective training, poetical clubs. 143

SECTION II.—Educated natives, results of the English system, unsatisfactory careers. 145

CHAPTER VI.—FESTIVALS OF THE PEOPLE.

SECTION I.—Semi-Social, funeral ceremony, marriage, Mangni, Mehdi and Barat.... 149

SECTION II.—Religious festivals, *Mohamedan*, Ramzan, Bukreed, Nowroze, Mohurrum, its history, anniversary, burial of the Taziahs at Kerbula; *Hindu*, Basant, Holi, Dewali, Ramlila, Asnan. 153

CHAPTER VII.—PAGEANTS OF OLD LUCKNOW.

State-entry, Royal banquet, illumination and fire-works, Grand-Durabar, Royal procession. 161

CHAPTER VIII.—ARTS.

General nature, Jewellery, Embroidery, Pottery and Clay-modelling, Sculpture and Wood-carving; Painting, Nature, History, Present condition; Photography. Architecture; Music, Nature and Classification; Dancing, Dramas, Poetry, General remarks. 172

PART III. ARCHITECTURE.

CHAPTER I.—ARCHÆOLOGY.

Defective knowledge, Ancient cities, Antiquarian records and remains, Eight epochs and styles, Manua, Nagraon, Bhuddhistic style was the outcome of Aryan civilization, Attempt of modern archæologists to derive everything Hindu to the Grecian influence, Bhars. 190

CHAPTER—II.

History of Lucknow-architecture, city and country styles. 202

CHAPTER III.—DOMESTIC ARCHITECTURE.

Bania house, Richman's house, Hindu, Mohameden; Zenana, Palace. ... 206

CHAPTER IV.— GENERAL CHARACTERISTICS OF LOCAL ARCHITECTURE.

Lucknow-buildings not generally appreciated, Ruskin's three virtues, Fergusson's eight principles, Mehmars, revival of native architecture. 210

CHAPTER V.—CLASSIFICATION AND DIFFERENT KINDS OF LOCAL BUILDINGS.

General principles, Facade, Pillars, roofing, Dome, Musjid, Emambarah, Mukbarah, Baradari, Hammam, Darwaza, Bagh, Houz, Pool, Killah, and Serai ... 217

CHAPTER VI.—THE CHIEF BUILDINGS OF LUCKNOW.

Section I.—Palaces, Punch Mahullah, Doulat Khana, Farhat Buksh, Chhutter Munzil, Moti Mahal, Kaiserbagh, Residency. 229

Section II.—Tombs and Mosques, two Juma Musjids, the great Emámbárah, Hosseinabad and Huzrutgunge Emámbáràhs, Shah Nazuf, Huzrut Abbas ki Dargah, Golagunge Mukburah. 238

Section III.—Gardens, Chinhut, Charbagh, Moosabagh, Dilkhosa, Padshahbagh, Seconderbagh, and Alumbagh, conclusion 246

THE

PICTORIAL LUCKNOW

INTRODUCTION.

Lucknow is situated on both banks of the river Goomtee, on an undulating plain. Its extreme length, excluding the Cantonment, is nearly six miles, from the Canal on the East, to the *Moosabagh* on the West. Its breadth is about four miles from the same Canal on the South to Aligunge on the North. Its present population is approximately 2,60,000; while under the native regime it counted as many as 900,000 souls.

The mean level of the city is about 370 feet above the sea. Its climate is generally dry and healthy, though lately it has comparatively deteriorated. The temperature ranges from 30° to 120° F. in the shade; and 170° in the sun. The hot season lasts from April to June, when the rains set in and end in September, after an average fall of 30 inches. The sickly months are August and September.

"The mornings in the hot season, at which time the wind blows from the East and changes to the West about midday, are generally cool and pleasent till the middle of May. The hot winds" (which then set in), "carry along with them clouds of a fine light grey sand, which enters every crevice, and being hot and dry warps and cracks furnitures when exposed. During its height, travellers occasionally fall down dead. North-Westers occur during this season just after an easterly wind, and usually come on in the afternoon, being often preceded for a day or two by some dense clouds in the North. In some of these dust-storms no rain falls;—hence the name of *dry-North-Westers*; but generally there is considerable rain and great damage to buildings and trees caused by them. When the wind occasionally blows from the east, in the hot season, the air is more free from the dust, but is clogged with watery vapour brought from the Bay of Bengal; and sometimes the heat is more oppressive from its clammy dampness," as well as "during calms in the rainy season. The annual fall of rain within the last 70 years, has varied from 70 to 30 (15 in 1881) inches, and from four to two months in duration. On an average of five or six years, it has been steadily decreasing;" owing undoubtedly to the clearing of the forests. "Hoar-frost occurs almost every year. Towards the end of the rainy season, the air is highly transparent, affording sometimes a distant view of the Himalaya mountains," nearly 200 miles far off. General Nott's Life, Appendix.

The best time for the tourist to visit Lucknow, is at the close of the rainy season, when the city can be seen to its greatest advantage, having a clear atmosphere, and a beautiful mantle of bright green grass covering the ground. The convenient way to inspect the buildings and the historical places, is to follow General Havelock's route from the Railway Station, that is, to proceed North-East by the side of Begumkothie, Martiniere, &c., to Secunderbagh, and then to turn westward to the Residency, Mutchhibhawan, &c.

The City may be assumed as divided into four parts :—(1) the Native Town, (2) the Royal Quarters, (3) the Civil Station, and (4) the Cantonment. The native town has no system in its street-architecture, which is indescriminately composed of hovels and good-looking houses. The lanes generally follow the bed of crooked and dirty Nullahs; and this portion of the town has a most uninviting and unsanitary appearance. It extends from Saadutgunge to Hosseingunge. Of this, the Chouk is a good specimen and needs but a cursory inspection.

The Royal Quarters extend from the Hosseinabad to Huzrutgunge, being flanked on the North by the meandering Goomtee. The streets are straight and broad; and the buildings lend beautiful effect to the general view at a distance. Of this, the greater part was demolished in 1858, after the final capture of the city. Only some isolated palaces or groups remain in a state of decay. These are Hosseinabad, Mutchhibhawan, Chhatter-Munzil, Moti-Mahal, and Kaiserbagh. The ensemble, before the great demolition, was quite fascinating. As seen from the Iron-Bridge, "the city seemed one mass of magestic and beautiful buildings, of dazzling whiteness, crowned with domes of burnished gold, while scores of mínárs, many of them very high, lent to the scene that airy grace, for which they are famous." Mintern. "The sun is setting, and the noises of the great city are subdued for a moment. The deep green gardens lie in shadow. But all around us, far and near, the gilded domes are blazing in the yellow glow. The scene is lovely, as the outer gate of Paradise." Tailor.

The Civil Station lies between the Moti-Mahal and the Canal. It has a complete country appearance; and though its archictecture is not pleasing to the oriental eye, its numerous streets with parks and gardens interspersed everywhere, and an almost dustless atmostphere, have made Lucknow famous as the garden-city of India. "Hundreds of acres, once occupied by houses, have been turned into market-gardens. Swarded parks, vistas, rides, and drives, far prettier than those of the Bois-de-Bologne, spread out, where once was street, bazaars, and palaces." Russel.

The Cantonment lies on the South-East side of the Nasir-ud-din Hyder's Canal. Its architecture has no commendable feature; its "white-washed ugliness" is patent to those, who care to see the barracks, whose appearance has nothing ornamental or skilful in them.

The panorama of Lucknow has a most enchanting effect, even now after so much demolition of the better half of the city. The demolition extends from Hossainabad to the Tarawali Kotti, a space of 5 square miles. There is not too great an assemblage of houses, trees, or open grounds; each serves a proportionate and beautiful relief to the other. The Chief points, whence views should be seen, are the Martineare, Chhutter Munzil, Residency-tower, Saadut Ali's tomb, and the great Emambáráh.

The growth of the city may be thus briefly stated. It was founded by Lakshman of *Ramayan*, on the elevated spot, now known as Lachman-tilah—(mound), overlooking the Stone-Bridge. Here a Brahman community continued to flourish, till a Mohamedan colony came and established itself in about 1450 A. D., under Minà Shah, a renowned saint, whose demolished tomb may still be seen near the Chouk. Lakhna, a local Ahir by caste, designed and built a fort for the colony, since known as Killah Lakhna, and then Mutchibhawan. The immigrants lived on terms of perfect fraternity with the old Hindu residents; and the Brahmans were not molested in their religious offerings to the sacred orifice of the subterranean passage, said to be connected with Ajodhya, distant about 70 miles. In 1530 A. D., Humayun, emperor of Delhi, while flying from Shere Khan, afterwards Shah, came here and saw the prosperity of the local Shaikhs, who contributed 40 horses and 10,000 Rs. for his relief.

In the reign of Akbar the Great, the town improved and extended to what is now known as the Akbari Darwaza, west gate of the Chouk. The local Bajpei Brahmans were encouraged, with a royal favor of one *lakh* of Rupees, in their religious sacrificcs and offerings to the sacred orifice. Alamgeer, or Aurungebe as known to the European public, however, stopped it by building a Mosque over the place, which may be still seen as a sample of the old style of the ecclesiastical architecture.

Saadut Khan, the founder of the Naishapurí dynasty, did not add any improvement to the town, where he simply took Punch Mohalla and Mutchhibhawan on rent of 535 Rs. His two successors had their seats of Government at Fyzabad or in camp. But in 1775 A. D., Asuf-ud-doulah came here and made the town the capital of his extensive dominions, as a more central position. He adorned the western part of the present city with palaces and gardens; while his brother, Saadut Ali Khan, did the eastern. The former built Doulut-Khana, Moosabagh, the Great Emambarah with Roumi Gate and the Musjid, Goomtee Bridge (stone), Charbagh, Bibiapur Kothie, and Chinhat garden. The latter erected the old Residency, since known as the Banqueting Hall, and Hospital of the mutiny time, the Lal Baradari, Dilaram, Dilkosha, the Golagunge mausoleum, &c. General Claude Martin added Farhat Buksh and La Constantia. Gazee-ud-din-Hyder erected Moti Mahal, Shah Najaf, two tombs of his parents, Khurshed Munzil, or 32nd Mess House of the mutiny time. Nasir-ud-din-Hyder built the Chhutter Munzil, Secanderbagh, Tarawali Kothie (observatory), Badshahbagh, and Welayetibagh, and commenced the Kerbula (tomb) and the Canal, which he left unfinished. Mohamed Ali Shah constructed the Hosseinabad buildings, and the Iron Bridge; Umjud Ali Shah did the Begum kothie palaces in Huzrutgunge and the

Chhota Emambarah; and Wajid Ali Shah, the Kaiserbagh and Alambagh.

Besides the buildings, above enumerated, the nobles raised many castle-looking palaces;—Maharajah Tikait Rai, Rajah ke Bazár; Aga Meer, the Serai and Deurhee, named after himself, and the mansion of late queen Malka Zamáni, and Noor Buksh and Zahur Buksh; Roushan-ud-doulah, the Kaisar Pasand; Monawar-ud-doulah, his uncle Hakim Mehdi's tomb; Amin-ud-doulah, his palace and bazár; and Ali Naqi Khan, his palace near Gowghat.—The city attained the greatest dimensions, during the last reign, and covered the whole area, which had been once the sites of sixty-four villages; in some Mohullahs, the names of the old villages may be traced; in others they were supplanted by those of the founders.

After the annexation of Oude, and especially the great rebellion, the better portion of the city was demolished; and the old splendour and majesty of Lucknow are now irrevocably gone, in spite of such buildings as the Bulrampore Hospital, the Canning College, and the Wingfield Munzil, or Dharmshala, that are clumsily and inartistically raised from time to time. "Lucknow has been fairly improved off the face of earth.........and has fallen from its high estate......They are like oceans, beneath which thousands of wrecks lie buried......Most remarkable changes have been effected in the neighbourhood and in the city by wholesale demolitions; but some have been done, which can be scarcely justified, unless it be maintained, that it is our duty to keep alive bitterness of feelings, and to remind Mohamedans that they are subject to a race, which dispises what they reverence, and desecrate what they consider holy......The stolid indifference to native feeling manifested in the treatment of the Emambarah" (in the Fort Mutchhibhawan) "cannot be justified at all. Store away guns and ammunitions there if you like; use the Mosque as Church or Chapel; but keep the place in decent order, root out the grass on the roofs and remove the number and inscriptions in black and hedeous white-wash on the walls of the buildings. If we ever lose India, it will be from want of sympathy." Russel's Royal Tour of the Prince of Wales in 1875-76.

The Naishapuri dynasty of Oude commenced in 1732, with *Saadut Khan*, who was Subadar here,-tributary to Delhi. His nephew, *Sufder-*

Jung became Nawab-Vizier (Viceroy-Premier), and severed the Mogul bondage. His son, *Shujah-ud-doulah*, maintained the independence, and entered into British friendship, (Atkinson's Treaties Nos. I to V). *Asuf-ud-doulah* grew more intimate, by ceding Benares districts, with the fashionable foreigners; (Treaties VI to IX); and interference and disorganization were the consequences. But re-action culminated in a conspiracy, which begat a counter-movement; and *Vizier Ali* fell in the attempt to restore the former freedom. Poor *Saadut Ali* was made to yield money (by treaty of 1798) and more than half of his territory (by that of 1801) not only to buy but to keep British alliance; and Oude was a Protected State, being bereft of political and military powers. Now Colonel Baillie bullied him out of his brain; interference was hard upon him; and his ably reformed administration could not be perfected and consolidated. But *Gazee-ud-din* had respite and lent 3½ crores to the Company for his friend, Lord Hastings' sake; he assumed the title of King, and his subjects were temporarily happy. Resident Ricketts, however, refused the services of the Company's troops, which were paid by and kept for Oude; and Aga Meer, the Khansamah-Vizier, created a new local army. *Nasir-ud-din* was an Anglicised despot; and the English cries for reforms and intervention continued with greater force. But Hakim Mehdi came to the rescue; and Lord Bentinck attended not to the exaggerated and highly colored accounts of the misgovernment of the kingdom. But the Company's thirst for interference revived, which terminated in a revolution, by the unauthorized treaty of 1837 with *Mahomed Ali Shah*; and British annexation was defined and anticipated. *Umzad Ali Shah* gauged the situation and preferred orthodoxy. After a trepidation of 20 years of questionable peace and policy, the annexation was unceremoniously realized and carried into execution in February, 1856; and treaties of friendship and obligations of loyalty were trampled under foot. Persecuted *Wajid Ali Shah* retired without opposition and was pensioned off with 12 lakhs at Calcutta. The introduction of the new rule, however, dissatisfied the people; and a great rebellion was the consequence. War and commotians followed; and Oude-misery was at its culminating point. British sovereignty was restored; and pauperism of the province is a noted thing.

Shujah-ud-dowlah 1753.
Mohammud Ali Shah.
1837
1847-56.

PART I. POLITICAL HISTORY.

CHAPTER I. MOHAMEDAN PERIOD.

A brief history of the late Oude dynasty (Period, 1732 to 1856 A. D.)

Saadat Khan (1732 to 1739).

Mohamed Ameen Saadut Khan Burhan-ul-Mulk, was the founder of the late dynasty in Oude. Coming as a merchant, from Naishapore in Khorasan, in search of employment, he went to Azimabad, (Patna), where he remained for sometime the guest of the Subadar (governor) of Behar. Thence he repaired to Delhi, and took service under the Governor of Gujerat. Incuring, however, the displeasure of his new master, he returned to Delhi and entered the imperial service, in which, by the strength of his merits, he rose from being an unimportant horseman, to the commandantship at Biana, and became Governor of Agra in 1721 A. D. Having delivered Mohamed Shah from the tyranny of the two Syed brothers, by assassinating one and defeating the other, he was in 1732, rewarded by the emperor with the Subadarship of Oude.

After having prepared himself with money, means and soldiers, by first going personally to ask assistance, to the Governor of Akberabad (Agra), then to those of Barielly and Furrukhabad, he came down the Gangá (Ganges). Here he had a propitious sign, for a fish leaped out of the water into his dress; and henceforth it became the royal insignia of Oude. Landing at Mehdighat, he entered the province, and approached Lucknow, the stronghold of the turbulent Shaikhs. Resting for a while at Kakori, he, in spite of opposition, entered the town, and by a strategem occupied Mutchhibhawan, the old citadel.

Settling terms with the Shaikhs, and other local chiefs, he set out on a tour of revenue-collection throughout the Soubah, as far as Gazeepore. Many old Rajahs either resisted or submitted to his exorbitant demands. The turbulent Rajah Balwant Sing Khichar, who had twice defeated the imperial army, made a sudden and furious onslaught on him, but was at last killed by a friendly Hindu. The trans-Gogra Rajah of Gondah successfully resisted his army, till he was pacified with very easy terms.

After thus settling the province, he began to return ; but in the meantime Mulhar Rao with his Mahrattas had invaded the Doab. The Nawab immediately advanced with vigour and repulsed him in an action.

Puffed up with these successes, he returned to Delhi, and was ambitious of becoming the prime-minister of the empire ; but failing in his aim, he, together with the old Nizam-ul-Mulk, is said to have invited Nadir Shah, his countryman, then at Cabul. The invader came ; and Saadut, feigning to oppose his advance, became his prisoner. Then the conqueror would have gone back to his Persian empire, on being indemified with only two crores of Rupees. But Saadut, finding himself outwitted by the Nizam for the invader's favor, said "why so low an indemnity ? I alone can give two crores from my small province." Thereupon Nadir Shah marched downward and entered Dehli with the local emperor (Mohamed Shah) as his prisioner. Then followed the terrible massacre and plunder of the city, by the heartless conqueror ; and his cupidity and thirst for human blood were fully satisfied for three days.

Being personally insulted by the haughty Nadir, Saadut took poison and died in 1739 ; while the old Nizam, his co-partner in treason, feigning to expire, evaded the promised suicide. Saadut was a man of great administrative ability and a noted artillery officer, being widely known in his age, as the *Bhorhmuja*, parcher of shot and shells literally.

Sufder Jung (1739-1753).

Mansur Ali Khan Sufder Jung, his nephew and son-in-law, after paying the two crores, promised by his uncle, was elected the next Subadar by Nadir Shah, who made him almost independent of the Delhi Government. For this reason, on the retreat of the invader, a quarrel took place with his master, Ahmed Shah, the next emperor. Sometimes after, however, peace was concluded ; and Ahmed Shah with Sufder Jung, who was now made the premier of the empire, began a tour of inspection throughout Upper India. On his return the Viceroy-premier (Nawab Wazir) placed Newal Rai, his lieutenant at Kanouj, as a check upon the refractory Ahmed Khan Bungush of Furrukhabad. But no sooner had the king and his Vizier reached

Delhi, than the Pathan chief marched against the Rajah, and in a battle that ensued, killed him.

Thereupon the emperor and Sufder Jung hastened, with a large but undisciplined army, to chastise the rebel. But before they could reach Furruckhabad, they were surprised and attacked with fury by the enemy. The emperor was the first to fly; and Sufder Jung, though he sustained the battle till night, was at last compelled to retreat towards the Chumbul. The victorious Pathans invaded Oude, but were repulsed by the loyal Shaikhs of Lucknow. The Bungush then turned towards Allahabad, which he captured.

Next year, Sufder Jung advanced with another army against Ahmed Khan, but was again defeated and wounded. With a broken heart and empty treasury, he retreated towards Delhi, and was in despair as to how to improve his affairs. But his high-spirited Begum came to his help, encouraged him, and advanced him her private money. With these fresh sinews of war, he procured the aid of Mulhar Rao, the Mahratta, and for the third time marched against Furrukhadad. Here he completely defeated the enemy, who, with 60,000 Sepoys and 30,000 Pathans, had advanced to resist his now victorious arms. The city was then beseiged; and the garrison, being short of provision, surrendered at discretion. A treaty of peace was then made; and almost the whole estate was annexed by the Nawab-Vizier.

After thus successfully concluding the war, Sufder Jung returned to Delhi. But the emperor was annoyed with him, through the intrigue of the infamous Gazee-ud-din. So he could not but encamp outside the city; and a civil war was the consequence. It continued for six months, during which the streets were inundated with blood. At last, through the intervention of some of his influential relatives, peace was restored; and Sufder Jung, retaining the title of Vizier, returned to Oude, as an independent ruler. After sojourning for some times at Lucknow and Fyzabad, he finally selected Pánparhghát as the capital of his dominion. But before he could complete the building of his intended seat, he died in 1753, of fever, which he contracted from the unhealthy place. He was an able viceroy, if not an able premier. His financial administration was successful.

Shujah-ud-doulah (1753—to 1775).

His son, Shujah-ud-doulah, succeeded him. But having enticed away a Khettri girl, he considerably endangered his position. He would have been dethroned, but for the Begum, his mother, who compromised the matter and pacified the indignant parties. The new Nawab-Vizier fixed his capital at Fyzabad; and palaces, trades, and population grew on all sides.

SHUJAH MAKES WAR WITH THE ENGLISH.

Ali Gohar, the heir-apparent to the Mogul throne, came here, after his heroic escape from the firm grasp of the infamous Gazee at Delhi, and took refuge with Shujah-ud-doulah, who received him with cordiality and respect due to his exalted rank. He also aided the prince with men and money, for his projected invasion of Behar and Bengal. While Mohamed Kooli Khan, governor of Allahabad, who was his relative, was absent with the Shahzada in Behar, Shujah-ud-doulah took possession, by strategem, of that important fort; and when M. Kooli returned to protest against such treachery, he received him with apparent cordiality and is said to have secretly got him assassinated.

When Ahmed Khan Abdali, the King of Cabul, invaded India, and headed the Mohamedan confederacy against the Mahrattas, Shujah-ud-doulah reluctantly joined him, and with uncommon bravery fought in 1761 at the battle of Paniput; for which reason he was famed as the Rustom of Hindustan. Flushed with this success, he returned to Oude, and joined Ali Gohar, now *Shah Allum*, at Allahabad, where he was made premier by the emperor.

Nawab Ali Jah, better known as Meer Cassim of Bengal, came here and complained of the injustice he had suffered at the hands of the English merchants of Calcutta, who were then rapidly rising from mercenary to political importance.* The Nawab Vizier addressed a letter to them, ordering, as premier of the empire, the restoration of the Ex-Nawab-Nazim; adding that Behar should be ceded to him for his trouble of intercession. The English not obeying, he, with the emperor and Meer Cassim, invaded Behar, and defeating an English army, laid seige to Patna, with great vigour (from 3rd to 30th May 1764.) But not succeeding in the capture of the town, and the rainy season setting in, he retreated to Buxar. The Company's army, reinforced under Munro, advanced and on 23rd October, 1764, attacked the proud invader. The Nawab-Vizier, though he fought with great bravery and sustained the battle till night, was at last compelled to retreat; because his generals and allies did not co-operate with and some even deserted him. He was himself wounded early in the morning, when he charged and drove back his enemy.

The victors advanced, and getting a legal status for their political situation, by a *firman* they had got from the emperor, now almost their prisoner, invaded the Nawab-Vizier's dominions. Shujah broke the

---

*Cassim Ali fled for refuge to Shujah-ud-dowlah, taking with him 385 elephants loaded with treasure. The exile offered Shujah a lakh of Rs, for every day's march, and half that sum for every halt, as long as the war might last, with three millions sterling, and the cession of the Patna district, on the recovery of Bengal, if he would join against the English. But Cassim Ali, desiring to have two strings to his bow, offered at the same time, a large bribe (?) to the emperor for his own appointment to the Viceroyship of Oude, in supercession of Shujah-ud-dowlah. The latter intercepted Cassim Ali's letter and forthwith placed him under restraint, after gaining Sumroo and other military officers with their troops. *Sir Henry Laurence.*

bridge over the Karumnassa, the Rubicon between Bengal and Oudh, in order to stop their advance; but the English forded it successfully a little southward, and beseiged Chunar, from which, however, they had a severe repulse. They still advanced and blockaded Allahabad with the greatest difficulty; for the Nawab-Vizier, by flanking movements, endangered their lines of communication with the base of their opperation, and attempted to seige their boats and the King. Still they persisted in the blockade;—and the famine-striken garrison at last surrendered at discretion.

Occupying this important fort, the British General inundated the Doab with the tide of invasion, and sent a detachment towards Lucknow. But shortly after, this and other out-lying forces were withdrawn and concentrated; for Shujah-ud-doulah, making Bareily as his base of operations, and re-organising his army, and with the aid of Mahrattas and Rohillahs, again advanced to drive out the enemy. On 3rd and 22nd of May respectively, two obstinate battles were fought at Kurrah; and the Rohillahs, deserting, or not heartly assisting him, the Nawab was ultimatelly defeated.

Now being on the extremity of his affairs, he sent proposals of peace, through two English officers, his prisoners of war, to the enemy, who, being in want of money to keep or extend his conquest, respectfully received him; and a treaty of peace was concluded on 16th August, 1765, at Allahabad. Fifty *lakhs* of Fyzabad Rupees were fixed as a sum for the indemnity of the war. As none of his rich Sirdars contributed their portion even on loan, Shujah-ud-doulah had to raise this enormous sum with difficulty from the private money and sale of ornaments of his wife, *Bahu Begum*, who gladly placed all her valuables at his disposal. For this reason he was greatly annoyed with his Sirdars; instead, Bahu Begam had all his favours and was rewarded with a large *Jagir* in Gondah and Bahraitch; and the surplus of yearly incomes over expenditure was given her every time it was found out. Hence she was so rich.

His English friends now tried to impress upon him the importance of a commercial treaty, to which, however, he did not agree, "Shujah-ud-doulah is extremely averse to the establishment of Factories in his dominions, which he considered as laying the foundation of a future rupture; the great abuses committed by the company's servants and extraordinary extension of privileges originally granted to the English, had been productive of much confusion and bloodshed in Bengal." Thus wrote Clive to the Court of Directors on 3rd September, 1765. "Poor Shujah! he did not know that the temporary charge of Rs. 2,10,000, he paid for an English brigade, became the root of all the subsequent misfortunes in Oude. In fact, it was the thin part of the

Company's wedge, imperceptibly introduced in his dominions; and what he feared in one quarter happened in the other !"

After the conclusion of the treaty, he returned to Fyzabad. Dismissing his Moguls and punishing his traitors, * he re-organized and reformed his army after the French manner, restored his finance, and consolidated his dominions. Next year a conference was held at Chhupprah by Lord Clive, with a view to preserve the balance of power; to this, the representatives of all the States attended. Shujah-ud-doulah, as Vizier of the Mogul empire, was made arbitrator of mutual differences, and he was especially requested to watch the growing power of the Scindia. That important trust he performed with credit; but when he prepared his army for this other and severer task, that is, to check the Scindia, the Company took alarm; and a deputation was sent from Calcutta. A meeting was in November 1768, held at Benares; and the Nawab-Vizier, to please his English friends, nominally reduced his army to 35,000 men. He was especially bound by treaty not to drill more than 10,000 of his army after the European manner of instruction. †

The next event of importance was the restoration of *Shah Allum* to the throne of his ancestors at Delhi, by the Mahrattas. The Nawab-Vizier aided the emperor, ‡ when he made, in 1771, the royal progress from Allahabad to the Mogul capital. On this, the English Company, who opposed the emperor's return to Delhi, nominally confiscated the royal domain, and sold the Doab to the Nawab-Vizier for 50 *lakhs* of Rupees;—for which purpose Warren Hastings came to Benares to meet and bargain with his Excellency. As a further mark of friendship, a

---

* Of Bulwant Sing of Benares and the Rohilla Chief of Furrukhabad, Shujah could not touch a hair; as they were by the treaty, under the special protection of the Company. And when he "seized Maharajah Beni Bahadur, and caused his eyes to be put out, an attempt was made to procure British interference in his favor, but the reply given was that the Vizier was master within his own dominions." *Sir Henry Lawrence.*

Article 9 of the treaty of 1865 expressly stipulates that "all the relations and subjects of His Highness, who in any manner assisted the English during the course of the late war, shall be forgiven, and no ways molested for same."

† When the views of the deputation were communicated to him, the Vizier objected to their conditions, saying he had not in any shape impunged the former treaty. He insisted, that he was not restricted to any particular number,—and then enlarged on the state of the troops in former times. The same demand, he added, might with equal justice be made upon the Rohillas. After much discussion, he declared with firmness, that he would never willingly reduce his forces below 35,000, of which 8,000 should be horse. He intimated his intention to go to Calcutta, unless the point was conceded. The Company, being most anxious to avoid all risks of a war, which might be hazarded by imposing conditions, "too mortifying for his haughty spirit," agreed to whatever the Vizier conceded. On this transaction, the Court of Directors remarked that, "with the professions of peace and friendship, you have inserted an article, which will not only give fresh cause of jealousy to the Vizier, but engages you likewise in disputes with other powers still more distant." At this time, the Vizier was pressed to dismiss all foreiguers, especially M. Gentil, a faithful French Officer of his. He refused compliance, saying that, "assure the English Chiefs, that I will be responsible that he shall never do anything to their prejudice." *Auber.*

‡ Shujah-ud-dowlah had been, a little before, re-instated in the Emperor's confidence. This unexpected reconciliation, between the Shah and the Vizier, received additional strength from the marriage, which was celebrated between one of the royal princes and His Excellency's daughter. So on leaving Allahabad the emperor put the Vizier in possession of the fort. *Auber and Atchinson.*

brigade (consisting of two European and six Sepoy battalions, with one company of artillery,) was lent to him, for a consideration of 2,10,000 Rs. a month. A permanent Resident was also appointed. Another sum of 40 *lakhs* of Rupees was stipulated as a reward to the Company for the conquest of Rohilkund.

After this transaction, Shujah-ud-doulah went towards Delhi, conquering all the intervening Mahratta forts, the strongest of which at Etawah, he blockaded till it surendered at discretion. Receiving the permission of the emperor for the prosecution of the projected Rohilla war, the Nawab-Vizier crossed the Ramgunga, and with the English brigade, which now joined him under Colonel Champion, invaded the land of the Afgan colony. The alleged cause of this invasion was that the Rohillas refused to pay the balance of 40 *lakhs, i, e.* 35 *lakhs*, for which sum the Nawab-Vizier had become guarantee to the Mahrattas, when they evacuated their country. The Rohillas under Hafiz-Rahmut Khan met the invader and obstinately defended their rights at the battle of Babul Nullah or Kuttra, which was fought on the 23rd of April, 1774. Their leader and some 4000 men were slain in the field ; and not till then were they defeated and repulsed. A second battle ending unfavorably, they finally fled to the northern mountains. At last a treaty of peace was concluded ; and Fyzoollah Khan was made the *Jageerdar* of Rampore. The rest of Rohilkund Shujah-ud-doulah annexed to his dominions ; and after the settlement of the conquered province, he appointed Saadut Ali, his second son, as its governor, with Bareili, as its seat of administration.

Returning to Fyzabad, he shortly after died suddenly at the age of 46 years, on the evening of the 26th of January, 1775, leaving his dominions at its greatest length and prosperity. He was a ruler of great ability and energy.*

---

* Dow, in his history of the time, describes him as " extremely handsome in his person, about five feet eleven inches in height, and so nervous and strong that with one stroke of his sabre he can cut off the head of a buffalo. He is active, passionate and ambitious ; his penetrating eye seems at first sight to promise uncommon acuteness and fire of mind ; but his genius is too volatile for depth of thought, and he is consequently more fit for the manly exercises of the fields, than for deliberation in the closet. Till of late, he gave little attention to business. He was up before the sun, mounted his horse, rushed into the forest, and hunted down tiger or deer till the noon of day. He then returned, plunged into the cold bath, and spent his afternoons in the harem among his women. Such was the state of Shuja-ud-dowlah's mind, till the late war (*i. e.* the campaign ending with the battle of Buxar.)........Stung with the loss of reputation, his passions have taken another course. His activity is employed in disciplining his army ; and he now spends more time at the comptoir of his finances, than in dalliance with the ladies of his seraglio. His authority is therefore established, his revenues increased, and his army on a respectable footing. But with all his splendid qualities, he is cruel treacherous, unprincipled, and deceitful".

Franklin and Scott, who were not like Dow, prejudiced against him by a private grudge, however, speak of him as " an excellent magistrate, a lover of justice, and anxiously desirous for the prosperity of his country... wise and dignified in character, affable, humane and generous......sincerely beloved by his own subjects,—even the sons of Hafiz Rahmut wept at his death."

Shujah-ud-dowlah used to love his Hindu subjects equally with the Mohamedans. He gave them grants of land and other encouragements for their religious practices and ecclesiastical establishments.

ASUF-UD-DOWLAH (1775-1797).

Mirza Amani, titled Asuf-ud-doulah, his son, succeeded him. According to its time-serving policy, the Company forthwith declared, that a treaty concluded with a father, becomes null, when the son succeeds; and so the new Nawab-Vizier, after a most tedious negotiation, reluctantly ceded the districts of Benares and Gazeepore worth 75 *lakhs*, and with a net profit of 23 *lakhs* annually to the British, ostensibly for the better defence of his dominions, but really for ousting of his younger brother, Saadut Ali, from his charge of Rohilkund. Having no cordial feelings with his mother, the celebrated *Bahu Begum*, whose advise he heeded not, he transferred his seat of Government to Lucknow, which he began beautifying with numerous palaces.

Sends presents to Delhi.

Shortly after, Asuf-ud-doulah sent a *peshcush* or offering to the emperor, with five thousand men. They arrived just in time to save His Majesty of Delhi from the evil designs of Zabita Khan; and this opportune aid secured for their sender the post of the nominal prime minister of the Mogul empire, in succession to his father. Jehander Bukth Shah, the heir apparent of Delhi, after his flight from the capital, having vainly endeavoured to restore the fallen fortunes of his family, took refuge for a time at Lucknow, and was received and entertained with great cordiality and respect. He retired on a pension to Benares, where he died in 1788, after vainly trying to induce Lord Cornwallis to support his cause.

Military reform.

In order to reform his army on a more effective footing, the Nawab-Vizier introduced many English officers into his military department. The English Brigade temporarily engaged for the Rohilla war, was made a permament charge on Oude, which was raised to Rs. 2,60,000 monthly or 31,20,000 Rs. annually. The introduction of the English officers, however, discontented the army and the Sirdars. While his Excellency was encamped at Etawah, in order to prosecute the Mahratta war with vigour, a portion of his army, that had been besieging Jhansi, mutinied against their English officers. An engagement took place between the Regulars called Sepoys, and the Matchlockmen; 2,500 of the latter successfully resisted and repulsed the charges of 15,000 of the former. At last the mutiny was quelled by the accidental explosion of a tumbril.

Some of these endowments are still existing in Aujodhya. To tap his religious tolerance and his alliance with the English, Hyder Ali of Mysore sent, in 1772, two emissaries with a letter. He wrote that, "it surprises me to find that your Excellency, while possessing so large an army and such ample resources, should submit to the yoke of the Christians. It would be more advisable for your Excellency to attack them on your side, while I assail them on mine, and by our united efforts destroy them." To this, Shujah replied, "Fanaticism in religion is for those, who have relinquished all interests in worldly affairs; but it would be culpable in persons, who, like us, have relative duties to perform towards thousands professing a totally different religion to our own, to show a preference for one sect over another. As for that large army and those ample resources which you have heard that I possess, they are maintained for the purpose of being employed against the enemies of the East India Company. Do not therefore expect me to use them otherwise."

English interference begins; bad results ensue.

That causes mutinies.

Another mutiny broke out, because of the machinations fo Mokhtar-ud-doulah, the unpopular minister and evil genius of the Nawab-Vizier; and a portion of the army was uselessly and ruthlessly butchered to a man. His Excellency, suspecting the fidelity of Busheer Khan, who commanded in Rohilkund, issued private orders for his seizure and execution. Busheer narrowly escaped, fled across the river, and proceeded to Agra, where he entered the serivice of Nejib Khan, the Rohilla minister of the emperor. Being jealous of him, Asuf-ud-doulah intended to join his epponents, the Rajpoots and Jats. But Resident Bristow dissuaded him to do so.

But the difficulties of the Nawab-Vizier were not at an end. Anoop Gooroo and Aumrao Gooroo, two *Gossain* Rajahs, under whom Shujah-ud-doulah had left the country of the Doab, openly shook off their allegiance. Fortunately, however, Asuf-ud-doulah, without entering into hostilities, succeeded in effecting their removal. Thus the affairs of his Excellancy grew embarrassed day by day, owing to his own weakness and fluctuating disposition, and the ambitious designs of his minister, Murteza Khan; while the Company's demands in the shape of *Tunkhas* or Orders on his Revenue, to the already large amount of 45 *lakhs* per annum, pressed heavily on the condition of Oude.

And conspiracy.

For these reasons, the discontented nobles began to conspire against the existing Government, especially against the minister. Saadut Ali was drawn into the plot with the hope, that he would be elected the next chief. Basant Ali, the eunuch General, the bravest soldier, and a man of extraordinary talents, invited the minister to a grand entertainment, and had him assassinated. Asuf took vigorous measures, and ordered the ennuch to be executed on the spot. On this, Saadut Ali mounted his horse, fled with precipation to Agra, and took refuge with Nujib Khan. The Nawab-Vizier, being thus in a moment deprived of his brother, minister, and general, knew not how to remedy his affairs, which fell into great disorders; while the troops were still in a very unsettled state, and discontents regarding the new arrangements and the introduction of British officers daily increased.

English interference.

Under these circumstances, the Calcutta Government forced upon him a Temporary Brigade, in addition to the permanent one, so as to ensure his safety from future dangers. To remodel and assist his administration, English farmers and adventurers flooded the country. Now it was, that Claude Martin, his Engineer, rose into importance, and had charge of the arcenal and other lucrative works; Colonel Scott monopolized the cotton and cloth trade; Hannay tyrannized over the trans-Ghagra provinces. "Lucknow jobs" were too tempting in those days of misrule and interference. Hence the Companys charges on the Oude Treasury grew in proportion. And as there was no limit to presents and allowances, salaries and extortions, the demands during seven years of Hasting's administration, rose enormously, and averaged one crore annually, while in spite of constant screwing, the receipts hardly amounted to 70 lakhs, leaving in 1781 a deficit of about 2½ crores. Sir E. Coote, the Company's Commander-in-Chief, drew 15,500 Rs. monthly, even while he was compaigning in the Carnatic. These exorbitant demands told very sadly on the finances of Oude Government—now bankcrupt, and on the condition of the people—now impoverished; while all, servants and transactions, were in debt and arrears. A severe famine was the consequence; and though relief-works were opened on all sides, as of the great Emambarah in Lucknow, thousands died in towns and villages; while rebellion broke out every where, as against Colonel Hannay, the tyrant of Gorakhpore. He came with a very large debt; and after three years, was compelled, by the Nawab's representation, to leave the land of his oppression, with 30 *lakhs* Rs. in his pocket.

"But he left behind him plenty of imitators, though on a less gigantic scale. These men, whether forced on the Nawab's service as revenue-farmers, or on military duty, seem to have been the curse of the country, which they plundered with a thoroughness and audacity, that were truly Verrine. They ill-treated and rackrented the Zemindar s in one case, and in the other, interfered with the course of trade, established markets of their own, abolishing those that were in existence, and collected the customs on their own account. Small wonder that the revenue dwindled." *Irwin's Garden of India.*

and extortions.

Before his connections with the English, the Vizier's dominions were luxuriant with prosperity and looked upon as the garden of India; but in 1779, they were reduced to deserts and waste lands, and the revenue, which had been more than 4 crores, now scarcely exceeded one. The military cost of the two brigades and the country troops under British officers increased to more than 80 and 40 *lakhs* respectively above the estimate; while the civil expences for the Compony's Residency and the Private Agency swelled to 6½ and 12 *lakhs*. These were not the only charges; there were other exactions in the shape of pensions, allowances, and large occasional gifts* to various persons, in the Company's service. The Nawab Vazier was over-burdened; difficulties and embarrassments grew thick in his paths; discontent and disorganization were the rule of his day. Poor Asuf! he could not *suborn* his relief even through the Private Agent; his Calcutta friends treated his entreaties and remonstrances with contempt and indifference.

* For example, a present of 11 *lakhs* was given to the British army for their action of 26th October, 1794, to quell an insurrection. The sum was thus distributed; a Colonel—16,400 Rs.; Lieutt-Colonel—13,220 Rs.; a Major—9,840; a Lieutenant—3,936; Conductor—1,312; and European Private—110. Not a *pie* of this extravagant throwing away of money like water was sprinkled on the poor Sepoys. An additional *lakh* was also given to the English widows of those who fell in the action.

On the recovery of the King of England from a dangerous illness, Asuf presented his Doctor with 25,000 Rs. and devoted another equal sum for charity in his Magesty's name.

"the support of my house-hold; in so much that the allowances made to the Seraglio and children of the deceased Nawab, have been reduced to one-fourth of what it had been, upon which they have subsisted for nearly two years past; the attendants, writers, servants, &c., of my court, have received no pay for two years past............." This representation, which events proved to be no exaggeration, were received by the Governor General with the highest indignation.

And to crown the Nawab-Vizier's difficulty, Warren Hastings came up on a money-making tour, and intended to stay for a time at Lucknow; but Asuf anticipated him, by himself hastening with a few followers to Chunar, (Chandalgurh), where a meeting took place. The Governor-General insisted on the immediate payment of the accumulated arrears. The Nawab said that he had given everything he could, and that "no further resources remained, and that he was without subsistence." At last Asuf soothed his exacting demands by a private present of ten lakhs of Rupees, and thus contrived him from a violent and impirous task-master into a warm advocate. An amicable arrangement was concluded, by which the Nawab was temporarily relieved of his unpleasant situation, by two mean resorts, through the Resident, Mr. Middleton, (1) by the spoliation* of the Fyzabad Bagums, his mother and grandmother, and (2) by the heavy extortions of 15 lakhs from Fyzullah Khan, the Nawab of Rámpore.

But still Asuf-ud-dowlah's distress decreased not; even now he could not provide for his own private expenses, still less for his relatives, many of whom were literally starving. A brother of his fled to Scindia's Court for a living. Consequently the Nawab Vizier again applied, and with tears besought the Calcutta Council for material relief. At last the hard heart of the Governor-General was moved; and Hastings came to Lucknow in 1784. The extravagant Residency establishment, costing 6½ lakhs a year, was abolished; but the Private Agency was retained at an yearly charge of 12 lakhs, of which Major Palmers' salary was 2,28,000 Rs. The Furrukhabad Brigade called also *Temporary brigade*, was ordered to be withdrawn. The ever-elastic arrear-accounts were adjusted and reduced to a reasonable limit, and preposterous demands were can-

* The Resident. after superceding the authority of the Nawab-Vizier, who recoiled from the proposed plunder, proceeded, with a body of English troops, to Fyzabad, on the 12th January, and occupied the Begum's palace. The Zenana was blocked up; and food was denied to all, the princesses and their attendants. Their two aged eunuch officers were seized, heavily fettered, dragged to Lucknow, confined and put to flogging. In this way, 76 *lakhs* of Rupees were extorted, which, added to 56 *lakhs*. taken before as loan amounted to 132 *lakhs*.

celled. These done, Hastings returned to Calcutta, and shortly after left for England.

But this second relief was as unsubstantial as before. The Furrukhabad Brigade, for example, was not withdrawn. The Nawab Vizier again cried, and sent Hyder Beg to Lord Cornwallis,* the new Governor-General at Calcutta. His Excellency, however, arbitrarily fixed or rather raised the annual subsidy from about 34 lakhs to 50 lakhs of ready money, on the principle that cash-payment makes good friends. Asuf-ud-dowlah yielded reluctantly to the decree of the Governor-General, whose awful presence at Lucknow, in October 1787, and bombastic lectures on the duties of Sovereigns, made the Vizier of the defunct Mogul Empire hold his peace, and smooth away his discontents by opium-eating. Hyder Beg was forced upon him as his minister, and abler men were thrown aside; he, however, died in 1795, throwing the affairs of Oudh into greater disorders.

The wheel of the Company's Government now again turned, because of its periodical changes; and Sir John Shore, afterwards Lord Teignmouth, appeared on the historical scene with altered mind and policy. Being solicitous of the Nawab's interest, he visited Lucknow in February 1797, and Tuffuz-ul-Hussain Khan smoothing his way, guaranteed protection from the supposed invasion of Zamàn Sháh of Cabul, on a consideration of 5½ lakhs of Rupees, in addition to the already very large subsidy. He gave him "a sight of good advice" and enforced two additional regiments, in compliance with the order of the Court of Directors, "owing to the late very great increase in their military establishment." He, however, failed to get Allahabad and the Doab, even on a lease; for which purpose, Maharaja Jhao Lal, the favourite minister of the Nawab, was forcibly taken away and imprisoned at Patna, because he objected to the increase of the subsidy and the addition of the two regiments. Tuffuzul Hussain was posted in his place as a reward for his subserviency to the Governor-General.

Asuf-ud-dowlah took this officious treatment so much to heart, that he fell ill and refused medicine, exclaiming that "there is no cure for a

* While here, he saw the notorious Lucknow jobs, contracts, peculation, excessive corruption, and the extent of delinquencies both at Lucknow and Benares, of the Europeans, who were saddled with friends not very distant from Government House, the confused manner of stating accounts, and constant practice of trumping up charges to extort every Rupee that it was possible to get from the Nawab-Vizier. Some of these evils he eradicated.

broken-heart," and, after a lingering desease, died on 21st September 1797. He was a ruler, liberal to extravagance and weak-minded even to helplessness,—the first cause of the decline of his successors and realm. Of all the sovereigns of Oudh, he is now most dearly remembered by the people. His affection for his subjects was such, that the Baniahs and shopkeepers, even to this day, repeat every morning his name as an auspicious incantation, before commencing their business. The celebrated distich,—

Jis ko na de Moulá.	meaning	Whom giveth not God (Moulá.)
Us ko de Asuf-ud-dowlah.		Him giveth Asuf-ud-dowlah.

is at the tongue of every body, native or foreigner. He was also a patron of arts and literature. With all his folly, he had fine qualities, attracted great men, and was served well.

VIZIER ALI (1797-98).

(FOUR MONTHS ONLY.)

Mirza Vizier Ali, his adopted son, succeeded him. Being of the anti-English party, which the exacting policy of the Company had raised against itself, the new Nawab-Vizier sent messengers all around to the different Chiefs at Gwalior, Poona, Delhi, and Lahore, to form a confideracy. Perhaps he would have succeeded, but for his private vice of licentiousness, which produced a host of enemies in his own house. Sir John was informed of his ambitious designs, and, suddenly coming to Lucknow, deposed him by a strategem on the pretext of illegitimacy.* The Nawab was deported to Benares on a pension of 1½ lakhs a year. There Mr. Cherry, the Resident, trying forcibly to take him away to Calcutta, was murdered by him in a fit of passion. The ex-Nawab-Vizier then, with a prince of Delhi, fled from the city, and making the forest of Butwal his base of opperations, organized an army of rabble. Occupying Goruckpore, he invaded Oudh; but unprovided with men and money, his starving army melted into straggling parties and disappeared in different ways. The campaign ended by the hot-blooded youth himself becoming a disguised fugitive. He fled through Lucknow to Jeypore,

* "We are bound to record, even more emphatically than before, our opinion that Vizier Ali was unjustly treated." *Sir H. Lawrence.* Mill says, that he was deposed with less ceremony and enquiry, than the question of a few pounds decided in a common court,

whose Rajah, on a threat from the Marquis of Wellesley, broke the traditional rules of royal shelter and hospitality, by betraying the ex-Nawab-Vizier to the enemy. Poor Vizier Ali lived the life of a criminal in an iron-cage in Fort William, as though an animal of show, till relieved by death in 1817.

SAADUT ALI KHAN—(1798-1814).

Saadut Ali Khan, the younger son of Shujah-ud-dowlah, was made Nawab-Vizier, on 20th January, 1798, by the revolutionary party, under the sanction of the Fyzabad Begums. Previously to this, he, having shown intelligence and ability from his youth, was by his father made deputy-minister to the Emperor, Shah Allum, while at Allahabad, and then raised to the Governorship of Rohilkund, after its conquest. Being recalled from Bareli by his brother, Asuf-ud-dowlah, and attempting a revolution by the assassination of Moktar-ud-dowlah, he fled to Agra; and thence retired to Benares on a pension of 1½ *lakhs* of Rupees. He visited Calcutta and cultivated friendship with the English. He could speak English very fluently. While on a second journey to the Company's metropolis, he received the offer of the Oudh *musnud* from Sir John Shore. He immediately retraced his steps from Rajmahal, which he had already reached; and entering Lucknow in company with the Governor-General, and throwing largesses to the people, who lined the road,—the first step towards acquiring popularity,—he assumed the reins of Government.

But a hard condition was exacted from him. As the Company never failed to take the best advantage of its traditional policy, when a Nawab is made, the subsidy was raised, at one bound, from 55½ to 76 *lakhs* of Rupees for 10,000 sepoys to be stationed in Oudh. The new Nawab-Vizier agreed very reluctantly to the hard terms of the new treaty;* and though he punctually paid the *kists* or the extraordinary quarterly instalments, the Company never kept their part of the contract, or shortly after forgot it. From the very commencement of his reign, he

* Money value of the treaty of 1798:—

By article 2	... 76 *lakhs*.	By article 9	... sum unknown.
" " 4	... sum unknown.	" " 10	... 12 *lakhs*.
" " 5	... 1¼ *lakhs*.	Total,	... 100½ *lakhs*.
" " 8	... 11¼ do.	Two unknown sums.	

After an old native Painting. "Choh-pani." (tea-water) between Saadut-Ali Khan & Col. John Baillie. P.C. Mookherji 8.8.85. Naini Tal

was also deprived of his political and military powers; and Oudh was degraded from its independent position to the level of the so-called Protected States.

Thus fettered by the manifold conditions, imposed by Sir John, Saadut Ali yet ruled his dominions with great tact and ability. All departments of his Government were organized; offices were reformed; and the services of able men were secured. Extravagant expenditure was put a stop to; and strict economy was the order of the day. The refractory *zemindars* felt his power; and the corrupt officials were compelled to disgorge their ill-gotten wealth. His subjects were happy; the middle class had ample employment; and the nobility, necessary comfort and luxury,—not extravagance. New palaces and markets were erected on all sides. The reign of Ilmas Ali Khan,* the Deputy-Governor of Doab and Western Oudh, was a pattern of native rule; while Hakim Mehdi, the Nizam of Gondah-Bahraich, was perfect of his class.

Thus far successful, the Nawab-Vizier was maturing his plans for introducing radical changes into his administration; when the Marquis of Wellesley entered the Company's stage, with all his greediness and aggressive policy. And as robbers do not practise economy with their abundant *kutcha* money, the noble Lord arbitrarily threw half of the military charge of the Company on the shoulder of poor and timid Saadut Khan, by forcibly introducing two divisions† of the British army into Oudh. To add to the latter's perplexity, his army was ordered to be disbanded; and two-thirds of his dominions were at once to be ceded. The Nawab-Vizier cried and protested against this most unjust and despotic proceeding, as contrary to the recent treaty, which was made permanent, and to be observed for ever. The imperious Lord heard him not,

* Mean Ulmas Ali Khan was the greatest and best man of any note, that Oudh has produced. He held for about 40 years districts, yielding to the Oudh Government an annual revenue of about 80 *lakhs* of Rupees. During all this time, he kept the people secure in life and property, and as happy as people in such a state of society can be; and the whole country, under his charge, was, during his life-time, a garden. He lived here (Meangunge, which he founded and built after his name) in a style of great magnificence, and was often visited by his sovereign, who used occasionally to spend a month at a time with him at Meangunge. A great portion of the land, held by him, were among those made over to the British Government, on the division of the Oudh territory, by the treaty of 1801, which were lightly assessed. *Sleeman.*

† 12 Battalion of Infantry and 4 Regiments of Cavalry were enforced at an additional cost of 54 *lakhs* annually. This sum, added to 76 *lakhs*, makes the total subsidy 130, for which 136½ *lakhs* worth territories were annexed. On this transaction, Mill remarks, that, "this was......an explicit declaration, that the military force, for the protection of Oudh, ought to be, at all times, even at the bosom of the most profound peace, at the utmost extent of a War-establishment;—than which a more monstrous proposition never issued from human organs."

and threatened to dethrone him, if he again dared to offer opposition. To avert this danger, poor Saadut feigned a pilgrimage and retirement to Mecca, but in vain; for then the Governor-General wanted to absorb his whole dominions. Still Saadut protested;—still he consented not. At last Lord Wellesley sent his brother to use the weight of his personal influence. But even yet the Nawab-Vizier was reluctant. Then the Resident, Colonel Scott, himself issued the order of occupation. The Company's soldiers flooded the country; and Rohilkund, the Doab, Chunar and Goruckpore districts, came within the *red line.* Finding at last his passive resistance fruitless, Saadut Ali yielded; and a new treaty was concluded on 10th November 1801, by which Oudh was bereft of territories worth 135½ *lakhs.* What was left could barely produce one *crore*; of the remaining dominions, he was not to continue master, but a responsible vassal, to be constantly exercised and controlled by the dictates of irresponsible Residents.

The Nawab-Vizier, sad and morose, prayed and vowed, at the shrine of Huzrat Abbas, for a change of the Company's Government. But the person he dreaded most, was near at hand; for the noble Marquis came and, in January, 1802, made his state-entry into Lucknow. The Governor-General lectured him as to the nature and limit of his duties and powers in a private interview; and the Nawab, in order to please him, built the Mundiaon Cantonment, and the Residency (old Banqueting Hall) for the comfort of the Company's army and ambassador. A guard of honor was attached to Colonel Baillie's establishments; whence was derived the name of *Baillie Guard,* so familiar since 1857.

Being now freed from further troubles, except that of the interference of the Resident, Saadut Ali again reformed his disorganised affairs, and introduced his celebrated contract–system; by which his remaining dominions were devided and duly proportioned into *Chucklas* and *Illakas*; and the work of revenue-collection was farmed out to different contractors, who, surrounded as they were with a complete system of double checks, had their robbing propensity completely nullified,—a system, that succeeded well under him, and was comparatively less oppreseive to the people, and more effective to Government, than that of the Company.

But he was in advance of his times ;* and the English understood him not. So Colonel Baillie, unable to comprehend his plans, interfered with all the details of his Government, and threw everything into disorder and disorganization. The experienced officers were removed; and young inexperienced Collectors were imported from the North-Western Provinces, under the Resident's patronage and favour. As a consequence, the revenue collections fell into arrears; and land-lords refused to pay, and, when pressed, rebelled. The Nawab-Vizier apparently submitted to the arbitrary proceedings of the Resident; but, as he had collected a vast amount of money, he had recourse to secret influence at Calcutta and London, for the removal of the despot. The private agency, employed by him, such as Major Ouseley, &c., succeeded so far, that his hard task-master, Lord Mornington, was recalled; and Lord Hastings came, decidedly the great friend of Oudh. The new Governor-General immediately journeyed towards Upper India to restore order and amicability. But meantime the Nawab's enemies scenting the coming changes, that might be most probably effected by his Lordship, had him poisoned on the night of 11th July 1814.

He was decidedly the Akbar of Oudh,—and though timid in nature, was not found wanting in all the transcendent qualities of an able ruler. He created a Reserve-Treasury, in which he accumulated and left 14, or as some say, 22 crores of Rupees. Shams-ud-doulah, his second son, was his *Naib* (minister,) and his third son, afterwards the third King of Oudh, was his financial minister;—both had his confidence and were of great assistance to him. But Gazee-ud-din, his eldest son and heir-apparent, being on terms of misunderstanding with his father, lived quite a separate and retired life.

GAZEE-UD-DIN HYDER (1814-1827).

No sooner was Colonel Baillie informed of the Nawab-Vizier's death, a few minutes after, than he hurried to the palace to crown his friend, Shams-ud-doulah. But Gazee-ud-din Hyder, being heavily armed for a

* "No person can read his replies to Colonel Baillie's demands, without being satisfied, that under kindlier treatment at the outset, much might have been done with such a prince. We are especially struck at his being in advance of the Bengal Government of the day, on revenue arrangements." Colonel Baillie's conduct towards him is well known; while "Colonel Scott could hardly be an acceptable ambassador .... his manner had nothing to compensate for the matter of the invidious duties imposed on him .... He did nothing for the improvement of the country. He was rather an obstacle in its way." *Sir Henry Lawrence.*

death-struggle for his birth-right, marched out of his private mud house, situated at the site, where his father's tomb now stands, and climbed the palace walls with the assistance of Aga Meer, his personal attendant. Gazee then seated himself on the ancestral *Gaddi.* Shams-ud-doulah, returning from the bath, a preliminary ceremony before proper coronation, to the *Lal-Baradwari,* or throne-hall, found himself out-witted by his elder brother, and the Resident powerless for the time being. Shortly after, he retired to Benares on a handsome pension,— thence to Calcutta to urge his claim to Oudh *Musnud.*

After the ceremony of coronation, Gazee-ud-din cultivated friendship with the Resident, and concurred with his views on the proposed reforms in the administrative affairs of Oudh. The *Ijarah,* or contract-system of revenue-collection, was looked upon as antiquated practice; and that of *Amani,* or trust with salaried collectors, was introduced into some districts, as a preliminary experiment. The new Nawab-Vizier chose his ministers as recommended by the Resident. And reforms were instituted, "being injudicious repetition of the mistakes, committed in the Company's territories, forcing upon the people institutions, foreign to their habits, strange to their notions, and repulsive to their feelings." And thus every attempt of the so-called improvements failing, "the new Nawab-Vizier withheld his confidence from the Resident and his ministers, who were the creatures of the former, and whose removal he now devoutly wished." *Horace Wilson.* Thereupon Colonel Baillie began to persecute the Nawab, as he had done his father,—to such a degree, that he even prevented the beating of the viceregal drum; because it disturbed his morning slumbers.

The relief was however, at hand; for on 8th October 1814, Lord Hastings, who had resolved to do justice to Oudh, arrived at Cawnpore, where he was visited by Gazee-ud-din. He returned to Lucknow, a few days after, with the Governor-General. He gave 2 crores and 10 lakhs as two separate loans for the prosecution of the Nepal War, which Lord Hastings declared immediately. Gazee-ud-din now submitted complaints against the imperious conduct of the Resident; but being frightened by the machinations of Aga Meer, the creature of the latter, retracted the statement. As a consequence, Hakim Mehdi, and other old and able officers were dismissed. Aga Meer became prime-minister, as a reward for his subserviency to Colonel Baillie. *

Lord Hastings, however, understood the Resident's intrigue, and ordered him to treat the Nawab as an independent prince, by a respectful urbanity and strict fulfilment of established ceremonials, not to interfere in his internal administration, nor to practise patronage and espionage any longer. But the phlegmatic Resident heeded not his instructions; for which reason, the Governor-General immediately removed him. The Nawab-Vizier was now left with uncontrolled direction of his administration. This abstinence from intervention was attended with the happiest results; and the people had unalloyed rest and contentment, which they had not known since the death of Shujah-ud-dowlah.

The Governor-General, returning from the Pindari war, in which Gazee had assisted him with cavalry and elephants, visited him at Lucknow, in March (4th to 10th) 1818; and to serve a double policy, made him quite independent of the imperial house of Delhi. In place of the premier of the defunct Mogul Empire, the Nawab-Vizier now became the *king* of Oudh; and the first royal coronation took place on 9th October, 1819, which cost a *crore* of Rupees, and which was celebrated with unusual splendour.† The districts of Khyreegurh and Terai, lately conquered from the Nepalese, were given to him by the Governor-General, for mutual advantages—and the second loan of one crore was cancelled by the bargain. Above all, the new *Padshah* was honored with the personal friendship of the Governor-General.

After this, no event of importance took place. His reign was peaceful and happy. He was just, liberal, and impartial to all. His leisure-hours were occupied with mechanics, arts, and literature, in which he took great interest. An elephant-carriage of his invention particularly attracted the notice of Lord Hastings. His Persian dictionary, which

* It is impossible to see this arrangement and not to discover, that the elevation of Aga Meer, is the reward of the influence exerted by him over the Nawab-Vizier to produce those incantations, which I have detailed............I believe some sort of intimidation is the practice used with the Nawab-Vizier. He does not seem deficient in intellect, but he appears weak in nerve." *Marquis of Hastings.*

† "Its object was an indisputable recognition of His Majesty's independence of any other power, by placing an effectual bar against the interference of any Government, either directly or indirectly, with the interior administration of His Majesty's Government." *Calcutta Gazette*, 28th October. 1819.

be printed and distributed gratis to the different libraries in Europe and Asia, was a valuable work and well known addition to oriental learning. But the latter days of his domestic life were embittered by the separation of Padshah Begum, his queen, and Nasir-ud-din, his son, heir-apparent and nominal minister, through the intrigues of Aga Meer, titled Moatim-ud-dowlah, the assistant but executive minister.

In November, 1825, Lord Amherst, the next Governor-General, visited Lucknow, and insisted on reforms. The King denied the necessity for any interposition into his affairs, which were as flourishing and successful as could be wished. Next month, a third loan of a crore was given to relieve the Company from its pecuniary difficulties. In the following year, a fourth loan of half-a-crore was also lent, though reluctantly; and the Company did not trouble him any more for reforms. Oudh was thus "periodically used as a wetnurse to relieve the difficulties of the East India Company's finances", (*Sir H. Lawrence*); and while benefiting its friends, it itself got involved in pecuniary difficulties.

In order to increase his income, Gazee ordered the Talukdars to pay enhanced revenues.* Most of them refused; and the King required the asistance of the British army, to compell the refractory Talukdars to pay their dues. The Resident declined to comply, unless, on a fresh condition, that he or his military officers be allowed to decide on the nature of Government-claims, before ordering the army to proceed for the recovery. Bitterly did Gazee complain of this unjust proceed-

*Great balances of revenue had occurred owing to the introduction of the *Amani* system, as enforced by the British Government, in place of the Ijàrah or farming out to contractors; and consequently many administrative evils arose from the innovation. "My past experience has fully convinced me, that we have at different times, caused mischiefs by merely urging the adoption of the *Amani* system, (without knowing, how it was to be carried into effect), especially when applied to large provinces, such as Sultanpore and Partabgarh.........The farming system has advantages, provided that the farmer be an intelligent and active man. *One* is that the farmer, not being at all interfered with by the Durbar, has thus the requisite power in his own hands, to keep the disaffected and turbulent part of the population in order, to the very great benefit of the peaceably inclined inhabitants of his districts; another is, that .... it is his interests not to apply the revenue-screw too tightly, or allow others to do so. Another advantage is, that in scanty seasons of rain, a wealthy farmer will always make advances to the Zemindars to enable them to dig wells, or in other ways irrigate a portion at least of their lands, that they may be enabled to live and to raise more revenue for the farmer's own benefit, in the following years. Some striking instances of this occured during the famine of 1837-38............When the Governor-General's camp passed up, forage was procured from Oudh, while at Cawnpore and all the way to Futtehgarh none was procurable in our territories. The fourth advantage is the *personal interest* of the farmer to prevent the soldiery and others (from plundering) the property of the cultivators; while the Amani Amil has none. Fifth is the *security* of the revenue, *Col. Lowe's Report.*

ing of the Resident. He urged that "all his difficulties have arisen from his entire confidence in the friendship of the Company. This induced him and his ancestors to disband an excellent army, till they scarcely left sentries enough for the palace ;.........and they have become unable, without help, to enforce payment of their ancient revenues. This also induced him to lend to the British Government all the money, which would have else enabled him to ease the people of their burthens ...." *Bishop Heber.*

On the 20th of October, 1827, Gazee-ud-din Hyder died a natural death. Though weak in nerve, he was not devoid of judgment or sagacity. He showed to great advantage in his correspondence with the Calcutta Government. He had a great mechanical turn, and was a patron of arts and literature. His reign was the happiest of all the latter Oudh sovereigns.

NASIR-UD-DIN HYDER (1827-1837.)

Nasir-ud-din became the next king. His first act was to take revenge on Aga Meer, the cause of his misfortune during the latter days of his father, who, however, just before his demise, had made a reconciliation between them. But this was of short duration. For the new king soon found that the British Government would not interfere with his choice of a minister, and that he might follow his own inclinations. This he ascertained from a private interview with Lord Cumbermere, the Commander-in-chief, who, at the time, came to visit Lucknow, after the successful termination of the second Bhurtpur sieze.

Immediately after, he dismissed Aga Meer, the minister, almost imprisoned him, and demanded repayment of sums, of which he was said to have defrauded the royal treasury. The ex-minister appealed for British protection. A military escort was sent from Cawnpore. The King reluctantly allowed him to depart; and Aga Meer, with 25 crores worth of property, carried in 800 carts and numerous camels and elephants, left the city in October 1830, and settled in Cawnpore, where he died two years after. There he established a press to attack the Oudh Government. He was a man of great tact, penetration and intrigue; and though of humble origin, was respected more than any other ministers by the Residents and other British officials. He it was, who organised a new Oudh army, when Mr. Ricketts refused to lend the Company's troops to suppress refractory Zemindars.

The dismissal of the minister disarranged the affairs of the Oudh Government. The new king wanted to become his own minister, but he being ignorant and inexperienced, Padshah Begum, his adoptive mother, through Fazleh Ali, managed his affairs. She was a good accountant, though not an able financier. But as the rule of women cannot be successful, unless they give up the Zenana and the veiling system, the Resident, Mr. Maddock, declined to have any communication with the king, until a respectable and a responsible minister should be nominated. After much hesitation, Hakim Mehdi Ali Khan was recalled from Farukhabad, and though opposed by Mr. Maddock as inimical to British influence, he was made, in 1831, the premier of the kingdom.

No sooner was he restored to power, than beneficial measures followed; the finances improved; the expenses diminished; the corrupt practices of the officers were checked; and the farming system was abolished for direct collection by officers, appointed by the minister.

In April 1831, Lord William Bentinck, while on a tour in the upper provinces, paid a ceremonial visit to Lucknow, and, at a private interview, severely remonstrated with the King, on his dissolute habits; and threatened to take over the management of Oudh, unless he reformed himself and his adminstration within a short time. And he informed him in the beginning of 1835, that he was authorised, by the Court of Directors, to assume the kingdom, when he might think proper. But the king heeded him not. His time was wholly engrossed among the five European associates of his dissipation, known as the barber, tutor, painter, librarian and Captain.* Hakim Mehdi, attempting to rouse His Majesty to a sense of his duty, and, at the same time, offending the Begums and the favorite courtiers, by the use of disrespectful terms, was at last, in August 1834, dismissed, and with difficulty retired to Farukhabad. Roshan-ud-dowlah then became minister; but though a man of good intention, he could not show much talent and intelligence; and the work of reforma-

*De Russet, Wright, Charles Mauntz, Croupley, and Magnes. Barber De Russet was the father of a merchant of the same name, who was killed in the Cawnpore Massacre of 1857.

tion, so ably begun by Hakim Mehdi, was not completed. Nor was it insisted on; for Lord Bentinck at last found that the condition of Oudh was not so bad as before reported to him.

In spite of the dissolute habits and prodigality of the sovereign, his people did not experience the effects of misrule;* nor were they oppressed, as was alleged by some Europeans. In fact Oudh was as prosperous as ever. "Whatever grievances the people might endure, they considered them light, in comparison with the unrelenting pressure of the revenue system of their neighbours, or the wearisome, costly, and vexatious process of their Courts of Justice" (*Horace Wilson*). There were, moreover, some satisfactory features in this otherwise despotic reign. Poor houses, Colleges, Hospitals, and an Observatory, and other useful public works were established and started. Slavery and Thuggee were suppressed. The Company too was benefitted with supplies of money. For these reasons, the threatened assumption of the Oudh administration, when sanc-

* The Government of Oudh is absolute, yet to its praise be it said, that, during the first eight years of my sojourn, I never heard of but one execution by the king's command; and that was for crimes of the greatest enormity, where to have been sparing would have been unjust. In cases of crimes, such as murder, the nearest relative surviving is appealed to by the Court of Justice; if he demands the culprit's life, the court cannot save him from execution. But it is rarely demanded; they are by no means a revengeful people generally. There are ambitious and cruel tyrants to be found; but these individuals are exceptions to the mass of the people. Examples of mercy, set by the king, in all countries, have an influence upon his subjects; and here the family of a murdered man, if poor, is maintained by the guilty party, or else relieved by royal munificence, as the case may require. *Mrs. Meer Hossein Ali*, 1830.

The people of Oudh are not worse governed than our own subjects. It is true, that things are not yet carried on with the regularity, which is practised in the British provinces; a rougher and more precipitous mode of proceeding is occasionally adopted, with the loss, sometimes, of a few lives in consequence; and the revenue officer, if he finds an estate very productive, will sometimes, demand a higher rent than was originally agreed to. Such are, I believe, all the real grievances they have to complain of; and individual hardship is thereby now and then caused. But the mass of the people,—I speak not of those in power, but of the landholders and peasantry,—are far more lightly taxed than those of the British dominions. The civil and criminal administration is certainly not worse than ours,—that is judging by the only criterion,—the difficulty and facility of enforcing a claim; the people are governed by their hereditary rulers, and benefited by the expenditure in the country of the revenue, that is raised, instead of being subject to a few foreigners, by whom as much wealth as possible is carried out of the country. Shore's *Notes on Indian affairs*, 1835.

The experience of the last sixty years has proved that the inhabitants of Oudh.........have evinced a steady preference to their own irregular Government, and to their own rough usages, over other governments and systems, which, according to our notions, ought greatly to be preferred by all classes of subjects. And I concur with J. F. Brown, then Collector and Magistrate of Jownpore, who wrote on 13th December, 1834, that " the cultivated portions grow very superior crops; that the districts of Fyzabad.........is indeed a perfect garden; that the original assessments are moderate. The people, though complaining of subsequent exactions, never emigrate into our provinces".........They have as many comforts, as few vexations of this world, as any equal numbers of persons in our own territories. *Colonel Low's Report*, 1841.

tioned by the Court of Directors, was not carried into execution by the Governor-General.

While the King was sick from the effects of excessive drink, some of the nobles, chiefly Roshan-ud-dowlah, dreading his vindictive spirit, had Nasir-ud-din poisoned on the night of 7th July, 1837, in spite of his precautions, when he had a presentiment of an unnatural termination to his life. He was of a despotic temper, an Anglicised autocrat,—but was generally liberal and kind-hearted. He was also a noted poet. Of the 10 crores, left by his father, in the reserved treasury, he spent all but 70 lakhs. The existence of such a semi-fictitious book as "The private life of an Eastern King," has prejudiced his character in the estimation of the European public.

MOONNA JAN. (three hours' King).

A few minutes after, Colonel Low, the Resident, was informed of the demise of the King. Throwing aside the non-intervention-policy, he went straight to the palace, had all the gates, leading to it, closed or thoroughly guarded, and sent for Mohomed Ali Shah, the uncle of the deceased, to be enthroned on condition of his signing a new treaty to be presented to him afterwards. But Padshah Begum,* who, (being on terms of misunderstanding with her son, the late King, had been living in Ilmasbágh with the heir-apparent, her grandson,) came out of her retirement, and, forcibly entering the palace by the Northern Gate, seated *Moonna Jan* on the throne of his father. The Resident and the British nominee were for a time in imminent danger. But troops came from the Mandiaon Cantonment to their help. The Lal Baradari was bombarded; the royal guards were bayonetted; many inoffensive men were killed; and everything was plundered, not only in the throne-hall, but in the

* Padshah Begum was a very noble and able queen, though her temper was generally imperious. "When Gazee-ud-din wanted to have Nasir-ud-din, in order to deprive him of his right to the throne, Padshah Begum fought for him with all the bravery of a heroine. She had armed her retainers, incited them by her example, and ultimately succeeded in baffling the king, but not until a bloody contest had taken place; and the Resident had been obliged to interfere to prevent further scandal.........But as Gazee had wished to act towards Nasir, so did Nasir wish to act towards his own son, (Moonna Jan). The mother of Nasir took her grandson under her protection, and refused to give him up. The king ordered her to leave the palace; she refused. The king then ordered his female sepoys to turn her out, but her retainers fought and routed them ....The Resident again interfered, guaranteed the life of the child, and she departed in content." *Private Life of an Eastern King.* She then lived a retired life with Moonna Jan at Ilmasbágh; and though again the king attempted to drive her out, she yet maintained her position.

Mohamed Ali Shah 1837-42

royal Zenana. The three hours' King and Padshah Begum were imprisoned, and sent to the fort of Chunar on a joint pension of Rs. 2,400, a month, a very poor sum in consideration of their claims, title and position.

MAHOMED ALI SHAH. (1837-1842),

Next day, Mahomed Ali Shah was crowned, and signed the new treaty with great reluctance, feeling, as he did, that he was signing away his kingdom from his children. An auxiliary army was enforced on a charge of 16 lakhs. The Police, judicial, and financial departments were to be remodelled after those of the Company, and, if the administration of these fail in any part, the British officers would assume the management of those districts, which might be especially ill-governed.

Lord Auckland, the then Governor-General, however, recoiled from this bold proceeding of the ambassador, observing that it was an improper time for it to be enforced, and adding that "it was not warranted by anything contained in the instructions issued to the Resident." So the Court of Directors annulled the treaty; but the king was never informed of the total abrogation of the treaty, even when the Governor-General came here, and was well pleased with a right royal reception. The intervention-policy was of course retained, even after many signal failures.*

*How British influence was appreciated by the people and the sovereign and what results were produced by it, may be shown by a few quotations from the highest authorities "The misfortunes of Oudh may be said to have commenced from that time, previous to which, we have Lord Cornwallis's own testimony, that this country was in a flourishing condition, and that it declined from the moment of direct interference by the English." *Shore*, 1835. "There is no estate in India, with whose Government we have interfered so systematically and so uselessly, as with that of Oudh. But this interference has been more in favor of men than measures...........There does not seem to be one measure, calculated to produce any lasting benefit to the people of Oudh." *Major Sutherland*, 1833. "*The authority of the native Government is greatly injured, and no general good is effected by our remonstrances. Such at least* has been the effect heretofore of interference of that nature during *the last three reigns*." Colonel J. Low's *Report*, dated 15th July, 1841. "British interference with that province (Oudh) has been as prejudicial to its court and people as it has been disgraceful to the British name......... It is the system that is defective, not the tools with which it has been worked. We have tried every variety of interference. We have interfered directly, and we have interfered indirectly, by omission as well as commission ;—but it has invariably failed. Our great error has been our interference in trifles... Another crying evil has been the want of any recognized system of policy in our negotiation with the Lucknow Court.........Every thing seems to have been mere guess-work and experiment." Sir Henry Lawrence. 1845. *Calcutta Gazette*.

A famine appeared at this time, which almost unsettled the collection of revenue. The King, being very old and sickly, and consequently unable personally to see and direct all the departments of his government, sent for Hakim Mehdi, the ablest minister Oudh ever had. The Hakim Saheb, entitled Montazim-ud-dowlah, returned again from Furruckhabad, and for the third time assumed the reins of Government, and restored everything to order and economy. But before he could mature his plans, death overtook the old minister, six months after his nomination. He was a man of great ability and intelligence; and his liberality was known throughout the province. He assisted and invited the oppressed Cashmirees (Mosulmans) to come down and settle at Lucknow;—and thus encouraged the local *shawl* industry. Lord Hastings noticed his able administration, of Gondah-Bahraitch as Nazim, when he made a journey in 1818, from the Oudh capital to Gorukhpore. Had the Hakim lived longer, or had he had time enough, in the last two reigns, to mature his system of administration, Oudh would never have been annexed, nor would its so-called chronic misrule have ever been heard of.

Monowar-ud-dowlah, the nephew of the late minister, succeeded to the vacant post; but though well-intentioned and free from corruption, he was not equal to his uncle, either in his capacity for work or in tact in transacting business. He was rather indolent, and pursued the general routine, laid down by Hakim Mehdi, and thus threw the whole burden of affairs on his able assistant. But the old king, himself possessing vast information, judgment, and knowledge of business, as Lord Aukland observed, the state of his kingdom was greatly improved. "He ameliorated the condition of the agriculturists, introduced reforms in the police, judicial and financial departments, encouraged commerce, constructed public works of great utility............and filled the exhausted coffers of his treasury." (Captain Bird). He also lent many lakhs of Rupees to the Company and otherwise assisted it, while involved in troubles in Afganistan.

Latterly Monowar-ud-dowlah resigned and went on a pilgrimage to Mecca. The King reverting to the old policy of the heir-apparent being made the nominal minister with an able and executive assistant, and the second son as "General Saheb" or Commander-in-chief of Oudh, as instituted by Saadut Ali, his father, he appointed Sooryia Jah as premier and Shurf-ud-dowlah as his Naib. But the two ministers generally lived on terms of misunderstanding with each other ; and public affairs were hampered in no small degree. But the King and the Resident neutralized their quarrels; and the Oudh Government was on the whole successfully conducted.

Thus after a reign of 5 years, the old King died on 7th June, 1842. He was a sovereign of great ability and experience; and his steady habits of business and his regularity in the payment of all his establishments endeared him to all his officers and servants.

AMJAD ALI SHAH (1842-1847).

Amjad Ali Shah, his son, succeeded. He followed the path of his father, and, though assiduously engaged in his duties, did not introduce any reforms into his administration. "Like his ancestors, he did all in his power to conciliate and secure the friendship and support of the British Government." (*Major Bird*). The only measure of improvement in his reign was the organization of the Oudh Frontier Police, costing Rs. 77,000 a year, which was placed under the direction of the Resident and his officers. Sundry other institutions were kept for the benefit of the Europeans at an yearly cost of Rs. 47,000. But the condition of the several districts became manifestly bad, owing to his marked inferiority to his father, both in natural talents and in knowledge of business.

After the conclusion of the Cabul war, Lord Ellenborough, not being satisfied with the manner in which the King was "going on," appointed General Nott as Envoy Extraordinary to the Court of Oudh. His Excellency, the General, came and faithfully discharged his duties, which were chiefly in connection with the payment of pensions to guaranteed families, complaints of Sepoys, apprehension and trial of Thugs and Dacoits, general advice to the King, settlement of boundary questions, and providing supplies for the Company's troops. In all these matters, the Oudh Durbar co-operated more willingly and efficiently than any other native Government; and the King was so much pleased with the suavity of the envoy, that a personal friendship sprang up between them.

Rajah Darshan Sing, the able and *Zabardust* Názim of Baiswara and Bahraich, in his over-eagerness to serve his royal master, went unasked to the Nepal territory to chastise the Rajah of Balrampore, who had fled there without paying the government dues. Thereupon the Durbar of Katmandu took offence and collected an army on the northern frontier, in order that, unless timely satisfaction should be given, Oudh might be promptly invaded, and its government chastised. On this, General Nott was authorised to prepare for the crisis ; and he was on the point of posting troops at Bahraich, Sikrora, Fyzabad, and Sultanpur with a strong body of reserve at Nawabganj, when, on the dismissal and banishment of the offending Názim, the Goorkhas were satisfied and the danger was averted.

His health declining, General Nott retired; and Colonel Richmond became the next Resident. He co-operated and assisted, with his advices the Oudh Government. He understood the feelings and the wants of the Durbar and the people, and conducted his duties accordingly. He was not like the unsympathetic Colonel Baillie and his class. When the Punjab war broke out, the Durbar cordially assisted the British Government with men and money; and Amin-ud-dowlah, the then prime minister, was publicly thanked for his services.

The King was strictly religious and wanted to reform his creed and society, which was now mixed up with Hinduism, according to the custom and manners of the primitive Mosulmans. He prohibited the faithful followers of Mahomed from buying articles of family-use and daily consumption from the Hindoo shop-keepers—thus putting all to great inconvenience and hardship. Mahomedans were compelled to become grain-dealers &c., after the manner of the Banias. Many of the Hindus thereupon embraced the State religion or were thrown out of their Government-service. Jagannath Bania was converted into Mahomedanism, titled Shurf-ud-uowlah, and though illiterate became an assistant minister. The high priest became all powerful in matters of State; and the King had his peace of mind, owing to his orthodox-mania, while the condition of his subjects considerably deteriorated.

The Resident calling the attention of the King to the bad state of his affairs, Manawar-ud-dowlah was re-appointed as a prime minister. He recalled Darshan Sing from his banishment and made him Inspector.

General, a new office, with a view to thoroughly reform and remodel all the departments of the administration.* But before this plan could be carried into execution, the Raja suddenly died; and the one able man of the time being gone, the work of thorough revision could not be completed.

Thus after an unimportant and uneventful reign of 5 years, Amjad Ali Shah died of a carbuncle on the 13th February, 1847. Though of an amiable character, which won him golden opinions from the people and foreigners,† yet he failed to effect administrative improvement; because of his inferiority to his father, both in capacity and experience, and of his antiquated orthodoxy, by which the old-fashioned priests influenced his mind into a narrower sphere of action. He had a liking for literature and translated Lord Brougham's treatise on Science, for the benefit of his subjects; for which the English author thanked his Majesty through Lord Ellenborough, and presented another treatise on Political Economy to be translated.

The legitimate claim of his eldest son, Mustafa-Ali-Khan Hyder, was set aside by *Zenana* intrigues. He was proclaimed a mad man, and was confined in a retired place. He was, however, a man of great gravity, determination and judgment. Had he become king, he would have proved a second Gazi-ud-din in principles and practice, and the annexation of the kingdom would have been delayed, if not averted.

WAJID ALI SHAH (1847-1856).

Wajid Ali Shah, the second son of the late king, ascended the throne, amidst volleys of cannon, songs of dancing girls, and acclamation of the people. The day after the coronation, His Majesty went

---

* On 30th May, 1844, the king conferred on the Rajah full powers over all his dominions with orders to make a settlement of the land-revenue, at an increased rate, and bring all waste land into tillage; to seize all refractory barons, destroy all their forts ; to put down all disturbances and protect high roads; to invite all back, who had been driven off by oppression; to muster the troops and report on the efficiency of all departments; &c. &c..—in short to reform all abuses and make the Government of the country what the king and his minister thought it ought to be. Darshun Sing went to work heartily at his Herculean task after his wonted way. But he soon became ill, and retired to his residence at Fyzabad, where he died on the 26th of August, 1844,—leaving his three sons, Ramadhin, Rugbar Sing, and Man Sing to fight among themselves for his property. Ultimately Rugbar Sing became Nāzim of Gondah-Bahraich; while Man Sing that of Baiswarah. *Sleeman's journal in Oudh.*

†He was on the whole something like a man of business, was free from debt, had his establishments and charity, *Zakát*, always punctually paid up. *Sleeman.*

in state to the shrine of Hazrat Abbás to ask a blessing from the spirit of the saint therein buried. The grievances of the old and infirm, who came on his way, were immediately redressed; and thus with all the ardour of a young student, he auspiciously commenced his reign.

Shortly after, Lord Hardinge, while returning from the Punjab war, visited Lucknow, and at an interview with the new king, dilated on the so-called chronic misrule of Oudh,* and lectured him on the duties of a sovereign; adding that if even now his administration did not improve within the two years of grace now given, the kingdom was to be assumed and governed by the infallible Company.

So incited to redouble exertion by his own preconceived desire and the warning thus given, the new king engaged himself assiduously, day and night, in improving his affairs. The old-fashioned Amin-ud-dowlah was dismissed and a young promising minister, named Ali Naqi Khan, was appointed. All the offices and departments were reorganised and supervised.

In order to strike at the root of the disorder in his affairs, Wajid Ali Shah at first turned his attention to the Military Department, to remodel his army into a completely effective and compact body. He wished to disband some of the old regiments, and raise fresh ones

*The chronic misrule of Oudh has been so often heard that a historian must test it before accepting its truth. It is a well-known fact, that during Shujah-ud-dowlah's reign, the country was well governed and the people were happy. On the succession of Asuf-ud-dowlah, English interference was enforced, and the condition of Oudh deteriorated proportionately, as Warren Hastings himself admited in an official minute before he came here in 1784. Saadut Ali Khan, however, restored Oudh to its former state and prosperity, as all the writers of the day attest. "An air of comfort pervades the greater part of the city............The poorer class of natives seemingly enjoy a degree of liberty fully suitable to their condition; and if, in the exercise of it, they at times overstep the bounds of prudence, their licentiousness is quickly repressed by the just and dreaded power of every superior." Sketches of India in 1814, by an anonimous friend of Colonel Baillie. "The Marquis (of Hastings) assures the Nawab (Gazee-ud-din) of his unqualified approbation and satisfaction at witnessing the high state of cultivation, in which he found the country, as well as its increased population and at the happiness and comfort of His Excellency's subjects." 1st April 1818.

"From the period you ascended the throne, your Majesty (Mahomed Ali Sháh) has, in comparison with times past, greatly improved the kingdom." Lord Auckland, July 8th, 1839. "The Oudh rulers have been no worse than monarchs so situated usually are; indeed they have been better than might be expected........they have seldom been cruel and have never been false.................. Among her ministers have been found as able individuals as are usually to be found in the East. *Sir Henry Lawrence.*

instead, to whose instruction and discipline he was in the habit of personally attending. But a hint of the displeasure of the Supreme Government was conveyed to him; and he was compelled to desist from this act of organisation, and could not thus suppress the evils of that department.

After this unsuccessful proceeding, the King desired to reform his Civil Department. His Majesty wanted to experiment upon the English system of administration, by first introducing it into the frontier districts. For this purpose, he, with the concurrence of Colonel Richmond, the Resident, sent Major Bird, the Assistant Resident, to Mr Thomason, the Lieutenant-Governor, at Agra, who matured the proposed plan of renovation. But again the Calcutta Government withheld its sanction, and thus prevented the work of reformation being carried out. Bitterly did the king complain, "should I approve of the *Amànì*, they praise the *Ijàrah* settlement; and should I speak well of the Ijárah, they praise the *Amâni* management." Thus the doctors disagree, while the patient suffers accordingly.

In October, 1849, Lord Dalhousie, the new Governor-General, with his favorite annexation-mania, sent Colonel Sleeman here as Resident, to prepare the way for "the great changes," that were soon to "take place" That great detective of Thugs, with his keen penetration, soon found that chronic misrule, in the little kingdom, was as rampant as ever. So he immediately prepared for "active service" for the reconstruction of the internal adminstration of Oudh. He began to interfere, in the face of solemn engagements, with the *personnel* of the Durbar, with the due course of justice and the workings of other departments. He established a complete system of espionage, and turned the Residency into a Court of Appeal from the decisions of His Majesty's Judges.*

*The root of this evil was two, the loan-system, and the privilege Sepoys had to complain direct to the Resident, against their king and his officers. "Loans.........are generally discreditable to the borrowers; in Oudh they have been doubly prejudicial. Most of them have been compulsory, and they have been the means of perpetuating and immeasurably extending the guarantee-system. The interest of each loan, whether from Nawab, King, or Begum, has been settled on the connections and servants of the several parties lending the money, with provision in each case that the pensioner was to be protected by the British Government. Thus for the sake of temporary pecuniary relief, have we established and fostered a system, which must vitiate any Government,—and is doubly destructive to a Native State. At Lucknow for years the Resident held public Durbars, where the guaranteed attended and pleaded against their own sovereign or his servants. Thus were the Monarch and his subjects arrayed against each other: thus was the sovereign degraded in his own capital.

"........But a still greater evil exists to the present day. The guaranteed are hundreds; the *Privileged*

He did not stop here, but like Colonel Baillie, the tyrant, descended to abusive personalities, to annoy the king and his officers. Without referring to the royal authority, even as a matter of formality, he arbitrarily did whatever he liked. He once threatened to declare the king a *rebel*; because His Majesty objected to dismiss and banish Wassi Ali, his able assistant minister. To crown all, he made a tour of three months, in the kingdom, without even asking the formal permission of the sovereign to do so, at a great cost (3 lakhs) to the Durbar:—receiving petitions and pretended complaints on the most liberal scale; remitting taxes, and otherwise overruling the long-instituted authorities of the country. Thus, instead of establishing good order and organization, which was his duty, he "unhinged the whole social and political system of the state." The persecuted king had no peace of mind.

Wajid Ali Shah, thus baffled in the execution of his much cherished projects of reform, or even in the discharge of his traditional duties, was sad at heart, and brooding over his misfortune, fell sick and grew weak both in body and mind. In despair, he retired from the cares of state affairs, leaving Ali Naqi Khan, to look after them. The prime minister followed the old line of business as a safer course.* Colo-

---

are thousands. Every British Sepoy from the Oudh dominions, can, through his commanding officer, refer fiscal or judicial case to the Resident............... the plan works badly. Zemindars throughout the country will buy, beg, borrow, or steal the name of a British Sepoy, in the hope of their gaining attention to their petty claims ....We are indeed of opinion, that much as Oudh Government is molested and degraded by Sepoy's claims, true or false, the men themselves are rarely benefitted by the Resident's interference. Litigation is provoked; hopes are excited, and eventually the party, who would, if left to his own resources and the practices of the country, have arranged and compromised his quarrels, is led to his ruin." *Sir H. Lawrence.*

*Several experiments have been made of converting the contract into the *Amáni* system over extensive districts of Oudh; but the result has always been the same,—a falling off in the revenue, and disappointment to the Government and people. These experiments have been made at the earnest representation of the British Government and its Representative. Under Ghazee-ud-din, while Col. Baillie was Resident, the contract-system was converted into *Amáni* all over Oudh; but in two years, the attempt was given in despair, and then the whole country was given to contractors. Under Nasir-ud-din Hyder, while Hakim Mehdi was minister, and Mr. Maddock and Col. Low, Residents, a similar attempt was made on an extensive scale, but with the same results; in less than two years all that was *Amáni* was given to Contractors. Under Mohamed Ali Shah, the experiment was again made on an extensive scale, while Cols. Low and Caulfield were Residents. The minister, Shurf-ud-dowlah, to gratify them, made districts, yielding an annual revenue of 35 *lakhs* of Rs., *Amáni*, and did all in his power, to make the system work well. In two years he was superceded; but his successor, Amin-ud-dowlah did all he could to sustain the system. He was soon removed, and under his successor, (Ali Naqi Khan) the system soon became nominal, and then gave place openly to the old one of contract. *Major Bird.*

nel Sleeman wanted to get him especially dismissed, and Golam Yayea appointed in his place, as a willing instrument for the introduction of his proposed scheme of reforms for thoroughly reorganizing the kingdom by British administrators, with subordinate native officers, the surplus-revenue being left for the living of the nominal king and his Court.*

But the Governor-General intended otherwise;—he was determined to have the annexation of Oudh as the crowning piece of his administration. He recorded, "from the date of the treaty of 1801 to the present day,...... each successive ruler has passed his lifetime within the walls of his palace, or in the gardens round his capital, careful for nothing but the gratification of his individual passion." The king retorted in his *Reply* and *Da-*

---

* The scheme of British management, which Colonel Sleeman advocated, was to have a Board of Regency with the Resident as president, the members, of which the number should be three, being chosen from among the royal family, such as the brother of the king, known as the General Saheb, Mousan-ud-daulah and the heir-apparent. Each should have his respective duties,—one to be at the head of the revenue department, a second, at the head of the Judicial and Police. This board was to form a council to deliberate and decide about measures of legislation and administration. The Governor-General was to sanction all important measures, such as nomination and removal of members. Estimating the civil and fiscal expenditure at 22 lakhs, military, 26, families and dependants of former kings at 12 lakhs, house-hold of the present king at 15 lakhs, amounting to a total of 75 lakhs a year, there ought to be a surplus of at least 25 lakhs of a revenue of about a *crore.*

While on this subject. we might as well quote in what way Lord W. Bentinck, Col: Low and Sir Henry Lawrence wanted Oudh to be taken and governed. "Acting in the character of guardian and trustee, we ought to have an administration entirely native,—an administration so composed as to individuals, and so established upon the best principles, revenue and judicial, as should best serve for immediate improvements and as a model for future imitation; the only European part of it should be the functionary, by whom it should be superintended; and it should be only retained till a complete reform might be brought about, and a guarantee for its continuance obtained, either in the improved character of the reigning prince, or if incorrigible, in the substitution of his immediate heir, or in default of such substitute from nonage or incapacity by the nomination of one of the family as regent, the whole of the revenue being paid into the Oudh Treasury." *Lord William Bentinck.*

In taking the management of any part, we should deviate as little as possible from the old usages and forms. The general system of the native government, *in its theory,* is well suited to the genius and habits of the people of Oudh; *in practice* it often fails to produce good results, owing to the fewness of honest men in authority. *Colonel Low.*

Let the management of all be assumed under some such rules as those, which were laid down by Lord W. Bentinck. Let the administration of the country, as far as possible, be native. *Let not a Rupee come into the Company's coffers*.........Give as quickly as possible a light assesment for 5 years, fixed, as far as possible, by the people themselves; that is, let the one-and-quarter million (or there about) the country may be supposed able to bear, be sub-divided, in a great assembly of the people, among the five districts; and then let the districts, Pergunahs, and village-quotas similarly told of, under the eye of British Superintendent ....All cases (civil, police, and claims,) should be made over to *Punchayets,* superintended by the best men in the land...... *Sir Henry Lawrence*

Oudh ought to be under such a system a garden; the soil is finest in Oudh; so are the men; and there is no want of an educated class for civil office; on the contrary they abound almost as much as the class of soldiers. *Sleeman.*

coili in Excelcis, that the non-fulfilment of the treaties was caused, not by him or his ancestors, who had faithfully abided by them, but by the servants of the Company themselves; and that the administration and condition of Oudh were what they ought to be, nay better than those of the British dominions; adding "I had boxes for the reception of complaints and petitions in the public streets; and on referring to these petitions, I found that our long-established Courts of Justice was unimpeachable, and that justice was administered to the rich and the poor in conformity to the precepts of Mohamedan Law." But Lord Dalhousie was not moved; he wanted to have his favorite policy carried into execution, with a secrecy and obstinacy, peculiar to himself. On this, the conscience of the Resident was aroused. Protesting against this aggressive measure and prophesying a great rebellion as its natural consequence, he retired from the service and resigned in great disgust.*

General Outram succeeded him; and while he was preparing for the *coup-d'-etat* of annexation, without personally going into the facts of the case, the Hanuman-Gurhi affray took place at Aujodhya. A certain fanatical Moulvi, Amir Ali by name, with his Mohomedans, attacked the local Hindus for the possession of a sacred piece of ground. But by the tact of Rajah Man Sing, they were repulsed with great loss. And when the king's troops approached, they were completely dispersed. This event served as an additional proof, in showing the weakness and rotteness of the native Government; and it was so laid down in the final report of the General to the Supreme Gevernment, showing that there was no other cure for the chronic misrule of Oudh than its complete assump-

*The system of annexation, pursued by a party in this country and favoured by Lord Dalhousie and his Council, has, in my opinion, and in that of a large number of ablest men in India, a downward tendency,—a tendency to crush all the higher and middle classes connected with the land. These classes it should be our object to create, and foster, that we might in the end inspire them with a feeling of interest in the stability of our rule. *We shall find a few years hence the tables turned against us.* In fact, the aggressive and absorbing policy, which has done so much mischief of late in India, is beginning to create feelings of alarm in the native mind; and it is when the popular mind becomes agitated by such alarm, that fanatics are always found ready to step into paradise over the bodies of the most prominent of those, from which injury is apprehended. I shall have nothing now to do at Lucknow. Lord Dalhousie and I have different veiws, I fear. If he wishes anythng done that I do not think right and honest, I resign and leave it to be done by others. I desire a strict adherence to solemn engagements, whether made with white faces or black. We have no right to annex or confiscate Oudh; but we have a right, under the treaty of 1837, to take the management of it, but not appropriate its revenues to ourselves. We can do this with honor to our Government and benefit to the people. To confiscate would be dishonest and dishonorable. To annex would be to give to the people a government almost as bad as their own, if we put our screw upon them.........Were we to annex and confiscate Oudh or any part of it, our good name in India would suffer, and that good name is more valuable than a dozen of Oudhs. *Col: Sleeman.*

General Outram

Loot. Kaiser-bagh.- March 1858.

From S.P. Hall.

The Prince of Wales receiving the veterans of Lucknow.

P.C.M. 20.2.83.
Camp Kharowli.

tion and incorporation with the British dominions. *

The Resident then went to Calcutta, and maturing the plans of the new adminstration to be introduced, as directed by the Governor-General, returned to Lucknow. Sufficient troops having been brought on the pretence of an impending Nepal war, he, all on a sudden, gave only three days' notice of the deposition and annexation to the reigning family, on 3rd February, 1856; and as the Company's decree was irrevocable, Wajid Ali Shah ceased to reign from the 12th.

Though whole Oudh was indignant at the unjust greediness of the British Lion, and was about to engage in a death-struggle for its right to govern itself, the king suppressed the growing excitement, and yielded to the inexorable mandate of the Company. But refusing to sign the proferred treaty and to preserve his self-respect, he shortly after left Lucknow, amidst the tears of the people, with the object of proceeding to London to complain against the unjust spoliation of his kingdom. The black ocean, however, frightened him, and being sick, dropped down and settled in Calcutta; while his mother, brother, ("General Saheb"), and his son, the heir-apparent, continued the journey on a royal deputation to

* The question whether the masses of the people of Oudh, in whose interest we believed ourselves to be acting, really desired to be incorporated with the Company's dominions, seems scarcely to have been raised at all in the course of the discussion.........Had they been allowed a choice, it is almost certain that they would still have chosen to bear the ills they knew, rather than to be brought under the rigid, irresistible action of the bureaucracy of foreigners, whose ways were not as their ways, whose principles and motives were generally beyond their comprehension, and whose laws and regulations, though not intentionally unjust, appeared to be hemmed in by every species of pit-fall and mantrap, from which a plain man, however innocent and well-meaning, could hardly hope to escape. *Irwin's Garden of India*, 1880.

"The disposition of the natives of Oudh is generally deemed unfriendly to us: in reality, I fancy not more so than those of our own territories." The difference is that with the latter it is suppressed by fear; while with the former it is open. They "are ever ready to evince their animosity towards those, who, in erecting their own government, shook that of the faithful to the ground." *Sketches of India*, 1814.

With regard to the people's desire to be placed under the British Government, Captain Locket fairly put the question to them, when the Jamadar, joining his hands, said with great fervency, " miserable as we are, of all miseries, keep us from that." *Bishop Heber*, 1824.

So far from their entertaining any such feelings (sighing for the blessings of British rule), I can inform my readers, that in one part of the Doab, not many months ago, the people, farmers and peasantry, held quite a rejoicing, on hearing a report, that that part of the country was to be transferred to the king of Lucknow. *Shore*, 1835.

The subjects of his Majesty of Oudh are by no means desirous of participating in the blessings of British rule. They are a richer, sleeker, and merrier race than the natives in the territories of the Company. Mrs. Fane Parks' *Wanderings of a Pilgrim*, 1831.

What Colonel Law has written on the subject, has been quoted before.

the Queen and Parliament of England. There they were on the point of gaining their object, when the great rebellion, that broke out next year, arrested the attention of the British nation; and in the din of alternate disaster, glory, and ultimate success, their claims were drowned and forgotten. They vainly knocked at the door of justice, till their very lives were worn out; whilst here in Calcutta, the king was confined at Fort William with great hardship, on the Panic Sunday, 15th July, when the Council saw so many ghosts around, that oscillating between action and in-action, it finally stumbled on such a mean-deed.

At last in October, 1859, Wajid Ali Shah, quite in despair, accepted the 12 *lakhs'* pension, offered by the Company for his maintenance; and separate provision was also granted to his collateral relations. "He had been allowed to retain the title of the king of Oudh, (a poor consolation and mockery of the term); but on his death, the title will cease absolutely; and the pecuniary allowance will not be continued on its present scale.........The king has been allowed no jurisdiction within his estate, but provision has been made for serving legal processes within its precincts through the officer, who is appointed as Agent with his Majesty on the part of the British Government. In March, 1862, an act was passed to exempt the king from the jurisdiction of the criminal courts, except for capital offences; to provide for his trial, if necessary, by commission, to exempt him from appearance as a witness in any court, and provide for his examination through the Agent to the Governor-General." *Atkinson's Treaties.*

Verily how is the great fallen! The king now smooths over his misfortune and hard-fate, by cultivating literature, poetry, and such cognate arts. As he is politically dead, impartial judgment may be now passed as to his high mental culture, liberal views, and kind-heartedness. His great active powers being thoroughly fettered as to his sovereign-duties, he was, as a natural consequence, compelled to feed his mind socially in the company of singers, dancers, Begums, and other professors of the fine arts. This taste he got and orientalized from the common practices of the British officials in the ball-room and theatre. Oudh has the fondest recollection of His Majesty; for the last is most remembered.

CHAPTER II.

Introduction of the Company's Rule and the consequent great Rebellion.

Meantime the Honorable East India Company reigns supreme over the land. Iron-rule succeeds that of silver. All establishments are dispensed with; armies are disbanded; native Offices are abolished. Much of the private property of the king and nobles is confiscated and sold at auction, at nominal prices. Many private palaces were appropriated; and the royal Begums were turned out, with insults, from the *Chhatter Munzil.* * The late native officials were arrested and were put under surveillance; and allowances, pensions and pay were atonce stopped.

Local custom and laws were trampled under foot. Foreign codification, with her constant companions, ignorance and over-taxation, reigns supreme; while the Dead Level School is in full swing. The foundations of property are relegated to primeval chaos; and it is not known who are the landlords and who the cultivators, with both of whom the new functionaries agree as little as among themselves. Wholesale demolitions of buildings, even religious, the so-called improvements in the city, are indulged in "too fast and too roughly;" and Bazaars and squares are levelled and cleared at pleasure; while the haughtiness, ill-breeding, and threatening language of the new rulers offend and insult all. *Kaye and Sir H. Lawrence.*

The nobles and Talukdars, civil servants and soldiers, artizans and citizens,—all equally suffer. Food and articles of daily use grow very high in price, as taxes increase in number. Suddenly tens of thousands began to rove about without employment or hope of subsistence. Families have to starve for days together, before a morsel of bread can be found or earned. Many commit suicide; many more sell their trinkets and ornaments; and not a few, their morality, and

*As a reward of such attachment and devotedness, and as a proof of the justice of your rule and Government, my property, movable and immovable, has been seized and confiscated, my palaces razed to the ground, and their rich furnitures and appointments destroyed. Never have you inflicted on your enemies, or upon those even, who have rebelled against your authority, such severity of punishment, such degradation and dishonour, as that with which you have visited my family, my relatives and dependants. *King's Complaints.*

their women their chastity, to drag their miserable existence along. And as the spirit of wine is triumphant, and the Excise-Department is luxuriant with many a temptation and allurement, vices and lies increase unchecked. "Families which had never been outside the Zenana, used to go out at night, and beg their bread" *Gubbins and Rees.*

So, discontents and complaints increased day by day. But redress and reliefs were not forth-coming. The delay, intricacy, and costliness of the new law, trouble the people. And to crown all, slow famine overtakes the mass, and imperceptibly carries away thousands. Thus even the passive portion of society is infected with dissatisfaction. All then wait patiently to make common cause in a revolution towards native rule. Lord Dalhousie's pet administration fails as completely, as those of Colonel Baillie and the officious friends of Asuf-ud-dowlah.*

Well those were the last days of the Company's existence; and as it happens in doting old age, it lost its reason, not only politically and militarily, but in the civil department as well. It dared to trample on the social and religious principles of the people. So the fuel of anger was added to the fire of discontent. The people recoiled from their loyalty and became patriotic to their own interests. They intrigued, united, and were confident of success. The *chapàti*, the lotus, and the impure greased cartridge gave the signal for explosion. Immediately (in June, 1857) the Sepoys break out; the disaffected chiefs join them; and the poverty-stricken people follow them. Every one unites in the common cause, forgets reciprocal enmity, and finds a good means of retribution for numerous and conflicting grievances. †

---

* What Hon'ble Shore predicted in 1833, happened in 1856, " No sooner have we taken possession, than at one blow, we have annihilated every existing establishment, whether for the administration of revenue, or of civil and criminal justice; we have pronounced the natives, in the mass, to be corrupt and incapable. and dismissed them all from their situations—however respectable and however qualified they might be to discharge their duties with fidelity and efficiency. In the attempt to supply their places by English agency, we have usually appointed about one-third of the officers required. Our next step has been to raise the taxes to a much greater height than was ever done by their own government; the larger land-holders, who possessed establishments of servants, elephants, and horses, being especially marked for plunder;.........and this course has been persisted in until we have succeeded in reducing almost all the landed proprietors.........to a happy equality of pauperism. They may now rest contendedly, *Qui procumbit humi, non habat unde cadat*"

† The Mutiny broke out at Lucknow, on 30th May; Seetapore 3rd June, Mulloan, 4th; Mohumdee and Fyzabad on 8th; Sultanpore and Dariabad on 9th; and Salone, Secrora and Gonda on the 10th June.

The Christians are rudely awakened from their sound sleep, and quite taken unawares. They fly into places of refuge; some succeed, while others fail, and are caught, imprisoned and slaughtered with innocent babes, and women,—as if their enemy or their future punishment, the rebels think, would cease by the massacre of a few fugitives. Then the storm-wave, with accumulated force from Fyzabad and Nawabgunge, rushes towards the devoted city, under Moulvi Ahmed Ullah Shah, and Meer Barkut Ahmed.

On the morning of 30th June, Lawrence Bahadur, who has come in last April, too late to resist or suppress the rising torrent, launches a little army towards Chinhut. It makes a good dash on the enemy, who, however, outflanks it by the Aligunge division. So it disastrously retreats, and with great difficulty, finds a secure asylum within the temporary stockade of the Residency. To chase the fugitives, to surround the *Baillie Guard*, to open fire on it from all sides, and to plunder the city, are the work of an instant for the now ubiquitous enemy.

Then the rebel-chiefs organize a constitutional government under that of Delhi; and Saliman Kader declining, Brigis Kader, a son of the Exking, aged about 10 years, is forcibly made *Nawab-Vizier*.—not king —of Oudh, with Huzrut Mahal, his mother, as regent, with little boys as body-guard, Sharf-ud-dowlah as Vizier, Maharajah Balkishen as financial minister, Hisham-ud-dowlah as Commander in Chief, and Mummoo Khan as *Naib*. Monawar-ud-dowlah was imprisoned, because he refused to become the prime minister of the rebel government; and so he was looked upon as a spy of the now accursed Company. *Chuckladars* and other officials were appointed according to the old native system. The *Durbar* then sent out orders to the *Rajwarha* to come in with their allegiance and militia. The mint was re-established; and from the royal furniture and ornaments, silver and gold were extracted and coined as money. A common foundry was erected, and old guns were repaired; while gun powder, shot and all else were manufactured on every side. The Commissariat Department is looked after in right earnest, and troops are enlisted on a prodigious scale; while the Pandays, Sepoys, and Badmashes rule the day.

Thus prepared and organaized, the Durbar adapts an aggressive policy. Mehdi Hussein is appointed Nazim of Gorakhpore, which he occupies with a large force. Rajah Jeya Lal, the *Nawab-maker* of the day, and son of old Galib Gunj, is commissioned to rule over Azimgurh and Jounpore; and another big fellow is despatched to invade Allahabad and old Kurrah. Rajah Koer Singh of Jugdespore and Rani Luchmi Bái of Jhansi are complimented on their success. Nana Saheb is confirmed in his post at Cawnpore; though shortly after, a controversy arises; for the Maharajah maintains his right as Peshwa of the old Mahratta empire; while the Oudh government acknowledge him no more than a great Nazim of the Doab. Khan Bahadur of Bareilli was also confirmed in his governorship of Rohilkund; and mutual advice as to future action is taken and given. An ambassador is then sent with presents to the momentory emperor of Delhi, for whom the western Doab is reserved and not invaded. And last of all, Nepal was applied to for aid.

These done, the Darbar looks to the Baillie guard, where the British flag still waves majestically and defiantly. The bombardment then gets warmer and well-sustained, though pointed too high to be effective. New batteries (*Moorchas*) are erected; and all the surrounding houses are loopholed for musketry-fire; while the Negro-ghosts, on the tops of Johannes-house and the Clock-Tower endanger the interior communication of the garrison. Sir Henry Lawrence gets mortally wounded; Major Banks killed; and many others meet untimely-death. The women, children, and other non-combatant inmates were thrown into utter confusion and consternation; for roofs, walls, and all are thrown down, one by one, causing horrid exposure. They fly into underground rooms and the Begum-kothi for greater safety.

But the military stood firm; for pure British blood ran in their veins;—that blood, which had persevered and at last conquered Napoleon the Great. No fire, however intense, could subdue, much less destroy them; for Vulcan is their ever-obedient slave. No mining could extinguish them; for their counter-mining was a more effective reply. No bayonet charge could dislodge them; for British bayonet charges are celebrated throughout the world.

Days pass on; the enemy cannot make any impression. At last the Begum Queen reproaches her *Sirdars*: "ye wretches that plunder the city and destroy my people; ye that trample the weak and fly from the strong, and ye clamour for pay and reward? How can I pay, when the

Treasury is within the Baillie guard ? How can I promote you, when the British flag flies triumphant over the Residency ? How can I reward you, when the enemy is as fear-striking as a lion in his den ? And yet ye brag and boast, ye murderers of innocent babes, killers of unresisting women, and massacre-agents of the weak fugitives and prisoners. Shame and thousand times curses upon ye, that have made the *Moorchas* your sleeping houses; while my brave soldiers die unsupported. Go away, ye barking dogs, and do not show your black faces, until better deeds prove that ye are men."

Thus shame-ridden, the *Sirdars* go out of the Durbar-hall, levy contributions on the city, and roll in luxury and debauchery at night; of course, they mean business for the morrow. They rise late in the morning, drink *bhang*, leisurely advance towards their respective posts, and bawl out from a safe distance, to encourage their men: " *Chalo Bahadurs*, advance ye brave; storm that Residency, Gubbins' bastion, the gate, the Redan, and all. To die there, is to have at once paradise with *houries* and ever-lasting happiness; and to win, is to be the lords of riches and fine *Jageers* and what not." The Bahadurs yell and advance; some redhot balls however appear to receive them; and the brave run back most cowardly. The Sirdars shout again, *Chalo Bahadurs;* but the brave have not the heart to advance, for the place is too hot for them. And thus this day's work and duty are done.

On the 20th of July, however, the enemy, under the personal direction of the Moulvi and Begum, make a supreme effort; and the momentum of attack is delivered. All their batteries vomit forth shells; their mines explode furiously; and their loop-hole firing is tremendous. They now advance in close columns. Gubbin's bastion is reached, and ladders are applied to the walls. The foremost and forlorn-hope ascend the parapet and are immediately shot down. The Redan and the gate have their share of the attack; and the other posts are not free from trouble. The enemy think themselves victorious ;—the Hindoos yell the war-cry "Jay Mohadeoki," the Mohamedans, "Allah ho Akbar". But the garrison within does not despair. They collect and defend their positions most manfully. Hand-granades make fearful execution. Some timely sallies and opportune bayonet-charges quail the enemy and break their compact formation. They retreat, fly, and melt into straggling parties, and out of pure despair, pour out a flood of abusive curses on the *Gorah* and the *Firingee.*

Thus gloriously did the garrison pass three months. But meanwhile there are great sufferings and diseases within. Cholera with plague of flies reigns supreme. The groans of the sick and wounded, the cries of the children, bereft of their mothers, the sobs of young beauties, suddenly deprived of their sweethearts, and the sighs of the ladies, who have lost their husbands, make and raise an awful hum, which deadens the heart of all. "Help, help, help;"—no help appears. "Relief, relief, relief;—ah, when will it come?" "Oh, it will come to-morrow or the day after." But alas, the hope of relief recedes into ever to-morrow or the day after!

At last, on the memorable 25th of September, as day dawns, they hear a faint sound of cannon-firing towards Alambagh. "Oh, the Relieving Force is coming, and we are saved." "And see through field-glass with what majesty British soldiers fight." Now they storm the Charbagh bridge; now they spring on their right flank, and seize the Choupera; now they slowly advance *via* Shah Najaf road, and gain space. "But those iron-hearted Highlanders, where are they gone?" Oh, they have lost their way. But lo! they make amends; they rush in direct through Huzrutgunge and Chhutter Munzil palaces, amidst the rain of fire, balls, and bullets; and though behind all, they reach Baillie Guard,—the first of the reinforcement, with two heroes, in the person of Outram and Havelock. A cheer greets them, that comes from the inmost heart.

Occupying Chhutter Munzil, the victory-inflated garrison makes ardent consultation for the capture of the city. The rebels, however, though at first panic-struck, take heart again, and pour in iron-fire all around; for now Nana Rao of Bithoor is among them. The rear-guard of reinforcement suffers tremendously; while provision, transports and amunition are all lost. The Doolies with the wounded are abandoned in the fatal courtyard of the Khas Bazaar. A party become fugitives in a side-room, and bravely maintain their position for two days. And General Neil meets a glorious death at the Tiger gate. If man is to die, that is the happiest moment of his, when he expires in the triumphal performance of his duty. His soul then sleeps serene.

The garrison again finds itself confined and couped up. Their difficulties again increase. Rations are reduced; their hunger is not satisfied by any means. Their clothing is as dirty as before, and every thing is filthy and of bad smell in the extreme. The gossippers cannot indulge in their talk; the gluttons in their greed; and the fashionable in their show. No news can they get from the outside world, except through the semaphore signal and a very few successful *cossids* (spies) chiefly Ongod. All, however, patiently wait on; but Kavanagh under the guidance of Kanoji Lal, assuming the garb of a *badmash*, crosses the Goomtee, enters Mutchibhawan by the Stone-bridge, penetrates the *Chouk* and safely passes out the Akbari gate. Missing the way, however, he makes a long detour, crosses the *Canal* by the Hosseingunge bridge, and successfully joins Sir Colin Campbell, who has already advanced to Bunni Banthura, and to whom he communicates the plans of relief of the city, and his local experience.

The Commander-in-Chief then marches hitherward, and takes Dilkhosha and Constantia. As he advances, the enemy retreats. But the Sikhs and Sepoys stand faithful to their position and offer a stubborn resistance at Seconderbagh. The fortified garden is however breached and stormed. A hand-to-hand fight ensues; and the devoted garrison dies a soldier's death. Only about 400 escape by the northern gate. Then the Shah Najaf is attacked; but the assailants are repulsed. The Naval and the Royal marines open a tremendous bombardment for hours together; but to no purpose. The rebels manfully maintain their position, and many times repulse the storming party. The Sepoys fight capitally when under cover. Their musketry fire tells dreadfully and with deadly effect. At last Campbell gets furious and harangues his army;—"Highlanders and Royals, British soldiers and sons of England! The prestige of our arms is celebrated throughout the world. Your ancestors fought bravely in the Peninsular War, and covered themselves with glory on the ever-memorable fields of Waterloo. Ye yourselves fought gloriously with me in the Crimea; and the impregnable ramparts of Sebastople could not withstand our irresistible storm. China and Persia, Cabul and Burmah, Punjab, and Nepal felt our power; Mooltan and Gwalior, Seringapatam and Bhurtpore, Malown and Delhi and other impregnable strongholds yielded to our charge, as though made of paper-walls. And now you allow the same great prestige to fall down and resolve into nothingness, before a common brick-wall? Nay, advance again;—mother England expects her sons to do their duty; and victory will follow as our natural legacy."

The excited Highlanders and all again advance and make a supreme effort; but again they meet with a stern repulse. At last rocket-fire is resorted to, which penetrates and searches every covered creek and corner of the position; and the garrison imperceptibly evacuates the tomb, at the first fall of darkness. Then the Sikhs and Highlanders capture the empty place by one climbing a neighbouring tree, and the other breaching or sapping an old fissure in the back-wall. Next morning the almost defenceless position of Khurshed Munzil is cannonaded, and though evacuated by the enemy, the victors have not the heart,—after the hard lesson of yesterday,—to occupy it, but after full three hours' bombardment. Then Moti Mohul is occupied after some hours' shelling;—when, on 22nd September, four heroes, Campbell and Grant, Outram and Havelock meet on the ground of their glory, to hold mutual congratulation on the memorable event of the *Relief of Lucknow.*

Then the pent up garrison is extricated and makes a safe retreat in the darkness of the night. Many, chiefly Gubbins Bahadur, (the Financial Commissioner), remonstrate against such a retrogade movement; adding, that "we should conquer the city, inflict on it retributive justice; and should not leave hold of our position, of which we have made so much good". The Commander-in-Chief replies, "dont you know that this kingdom has been taken most illegally and unjustly? It should be restored to its rightful ruler." Thus saying, he continues the retreat, eaving, however, a little army under Outram at Alambagh.

Meantime the Begum, Penthiselia-like, stands undismayed on the ramparts of Kaiserbagh, and sees with despair her Sepoys flying westward, while her enemy is retreating leisurely eastward. She gets furious, not as much caring for the *Feringees*, that are going off, which is a matter of pleasure to her, but the treasures, that are being taken away. She however loses not her heart; and crying shame and pouring a flood of abuse on her coward army, after the fashion of women, personally encourages, by her example, those, who remain faithful to their duties at the *China-Basaar* Moorchas. By her own hands, she rewards the gunners, there and then, at the rate of Rupees 5 for each round, in order to stop the exit of the enemy, or at least to retake the treasure. But her antagonists retreated safely all the same; for a great mass of locusts cannot be prevented in its movements by the pelting of a few stones.

The rebel Government of Lucknow now began to assume a more settled aspect. The martial law of the Sepoys was now over; and no more complaints of robbery, outrage, and plunder were heard. The people resumed their usual jovial way of living. They forgot their past sufferings; neither did they care for the coming dire storm. They had their wished-for happiness and fool's paradise for the time. Prince Feroze Shah of Dehli came here as a fugitive, and was received with honor and respect, by the Durbar, who thus got an accession of strength. Occasionally an army of monkey-mouthed Bahadurs went out and attacked the Alambagh position, but were well handled and repulsed; and the *Hanuman* heroes had their reward of desperate rashness either in death or in imprisonment, to be laughed at and spat upon by the unfeeling *Sikhs* and infidel *Gorahs*. The Begum and the Moulvi, who had personally directed the movements of attack, saved their lives by a timely retreat.

But a civil dissension had sprung up between the Begum and the Moulvi, respectively the peace-party, and the war-party. The former wanted to conclude the war by an honorable peace, and to retire from the troubles of political life on a pension for her son; making over the Government of Oudh to the English to conduct as they might think proper. But the latter advocated the prosecution of the war to the knife and to its bitter end, before he would yield an inch of ground of the faithful to the infidel. Not only that, he entertained the ambition to become independent king of Oudh, and if possible, of Hindustan. He pretended and proclaimed himself to be a prince of the Carnatic, though many knew here, that he was of very humble origin from a poor old Moulvi of Gopamow, who had been tutor to the Nawab of Arcot. The rebel Sepoys sided with him; for he lived a very simple life, and had winning manners; while the old soldiers of the late dynasty and the *Rajwarha* were with the Queen. She, however, getting disheartened at so many reverses, sent overtures of peace, through Rajah Man Singh, to Outram. The General declined to enter on her terms. Had her application for submission been favorably received, and peace amicably settled, much subsequent bloodshed and troubles, suffered by the people of Oudh, would have been saved; and both the conqueror and the conquered would have been happier, the former for his good name, and the latter for their loyalty.

No sooner had she heard that her terms had been rejected, than Hazrat Mahal, with the firm determination of a Semiramis, gave order to continue the war, made up her quarrels with the Moulvi, and made further preparations for resistance. All the palaces and Emambarhas were fortified; trenches were dug across every road, at every turn, especially those of Aminabad, Hossaingung, and Huzratgung; and three lines of defence were raised by enormous labour, along the Canal, by the side of the Begum Kothie and the Khurshed Munzil, and Kaiserbagh. And to encourage her men, the Queen, riding on an elephant, personally superintended the rapid prosecution of the work; while the fanatic priests and *Faqirs* harangued the people and soldiers on the duty of their killing the Kaffirs and on the grievances they had suffered from the *Feringees*. And to crown their united efforts, Moulvi Ahmed Ullah, (otherwise called Dunkah Shah, because a drum was always beaten before him,) by a series of very skilful manœuvres, that bespoke a great general, attacked Alambagh from three sides, all at the same time in the night, and would have succeeded, but for the timely warning, conveyed by the spies to the garrison.

At last, on the 2nd of March, 1858, Sir Colin Campbell, after beating out Nana Saheb and the Gwalior contingent, from Cawnpore, and collecting an army with a capital seize-train, advances into Oudh, and relieving Outram at the Alambagh, sits before the devoted city with his head-quarters at Dilkhosha. He now beseiges Lucknow on three sides, with Outram on the right wing, and Jung Bahadur of Nepal on the left. Outram crosses the Goomtee by two temporary bridges near *Welaitibagh;* and though opposed by the Moulvi and the L'Martiniere battery, marches on triumphantly. But the *Gazees,* about half a dozen in number, from the *Chackerwali Kothi,* check his progress, and inflict a severe loss on the attacking party. The house is bombarded for several hours, and is then stormed by the Sikhs. With the greatest difficulty, one survivor only of the few foes was brought out of the dreaded rooms, put to tortures and burnt alive, most cruelly. The General now again advances, occupies the Padshahbagh, and pursues the enemy beyond his strength and so suffers. He then retraces his steps, stops, and finally settles at the *Iron Bridge,* the opposite end of which the enemy holds most tenaciously. Now his line of batteries of about four miles, vomit forth fire and balls, such as has never been seen before. Vertical and oblique, round and flanking, straight and cross—these direct and indirect fires tax to the utmost the tactical powers of the Panday and Pathan, Moulvi and Mogul. Red hot balls come from all sides and explode everywhere, while another great fire of four miles, from the Canal side, keeps up the front hotly engaged. The enemy, in short, is under double fire and is in a dilemma.

Lord Clyde then orders his centre to advance; and the Martiniere, which has been hitherto troubling the head-quarters with its inestinguishable battery, is stormed and occupied. Gradually, the canal line of defence is broken through, and *Hyat Buksh* is reached. The enemy makes a stout resistence at the *Begum Kothi.* But a tremendons bombardment, breach, and a heavy storm, expel the defenders from their position with great loss. The intervening buildings are now sapped through, and the *Chhota Emambarah* is captured. The *Kaiserbagh,* the strong citadel of the city, is now approached and occupied from two points. And Goorkhas, Panjabies, and British soldiers and officers are drunk with plunder.

The Sepoys retreat and fly westward; and the citizens follow them. The city is now almost deserted by all, but some desperadoes, who lingered behind to protect and die for their home and family. Feroze Shah, attacking Walpole's position, retreats towards Seetapore. The exasperated Moulvi delivers a last attack upon the Alambagh, to cut off the besiegers' communications. But Jung Bahadur comes to their aid, repulses, and pursues him through the intricate streets and lanes and saves two English ladies. The Begum, with her son, flies on a palanquin, and occupies *Moosa bagh*; while the Moulvi leaves *Aga Meer ka Serai,* his head-quarters at the last moment, and fortifies *Huzrut Abbas ka Dirgah,* where he murders Shurf ud-dowlah, on the suspicion of his being an English spy.

Then were seen dismal scenes, the like of which were not known before. Many *Kahars* ran away for fear of their lives, after throwing away some silvery palanquin with fair helpless occupants. Many a charming Begum, with dishevelled hair and disordered garments, fled away in utmost fright; they, who never knew how to walk in the light of day, and expose themselves to the rude gaze of men. They throw away their jewelled ornaments in order to lesson their physical burden, or to escape the notice of the brutal plunderers, but in vain. Many a mother loses her dear sons and daughters on the way. In short, the awful incidents of that universal flight might be better imagined than described.

Meanwhile Outram came across by the Seconderbagh bridges, smarting on the check given by Lord Clyde, that he was not allowed to participate in the first glory of the capture of the city. The now ruined Residency was occupied, and the Engine-House massacre took place. Then the flood of occupation streams on in the streets and houses; the *Emambarha* is reached. Here and there, now and then, some isolated defenders, determined to die for their hearths and homes, fight and fall gloriously : while a few desperate fanatics make an unnoticed Thermopylœ in the coners of the streets and side lanes, and meet a martyr's death. Many of the non-combatants, women children not even excepted, who had lingered in their ancient home, were cruelly killed or maltreated, and their property most greedly plundered. Many committed suicide to escape dishonor, or fall into wells.*

Who can estimate the amount of rich *loot* the soldiers and all got in those days ? The reported vast hordes of Lucknow disappeared in a day. Those very rare and valuable articles, which could not be carried away conveniently, such as pictures, mirrors, chandeliers, costly furniture, statues, were all broken down or smashed to pieces, in a spirit of wantonness, never known before, when one Asiatic warred with another.

The rebels now intended to retake the city by combined and concentrated movements, with Rana Beni Madho attacking it on the south; Rajah Debi Bukhsh on the north-east, and the Begum and the Moulvi, on the west, from their fortified places at Moosabagh and Huzrat Abbas. But the scheme failed completely because of its impracticability. The Rana and the Rajah could not appear in proper time; and so Huzrat Mahal and Ahmed Ullah Shah, fearing their retreat to be intercepted, retired from their respective positions, to Bari and Boondi, after repulsing the storming parties of the enemy. By the 20th of March, the whole city came under British rule.

Then the gang of the prize-agents spread over the city, now depopulated, and *loot* out the already plundered houses; while the Engineers are busy demolishing the private buildings of the citizens from one end to the other : and Chandni Chouk, Smilegung, Golagung and other *Mohallahs*, disappear from the map. Military positions are strongly held at Muchibhawan, the Iron-Bridge-head, Baillie Guard and the fortified palaces. In short, the autho-

---

* Horrid sights encountered me, as we returned towards our camp. An old *fakir*, whom we had saved, was lying with his brains out. Many dead bodies which we had not noticed at first are now lying in the streets. After the Fusiliers had gone to the gateway (of tho great Emambarah), a Cashmeri boy came towards the post, leading a blind and aged man, and throwing himself at the feet of an officer, asked for protection. That officer,... ..drew his revolver and snapped it at the wretched suppliant's head. The men cried "shame" upon him. Again he pulled the trigger—again the cap missed ; again he pulled it, and once more the weapon refused its tasks. The fourth time—thrice had he time to relent—the gallant officer succeeded,—and the boy's life-blood flowed at his feet, amid the indignation and outcries of his men.

We hear with regret, that the women are sometimes illused, and Hindus commit suicide when they are dishonoured,—Cap. C. Johnson, who had been in charge of the parties employed to bury the dead, who are found all over the town, has told me some very affecting stories of the distress and miseries he has witnessed.

We permit things to be done in India, which we could not permit to be done in Europe, or could not hope to effect without public reprobation, and that our Christian character in Europe, our Christian zeal in Exetar Hall, will not atone for usurpation and annexation in Hindostan, or violence and fraud in Upper India.

Russell's Diary in India, 1858.

rities behave themselves most unfeelingly; as if the British do not belong to a race of rulers but to that of an enemy, pure and simple; as if they have not come to rule the subject nation, but to destroy and rob of whatever it has. At last the homeless and almost starving population is allowed to come in. The citizens, or what are left of them, enter Lucknow, and find their homes "improved of the face of the earth:" or bereft of every thing but the dead walls. Some settle with difficulty: while others emigrate out to Gwalior, Barodah, Calcutta, Hyderabad, and other places.

The grand Oudh army was now broken into columns; and General Grant went out to pacify the province. First he marched westward, and outmanœuvering the Moulvi, defeated him at the battle of Bari. The Moulvi retreated to Mohumdee, whence he, for a long time, harassed the English at Shahjehanpore, till at last he was killed by the Zamindar of Powah, who got half a lakh of Rupees as his reward. Of all the rebel leaders, in Oudh, the Moulvi was the most capable: and had he had better materials and men at his command, he would have succeeded with all his skilfully laid out plans.

Grant then marched eastward; and the Begum and Bala Rao, the brother of Nana Saheb, fled from Boondi, to the other side of the Ghagra. Then the obstinate battle of Nawabgunge was fought with the Raikwars; but our General prevailed at last. He next triumphantly progressed to Fyzabad, and delivering Man Singh from the seize of his capital, Shahgunge, by the rebels, marched to Sultanpore and cleared the district after some desultory actions while crossing the Goomtee.

Lord Clyde, after the Allahabad Durbar, in which the direct assumption of the Government by the crown was notified, and old John Company forfeited its existence, came again to the front; and the powerful chieftain of Amethie submitted to the terms of the Queen's proclamation, now issued far and wide. But Rana Beni Madho of Shankarpore, the Nazim of Baiswarha, refused, saying that he would not desert his king at the last moment of his need; but evacuated his fort and left behind his son to become the subject of the British Government. A battle was the consequence, which was well-contested on the field of Dhundhia Kherha. The English, as usual, were victors; and the Rana leisurely retreated, after repulsing the dashing pursuers, and joined the Begum at Bitowli, now the head-quarters of the rebel-Government.

Though opposed by a rebel force, General Grant succeeded in crossing the Ghagra at Fyzabad. A regular battle was, (on 4th January 1859,) fought at Kundakote, beyond the Bur-Ruptie; and being outflanked, the famished enemy could not sustain the double attack. Then followed the death-struggle between the Hussars and *Sewars* on the Raptee. The army of Bala Rao and other chiefs broke down; and all took refuge in Nepal. Bala Rao became penitent; but Nana Saheb was as defiant and abusive as ever.

Lord Clyde again went to the front in January, and organizing a system of frontier military posts, as recommended by Maharajah Man Sing, the so-called British ally of the time, returned to Lucknow; while Grant maintained a thorough outlook on the pent-up enemy, who, however, sometimes succeeded in breaking through the almost impenetrable cordon. Godadhar Singh, a rebel of the deepest dye, whose hatred to the *Feringee* was inveterate, and who had lost an arm at the relief of Lucknow, surprized the column at Secrora, by means of forced marches, and went on harassing or harassed, till he was killed at Bangaon, his last place of refuge.

Permission being given by Jung Bahadur, Grant entered Nepal; and the battles of Sonar and Serwa Passes were fought. At the latter place, on 21st May, 1859, the enemy opened fire with musketry from the hills on both sides and from the two last guns on the low ground. Though almost starving and in a wretched plight on account of pestilence, famine, and what not, the rebels with their wives and children, still fought desperately. Beni Madho said to his followers, "Rajpoots, friends, and members of my clan, our independence is gone, and I will not survive its extinction. Those, who wish to go home, leave me, your old companion in arms, and take whatever you like from this heap of all my money and jewels. Those, who do not, come forward and let us maintain our ancient reputation, either to conquer or to die." Very few took the money; and all, throwing it away at his feet, rushed headlong with their beloved chief, to the thickest fight, and gloriously died sword in hand. The nation, which could forego so much, and show such noble examples, deserved autonomy.

Thus ended the terrible rebellion, which had for a time shaken the British power in India, to its very foundation. Mohamed Hussain made his submission; Nana Saheb and Bala Rao died of dysentry in the Terai. The Begum and Brijis Kader became fugitives in Nyakote, and thence in Katmandoo. Mummoo Khan was captured and transported to the Andamans. Rajah Jeya Lal was hanged for the execution of some English prisoners. The rebel army dwindled into submission, or melted among the Goorkhas. The Taluqadars were rewarded or punished according to the amount of their allegiance or disloyalty, by enlarging or curtailing their estates; while the proprietory right of the whole of Oudh was confiscated by the new Government, a false step of the worst type, being one of the chief causes of the poverty of the province.

CHAPTER III. *British Rule,* (1859-82)

Chief Commissioners of Oudh.

No.	Names.	Assumed charge.	REMARKS.
1	Major-General Sir James Outram, K. C. B., ...	7th. Feb. 1856,	Officiated for Maj. Genl. Sir James Outram on furlough.
2	Mr. C. C. Jackson, C. S., ...	8th May. 1856,	
3	Major-General Sir H. M. Lawrence, K. C. B., ...	21st. Mar. 1857,	Dies of a fatal wound.
4	Major J. S. Banks, ...	5th July. 1867,	Killed in action.
5	Lieut.-General Sir James Outram, K. C. B., ...	11th Sep. 1857,	Transferred to Calcutta as Military Secretary.
6	Mr. R. Montgomery, C. S., ...	3rd April 1858,	Appointed Lt.-Govr. Punjab.
7	Mr. C. J. Wingfield, C. S., ...	15th Feb. 1859,	
8	Lieut.-Col. L. Barrow, C. B. ...	20th April 1860,	Officiated for Mr. Wingfield.
9	Mr. G. U. Yule, C. B., C, S., ...	4th April 1861,	Officiated for Mr. Wingfield.
10	Mr. R. H. Davies, ...	26th Aug. 1865,	Appointed addl. member of the Council of Govr.-Genl.
11	Mr. J. Strachey, ...	17th Mar. 1866,	
12	Mr. R. H. Davies, ...	9th Mar. 1868,	Offic'd for Mr. Strachey from 24th May 1867 to 8th Mar. 1868.
13	Colonel L. Barrow, C. B. ...	18th Jan. 1871,	
14	Sir George Couper, Bart, C. B., C. S. I.	8th Dec 1873,	Officiated for Maj.-General Barrow from 20th Apl. 1871 to 8th Dec. 1873, when he was confirmed.
15	Hon'ble J. F. D. Inglis, C. S., C. S. I.	15th Mar. 1875,	Officiated for Sir George Couper while on forlough.
16	Sir George Couper, ...	15th Nov. 1875,	
17	Hon'ble J. F. D. Inglis, ...	26th July 1872,	Oudh amalgamated with N. W. P., February 15th, 1877.
18	Sir George Couper. ...	15th Feb. 1877,	
19	Sir Alfred C. Lyell ...	15th April 1882,	

As soon as the city came under British possession, Sir James Outram, second to none in influence among military men in India, assumed supreme authority as Chief Commissioner in Oudh. He commenced to collect round him a civil staff, and proceeded to enrol police stations and establishment orders. But, shortly after, he was called away from these duties to Calcutta, in order to succeed General Low, as military secretary to the Governor-General.

The reasons of his being thus suddenly summoned away, are his disagreement with Lord Clyde on military matters, especially on the complete escape of the rebels from the city. Not only that, he disagreed with the Governor-General on the subject of the draft proclamation, which His Excellency wanted to issue to the landlords and people of Oudh; chiefly objecting to the clause of the proposed wholesale confiscation of the proprietory right on land in the province. On this subject, he was supported by the Court of Directors,—especially by Lord Ellenborough and Mr. Bright, who criticised in no measured terms the narrow-minded policy, Lord Canning wanted to pursue with regard to the punishment of rebels.*

* "The produce of the land of Oudh and of the industry of the people will be divided into two most unequal portions ; the larger will go to Government in the shape of tax, and the smaller portion, which will be a handful of rice per day will go to the cultivator of the soil......It has been stated in the course of the debate, that this sentence of confiscation refers only to certain unpleasant persons, who are called Taluqdars, who are barons and robber chiefs, and oppressors of the people. This is 'by no means the first time, that after a great wrong has been committed, the wrong doer has attempted to injure by calumny those upon whom the wrong has been inflicted." *Bright's* great speech in the House of Commons, on the 28th May, 1858.

The proclamation is thus criticised in the Secret Despatch of 19th April, by Lord Ellenborough.

Our letter of the 24th of March, 1858, will have put you in possession of our general views with respect to the treatment of the people in the event of the evacuation of Lucknow by the enemy.

2. On the 12th instant, we received from you a copy of the letter, dated the 3rd of March, addressed by your Secretary to the Secretary to the Chief Commissioner in Oudh, which letter enclosed a copy of the proclamation to be issued by the Chief Commissioner as soon as the British troops should have command of the city of Lucknow, and conveyed instructions as to the manner in which he was to act with respect to different classes of persons, in execution of the views of the Governor-General.

3. The people will see only the proclamation.

4. That authoritative will of the Government informs the people that six persons, who are named as having been steadfast in their allegiance, are hence-forward the sole hereditary proprietors of the lands they held when Oudh came under British rule, subject only to such moderate assessment as may be imposed upon them ; that others, in whose favour like claims may be established, will have conferred upon them a proportionate measure of reward and honor ; and that, with these exceptions, the proprietory right in the soil of the province is confiscated to the British Government.

5. We cannot but express to you our apprehension that this decree, pronouncing the disinherison of a people, will throw difficulties almost insurmountable in the way of the re-establishment of peace.

6. We are under the impression, that the war in Oudh has derived much of its popular character from the rigorous manner, in which, without regard to what the chief land-holders had become accustomod to consider as their rights, the summary settlement had, in a large portion of the land, been carried out by your officers.

7. The land-holders of India are as much attached to the soil occupied by their ancestors, and as sensitive with respect to the rights in the soil they deem themselves to possess, as the occupiers of land in any country of which we have a knowledge.

8. Whatever may be your ultimate and undisclosed intentions, your proclamation will appear to deprive the great body of the people of all hope upon the subject most dear to them as individuals,

This subject caused great discussion in Parliament; and the justice of the annexation was once more questioned. Indeed, the rebels were taken more in the light of an honorable enemy than any other; for as Sir George Couper, the then Secretary, puts it, "it was not until our rule was virtually at end, the whole country over-run, and the capital, in the hands of the rebel soldiery, that the Taluqdars, smarting, as they were, under the loss of their lands, sided against us." Besides they were under our rule for only about a year; nor did they acquiese in the annexation and the introduction of English sovereignty; nor did they pay allegiance. If proprietory right be assumed, "we are only at the commencement of a guerrila war for the extirpation, root and branch, of this class of men,

---

while the substitution of our rule for that of their native sovereign has naturally excited against us whatever they may have of national feeling.

9. We cannot but in justice consider that those, who resist our authority in Oudh, are under very different circumstances from those who have acted against us in provinces which have been long under our Government.

10. We dethroned the King of Oudh, and took possession of his kingdom, by virtue of a treaty, which had been subsequently modified by another treaty, under which had it been held in force, the course we adopted could not have been lawfully pursued, but we held that it was not in force, although the fact of its not having been ratified in England as regarded the provision on which we rely for our justification, had not been previously made known to the king of Oudh.

11. That sovereign and his ancestors had been uniformly faithful to their treaty engagements with us, however ill they have governed their subjects.

12. They had more than once assissted us in our difficulties, and not a suspicion had ever been entertained of any hostile disposition on their part towards our Government.

13. Suddenly the people saw their king taken from among them, and our administration substituted for his, which, however bad, was at least native; and this sudden change of Government was immediately followed by a summary settlement of the revenue, which, in a very considerable portion of the province, deprived the most influential land-holders of what they deemed their property——of what certainly had long given wealth, and distinction, and power to their families.

14. We must admit that, under these circumstances, the hostilities, which have been carried on in Oudh have rather the character of legitimate war than that of rebellion, and that the people of Oudh should rather be regarded with indulgent consideration, than made the objects of penalty, exceeding in extent and in severity almost any which has been recorded in history as inflicted upon a subdued nation.

15. Other conquerors, when they have succeeded in over-coming resistence, have excepted a few persons as still deserving of punishment; but have with a generous policy, extended their clemency to the great body of the people.

16. You have acted on a different principle. You have reserved a few as deserving of special favor, and you have struck with what they will feel as the severest of punishment the mass of the inhabitants of the country.

19. We desire to see British authority in India rest upon the willing obedience of a contended people; there cannot be contentment where there is general confiscation.

20. Government cannot be long maintained by any force in a country, where the whole people is rendered hostile by a sense of wrong; and if it were possible so to maintain it, it would not be a consummation to be desired.

which will involve the loss of thousands of Europeans by battle, disease, and exposure." And the Court of Directors, following the same line of argument, issued a resolution for the pacification of Oudh and other disturbed provinces, pointing to a line of policy, dictated by generosity and tempered by mercy.

These criticisms turned the Governor-General into 'Clemency Canning' of the day; and he now, deploring the administrative blunders of former years, began to hatch his favourite Taluqdari policy in Oudh, even though the confiscation of proprietory right on land was enforced in spite of all opposition. And in justice to him, we ought to admit that his Lordship, while curbing the inhuman thirst for blood of the vengeance party, saved Cawnpore, Dehli and Lucknow, from utter destruction, as strongly proposed by its influencial members, and "did much to mitigate the spirit of blood and iron, which pervaded its counsels;" for Sir James Outram, in his farewell address of 29th of March, recommended (1) entire exclusion of natives from judicial employment; (2) that there should be no appeal in criminal cases; (3) native bar and office establishments are at once to be abolished, and instead European sergeants to do their work; (4) any one found in possession of arms, one month after the proclamation, should be at once put to death;(5) that the lash should be freely used for all manner of punishments, and (6) military officers are only to be selected for carrying out the system he advocated.* But Lord Canning could not enter into, nor could he quite agree with the wisdom of this proposed model system; he quietly overruled his authority, and transferred him to the military Secretary-ship, from the civil line, in which he was found wanting.

Mr. Montgomery, who, as Judicial Commissioner of Punjab, had rendered admirable service to Sir John Lawrence, and was believed to possess a fair amount of the valuable qualities of sagacity, experience, firmness, and

---

* One cannot but remark the spirit of severity, almost ferocity, which inspires this memorandum, as an instructive illustration of the extent, to which even a great and good man may be overpowered by re-actionary impulses. If such was the effect of the mutiny upon Outram, what was to be expected of lesser men, when armed, as was *ex-officio* every Commissioner and Deputy-Commissioner in Oudh, up to the beginning of 1859, with irresponsible power of life and death? The system of administration imposed upon Oudh after re-occupation was the outcome of a deadly and ferocious struggle between alien races. *Irwin,* Thus the blessings of British rule was introduced to save the people from the chronic evils of the late regime.

conciliation, was selected on 3rd April, to fill the office of the Chief Commissioner of Oudh ; and on him devolved the difficult duties of the organization of the administration of the province,—aided by a staff of Judicial and Financial Commissioners, civil and military secretaries. Large discretionary powers were given to him with regard to the proclamation and other matters. It was proposed that as soon as any part of the province was conquered, Montgomery should at once bring it into order in relation to Judicial and Revenue officers. Oudh was to be parcelled out into four divisions, (each under a Commissioner) to be subdivided, each into three districts, which are to be placed under the charge of District Commissioners.

Shortly after the final occupation of the province, the whole proprietory right in the soil, excepting those of the six loyal Taluqdars, was confiscated by a proclamation ; and though it was apparently a technical, nominal and merely formal punishment inflicted on the people of Oudh, yet it must be confessed, that this impolitic measure produced a sea of troubles not only to the people, but to the rulers themselves. This proclamation was followed by another, by which the Taluqdars, or rather what remained of them, were invited to attend at Lucknow to receive, from the Chief Commissioner, grants of their proprietory rights in their respective *Taluks*, as they existed just before the annexation, based on a second summary settlement. Of thoroughly confiscated estates, Tulsipore was given to Raja Dig Bijay Singh of Balrampore, and Gondah to Raja Man Singh, both of whom were made Maharajahs for their conspicuous loyalty during the dark days of the rebellion. Some new Taluqdars were also created at the same time, as Maharajah Kapurthalah, a Punjabi, of Bahraich and Raja Dukhinaranjan Mookherji, a Bengali, of———. And with regard to the old Taluqdars, policy and justice alike forbade their being over-looked in the second summary settlement, which was completed before the middle of 1859. As they gave in their adhesion, they were invested with all the villages they had held in the last years of native rule, and the lists they submitted were confirmed after a summary examination by local officers.

In June, however, Sir C. Wingfield, who succeeded Montgomery, on 15th February 1859, reporting that distrust in the permanance of the settlement was widely diffused, recommended the formal accord by Government of India of its sanction to its finality or perpetuity. Accordingly on 10th October, the Supreme Government sanctioned the recommendation of the Chief Commissioner, directing him to prepare a list of *Sannads,* which Lord Canning himself distributed to 177 Taluqdars, on 25th October, at a grand Durbar in the Lal Baradari, conferring on them full proprietory right, title, possession; for which purpose His Excellency Lord Canning visited Lucknow on 22nd October in great state. He went through the principal streets, which were lined with troops (*Grant's* diary.) But though the Taluqdars had the power to dispose of their estates, according to their will, to whomsoever they pleased, yet the Governor-General subsequently passed final orders on the question of making primogeniture the rule of succession in great families: for much trouble ensues on the division of an estate among several inheritors. Accordingly a fresh clause was inserted in the *Sannads*; and 160 Taluqdars adopted the principle.

The form of administration now introduced was that of the non-Regulation system similar to that prevailing in the Punjab, being composed of a mixed body of civil and military officers. At the head, instead of a king, and the evils of a double Government, is the Chief Commissioner, who is immediately under the Governor-General in Council, and who is responsible for the supervision and control of all department except the Judicial, in which a Commissioner is supreme. The Judicial Commissioner is the High Court of the province; and from his decisions appeal goes only to Her Majesty's Privy Council in London. In criminal cases no sentence of death can be executed without his sanction; and he is responsible for the way in which justice is administered. But he has no executive powers. There was also a Financial Commissioner. The four Commissioners have judicial as well as executive duties to perfrom, subject in the former to Judicial Commissioner, and in the latter to the "Chief." As Judges, they have the powers of Session Courts on the criminal side, and in Civil and Rent suits they are appellate Courts. Under them are 12 District Commissioners, three in each division, who are representatives of Government in all its branches in their respective districts. A District Commissioner is the Chief Magistrate: he is on the civil side the highest court of original jurisdiction, and in many cases appeals lie to him from the decisions of his subordinates, who are Assistant and Extra Assistant Commissioners. He is responsible for the collection of revenue. Under him are generally four Tehsildars, who are in their respective Tehsils the principal revenue authorities; they also exercise judicial powers.

There are two Judges, the Civil and the Small Cause Court Judges at

Lucknow; in fact, these two and the Judicial Commissioner were the only civil officers in the province. At the head of the Police is the Inspector-General, who is also Deputy Secretary to the Chief Commissioner in that department; and under him are 12 District Superintendents, who are however under the general control of the District Commissioners, he only supervising in matters of discipline. There is also a city Superintendent for Lucknow. In the P. W. D, the Chief Engineer is the Secretary to the Chief Commissioner; under him are the four divisional (Executive) and 12 district (Assistant) Engineers; and to this Department is entrusted the execution of Public Works, whether of a local or provincial character. Jail are to a certain extent under the general control of the Magistrate of the district; but each jails has its own Superintendent, under the immediate control of the Inspector-General of Prisons.

While on the form of English administration, we might take this opportunity of devoting a little on that of the late native regime, which was not yet noticed in the hurry of the historical sketch. The constitution was that of a double Government;—one was of purely native principle, of which the governing body was executive; the other was the power of advice and control, exercised by the ambassador of a neighbouring ruler, who was generally called Resident. The former was represented by a Nawab-Vazir, latterly a Padshah, Viceroy or King, assisted by a Naib or Vazir, (minister). The Resident had an Assistant, Treasurer, Moonshi and office. The Moonshi used to read to him all vernacular reports from the king, and send word to his Majesty. This native principle of Government succeeded well so long as it remained pure, unmixed and not interfered with. It was the duty of the king to hear or peruse all documents and cases and make enquiries and send orders to Dewani with the seal of state affixed by himself. But as soon as the controlling and advising authority was taken over by a neighbour, the original administration failed, and the native ruler became a mere puppet; and his power, or what was left of it, was exercised by favourites, either of his, or the Resident's. A crop of evils naturally sprang up, as shown before. Below the king was his Vazir-i-Azam, prime minister, whose pay was 10,000 Rs. with large perquisites a month, and who executed all orders of the king and appeals of the people communicated to him by the Court of Dewani-i-Am. The Vazir had an Assistant minister. There was also a "General Saheb," or Commander-in-Chief, having about 50,000 troops to look after.

After the primier, comes the financial minister, whose pay was 5,000 Rs. a month and had perquisites from *Nazerana* and other sources. Next came *Bakshi* or pay-master general, on a pay of 150 Rs. a month;—his duty was to make payments and adjust accounts. As we descend in the scale of Government, we find a *Meer Moonshi*, who carried on the correspondence between the king and the Resident; a superintendent respectively of the Dewans of the king and Vazir; a treasurer in charge of the crown jewels and private money of the king; another of the Government treasury; a Kotwal or city magistrate; a superintendent of magazines aud commissariat; three principal Hakims and physicians; a poet and aid-de-camp; a superintendent of city news; and another of district news.

Instead of divisions and districts, Oudh was formerly divided into 22 *chucklas*, including Nizamuts, and Hoozoor Tehsils, the revenues of which were generally given out in contract. A Nazim, like the present Commissioner, was superior to *chuckladar*, who resembled the District Commissioner of the present day. The Chuckladars were of two kinds; (1) the *Lakanami*, or one who was under obligation to pay a fixed sum per annum; he received no pay or salary; (2) the *Amani*, or one who paid into the treasury whatever he collected, receiving a fixed salary. The Chuckladar could inflict any punishment short of taking life, but "as imprisonment was carried out only in Lucknow, it was no uncommon occurrance for a prisoner sent in, to be at large within a short period, and entering on a new career,.........might end erelong in the life prisoner being a rival Chuckladar."

"The chuckladars scattered over their districts subordinate agents, corresponding to our Tehsildars and *Thanadars*, giving them each a small body guard, from the class of mercenary soldiers, called Najibs. When they failed to realize Government revenue, the Chuckladars called in the aid of the king's troops, who were paid by him for this service; so that they sometimes get twice their pay. (Hutchinson's *Narative of the Oudh Mutiny*).

Attached to the chuckladars were *Akbar-nabish*, news-writers, who, being quite independent of them, had their duties to send daily reports of the Officer's proceedings, especially his misdeeds, if any, to the king, thus they were a kind of check on them. They, to the number of 660, attended on all officers in charge of districts, fiscal and Judicial Courts, corps and establishment of all kinds, and had faithfully to record all facts for official information at head quarters. Their pay was from 4 to 15 Rs. a month. The Cazi was the civil Judge, Registrar and Priest of the Mohamedans; and the Rajas (now Taluqdars) and Punchayats were respectively the national kings and Councils of the Hindus. The Taluqdars "apportioned out the waste lands to tenants for cultivation, decided the suits of his subject in his *Kachari*, and enjoyed a number of different rights in wild produce resembling the rights attached to an English manor." (*Oudh Gazetteer.*)

The Government demand was confined only to land revenue, which was altered according to the realization from harvest, and paid by two *kists*, half yearly instalments, while the Taluqdars had the undisputed possession of minor taxes. There was no legislature and changeable laws promulgated every year; but all followed the ancient line of customs and the dictates of their scriptures, which being old, well-known and simple, the people had no difficulty in abiding by them. Besides the military, there was no other coercive measures; for a Taluqdar, if deprived of his estates, got it back without much difficulty and delay. "The Nawabi principle was to drive no one to desparation. But with the British Government, a village once lost, is always lost." The total income was about 110 lakhs, which was expended thus: 38 lakhs, for civil and fiscal establishments and stipendiaries; 55 lakhs for military and police; and 15 for king's private expense; total 108 lakhs. Thus the income was well circulated and expended in the province, from which it was taken; and the people had enough employment and earnings.

But no sooner was the English rule introduced, than all the old establishments and institutions were done away with; and "where formerly 300 native chiefs executed their commands through the first handful of stalwart adherents, now 12 District Commissioners carry out the orders of the courts and the administration."

The province being now altogether free from all disturbing causes, the next great question after the organization of the administration, that presented itself, was Revenue and taxation. At the second summary settlement, the land tax was fixed at little over a *crore*. But the new Government was not satisfied with this; it grasped at all other possible means of income. Trade and manufactures felt pressure under the

Customs; while *Excise Abkari* hatched and obtained as much as possible from spirits and drugs, and the principle of levying the highest possible duties by taking the Sudder distilleries in every Tehsil, under direct management, was rapidly extended, even though strongly opposed by many officers, Abkars and village-venders. Great improvement in the manufacture, distribution transports and profits on spirits were effected, and consequently the habit of drinking among the people increased at no slow rate.

Next to these items were *opium* and *salt*, two important sources of income; and fraudulent manufacture and smugling were their natural results, even though indegenous salt was strictly prohibited to be used. Opium agencies were established at Seetapore aud Fyzabad, and a stimulus to its increased cultivation had been given at the enhanced price of Rs 4 per seer. Nor is least the item of *stamp* revenue, that is, taxation on dealing justice to the people; who tried to evade it to every extent they could. And to crown all, the *Income-tax* was introduced from 1st August, 1860, in anticipation of which a Trade tax was levied at about 2 Rs. per head in the province, and Rs. 4-8-0 in the city; besides there was an extra-duty on transit.*

All these sources of receipts amounted to about 175 lakhs; so that at one bound ¾ of a crore was added to what the native Government le-

---

The results of these new taxations are shown thus:—

The stamp is entirely novel to the people, who tried to avade it and so crime increased. The manufacture of salt in this highly saliferous province, has been entirely suppressed; and even the "Kharee" salt, for the use of cattle, was also prohibited; for which purpose the department was placed under the Commissioner of Customs, N-W. P., in subordination to the Chief Commissioner from December 1863. The Superintendent and his four Assistants who were appointed in May 1862, were dispensed with; and a separate establishment for 5 circles, under an Assistant Commissioner of Customs was organized; the sole object was the suppression of indegenous salt, and importation of foreign salt. As a natural result, great hitches occurred between this new department and the Judicial authorities. "The Magistrates naturally view with suspicion the evidence (and often there is no other) of the Custom's Chaprassees, who are rewarded from the fines, and have therefore a direct interest in procuring convictions.... ....The highly saliferous nature of the soil in many places affords almost and irresistible temptation to manufacture salt in small quantities for domestic use..........The assaults on the Custom's Chaprasies are more common in Oudh than in N-W. P."

As early as 1861, the political atmosphere was disturbed, owing to the undue severity and oppressive measures concerning the collection of the Trade's Tax. A leading article appeared on the subject in the *Oudh Gazette* in which one E. A. Commissioner was particularly accused. That Officer, without the permission of higher authorities, instituted an action for libel. Intense excitement was he the consequense. The defendants endeavoured in every possible way not only to bring home to plaintiff, acts of revolting brutality, but generally to throw discredit and odium on the officers of the Commission and their proceedings. In this they were aided by certain officers and men of the Police. The Civil Judge however decided in favor of the Plaintiff; the Police was condemned, and certain European officers were removed from their posts.

vied; to that total must be added local cesses, as that of education, roads, choukidari, Ferry, Patwari, &c. So that in the former regime the people gave a moderate land-tax to king and a little bazaar duties to the middle-men (Talukdars). They began now to pay not only for the possession of land, its produce, transit for its carrying, for sale and purchase, not only for necessaries, for luxuries, and for justice, but for many other ways and means of life. The duties of Government consist in protection, from external and internal enemies, their convenience and communication, for which purpose the old patriarchical sovereigns were content to take some simple taxation generally on land, which they spent in the country, reserving some surplus for future contingencies. The new civilized rulers exacted for the same duties much more than they needed ; and spent much more than they received for other than legitimate purposes, and got into debt. Thus many new evils ensued, to which the old native Government was never heir.

The fiscal arrangements with the Taluqdars being temporary, a permanent settlement for 30 years was deemed necessary ; and so from 1860, regular operations were commenced in Pertabgurh and Onao districts. The principles, on which these laborious works were undertaken, were to collect all information concerning land in order to establish some exhaustive data, on which to found the utmost *bearable* Government demand. The Settlement Report, otherwise called *Wajib-ul-wiz* or administration Paper, was to be divided into (1) History of the village, (2) Record of the present proprietors, defining their holdings and the distribution of Government demand on each separate tenure ; (3) collection of rents and rendering of accounts and payments of the Government demands together with village-customs and usages concerning them, (4) Right and succession, (5) Lumberdars, their appointments and removals, (6) Groves, (7) Rent-free holdings, (8) Rights of irrigation, (9) Abadies, serais and bazaars, (10) Grazing and manure, (11) Village servants, their appointments and renumeration, (12) Under proprietors, their nature and extent of their rights, and (13) Cultivators.

The system of surveys and settlement here employed, was similar to that in N. W. P. of which the necessary preliminary was the demarcation of village boundaries. An especially organized department under an officer under-took this work, on the completion of which he handed over the results of his operations to the Surveyer, being maps in scale 16 inches to a mile,—a list of the villages in each Tehsil, and a record showing the numbers of boundary pillars, the distance between them, and the engagements entered into by the Zamindars.

The Surveys then properly began simultaneously in two different ways by two distinct sections, one being presided over by the Revenue Surveyor, the other by the Settlement officer. The former was scientific and accurate as to total areas; the latter known as the *khasra*, or field survey, was practically one, upon which the settlement of Oudh was based. The professional survey, however, was generally considerablly ahead of that of the settlement officers; and in order to keep pace between the two, the establishment of the latter was greatly augmented; and the progress of the former was made slow. The Revenue surveyor, after verifying the boundary, as laid down by the Demarcation officer, measured the area of each village, and prepared two sets of maps, 1 inch to a mile, for a tract of country, containing 300 to 400 villages; the other, 4 inches to a mile, showing 10 or 8 villages in each. The Khasrah or field survey was conducted by Amins and other native officials, based on the Shahjehani *bigah*, which is equal to $\frac{5}{8}$ of an acre. This operation resulted in a village-map, which is 16 inches to 1 mile, and a field-register.

After the survey-work the settlement officer entered upon the scene, and the work of assessment proper now began. The principles of assessments were (1) to assess the province, village by village, and not estate by estate; (2) to fix the Government demand at one half of the average gross rental of each village; (3) this operation was to be guided, not only by the actual present gross rental, but by other considerations, such as the village rent-roll, prepared by the local accountant, different natures of the soil, personal enquiries, reference to former collections and payments to Government, the character and caste of the people, the style of cultivation, the capability of improvement, the comparative certainty of crops, vicissitudes of season, liability to flood &c. The assessment being framed on these considerations, the settlement-officer made known to the landowners the amount which he proposed to fix as the annual Government demand for a period of 30 years. After all objections had been raised, considered, and disposed of, engagements or *kabuliats* were agreed upon, entered into, and executed by the Zamindars, and were in due course reported to the superior authorities for sanction. After all these things were done, the settlement officer closed his labors by preparing for each village registers of (1) field-map, (2) house-map, (3) wells and tanks, (4) land in possession of co-sharers, (5) census-paper, (6) amount of each co-sharer's share, (7) land-custom regarding inheritance, irrigation, fisheries, groves appointments of Lumberdars and inferior village-servants. Besides settlement works, the officer had judicial work to perform, concerning suits on land, having unlimited original jurisdiction as well as the powers of the court of appeal and revision; he was thus the District Judge for all such suits.

The Settlement-operations began in 1860, in the districts of Pertapgurh and Onao; and thence on to Dariabad, Fyzabad on one side, and Lucknow, Hurdui, and other districts, on the other. The Settlement closed in 1877-78, when the operations lingered in Gondah for a considerable period; and the long talked-of amalgamation of the Settlement Officers with those of the regular line was effected in 1873-74, which caused block of promotion and consequent discontent. The percentage of Government demand on land has been fixed at 51.05; Taluqdar's profit = 16.87, sub-proprietor's and cultivator's at 32.08; total = 100. Besides the punctual payment of revenue, the conditions, on which the Taluqdars are allowed to have a permanent hold on land, are loyalty, the rendering of assistance to the police, in the preservation of order, and in the prevention and reporting of crime, the maintenance of village watchmen and accountants, and the agricultural prospects of their estates. If they fail in any way to fulfil these conditions, Government will take the management of their Taluks under its own control. For this purpose four classes of coercive measures, such as distraint, transfer, farm, and sale, were enforced.*

---

* The old *Shahi* Settlement was thus conducted :—In the month of *Asarh* (or the commencement of the rainy season), the *Amil* (or head collector of the Revenue) proceeds in person to every village under his management, assembles the *Assamees* (cultivators), and directs their zealous attention towards the cultivation of their respective division of land. To such of the husbandmen as are in distressed circumstances, advances of Taqavae (pecuniary loans) are made, in order that no part of the arable lands may remain neglected, or for want of means the cultivation relinquished, but that *Jins-i-Kamil* or grains &c. of high value may be cultivated throughout.

The *Amil*, having thus arranged, grants to each of the cultivators, a document under his seal, called *Putta*, in order that from the apprehension of a greater demand being made on them than the settled revenue, they should not neglect the husbandry, the Putta strictly binding the Government, that no advantage should be taken of increase consequent on agricultural improvements of the husbandmen.

(Bundobust). To ascertain the *Kham Nikasee* (or the gross assets) of a Mouzah, it is necessary that the fields, in their full harvest, be measured in the *Khariff* (winter) and *Rabi* (Summer) seasons respectively, showing the exact extent of the cultivation of each Asamee :—an estimate is accordingly formed of the produce, and the value of the different grains ascertained. The *Zemindars* and *Ryot* being assembled, a Moochulka (indemnity bond) is taken from them, that during the measurement they will, under no plea whatever, create any disturbance, or allow any part of the cultivated land to be left unmeasured.

But the Government demand, fixed by the settlement officers, was in many places much higher than the land was capable of bearing. The very numerous transfers of land, that were taking place, became a source of much anxiety to the officiating Chief Commissioner. Sir G. Couper recorded in the Administration Report of 1872-73, that "considering the great reluctance, with which natives part with land, (he) fears that the poverty of the owners, who are unable from the profits of their estates to make both ends meet, is the cause ;—the poverty aggravated by heavy law expenses. Litigation was costly, and in many cases unnecessarily so. The result of all is that most landholders are in debt, and many are driven to raise money by mortgage, or by sale of portions of their estates."

Accordingly the assessment was in many instances revised and reduced; but still the distress decreased not. Coercive measures were as ordinary as before, and many estates were assumed under direct management, called *kham*, for arrears of revenue. The system of granting Pattahs, which was enforced with a view to secure protection to sub-proprietors from extortion gave a great deal of trouble.* In the investigations concerning

---

An *Ameen* (overseer) then proceeds, attended by the Quanungoes, Mootsuddies, Patwaries, and Zemindars; and in the presence of the *Kesans* (cultivators) every field is measured by a *Jureeb* held at full length by a *Meerdeh* (land measurer) at each end, and a third *Meerdeh* is directed to attend at the centre to report the extent of the land measured. The Meerdehs are also made to execute a *Moochulka* against all dishonesty in measurement. As soon as each field is measured, the result or the *Ruqba*, is written down on the spot severally by the Quanungoes and the Mootsuddies, in a paper, which, when completed, is called *Khusrah* ... ..The khusrahs of the Quanungoes and Mootsuddies are compared together, (and) the signatures of the *Ameen*, Quanungoes and the Patwaries are affixed : thus the measurement is daily continued until the whole is completed.

The cultivation or produce of a Mouzah being now known, the value of the crops is easily ascertained, and a *Jumabundee* (assessment) accordingly formed, either *Mouzawar* or *Asameewar*, and Puttahs executed according to local usage.......The Revenue is payable by *Kists*, *i. e.* instalments. Having arranged these points the necessary Puttah on the part of the Government, and *Qabooliut*, on that of Zemindars are executed. A settlement of the above nature is made for one, two, or as far as ten years. Dacosta's *Dewan Pasand*.

The *Aain-i-Akbari*, thus enumerates the duties of an Amil :—

"He must consider himself the immediate friend of the husbandmen, be diligent in business, and a strict observer of truth, being the representative of the Chief Magistrate. He must transact his business in a place, where every one may find easy access, without requiring any mediator. The crafty and disobedient he shall strive to reform by reprehension.......He shall not be satisfied with receiving pecuniary fines in exculpation for murders and other capital offences. His conduct must be such, as to give no cause of complaint. He must assist the needy husbandmen with loans of money, and receive payment at distant and convenient periods. When any village is cultivated to the highest degree of perfection, by the skilled management of the chief thereof, there shall be bestowed upon him half a *biswah* out of every bigah of land, or some other reward proportionate to his merit. Let him endeavour to ascertain the quantity of land in cultivation, and make trial of different portions, in order to gain a competent knowledge of its various properties. He shall acquaint himself with, and maturely consider the conduct of former Amils; and if they appear to have been guilty of inconsiderateness or dishonesty towards the husbandmen, he must strive to remedy the evils they may have occasioned &c."

*The compulsory grant of Pattahs is looked upon by the cultivators as an official formulary more required by Government than desired by themselves, and has an injurious effect on the good feeling generally subsisting between landlords and tenants ; and in this opinion, the Chief Commissioner concurs ; for instead of reducing the amount of litigation and facilitating the decisions of summary suits, dormant claims, which might otherwise be allowed to slumber, are awakened ; and consequently suits have largely increased. The near approach of settlement stimulated litigation. (Administration Report of 1862-63.)

Maafi or rent-free tenures, many were resumed by Government, thus causing great hardship to those, who were deprived or curtailed of their old holdings; while the Court of Wards, a new institution, by which Government itself managed the estates of minors and incompetent landlords through its District Officers, though it effected much good individually, could not have its beneficial measures felt throughout the province, or even in a estate in all its departments. The Talukdars' Relief Act, enacted in 1870, instead of conciliating the debtors and creditors, made the gulf wider between them; and discontents were universal and at its height. In 1872, five Superintendents were appointed; but Government was not satisfied with the result; and the management of the encumbered estates were transferred in two years to Deputy Commissioners.

At last in 1873-74 when the Viceroy—Lord Northbrook visited Lucknow—a conference was held to discuss the nature and causes of the distress of the agricultural classes; and His Excellency at once empowered the Chief Commissioner to make certain remissions of land-revenue, which had a most beneficial effect. Considerable balances had taken place, "on account of losses sustained by the defaulter, by reason of either too sudden and immediate enhancement of the revenue demand, its too early introduction before subordinate rights in the soil had been settled, and before the shares in the liability for the revenue had been determined, and by reason of the recent bad seasons or for other causes, such as the rebellion, and double Summary Settlement.

Let us conclude the Talukdari business by enumerating the nature and classes of land tenures in Oudh. They are of two kinds;—I, held direct from the state, and II, held indirectly from the state. Direct holdings are subdivided into (1) Talukdari estates, (2) Zemindari or Mufrid estates, and (3) estates held in fee—simple. Indirect tenures are subdivided into (1) entire villages or entire shares of villages, (2) *Sir*, *Duswant*, *Nankar* and *Dehdari* lands, (3) groves, (4) *Birts* and *Shankallaps*, (5) *Marwati*, (6) lands held by village servants, and (7) Mosulman *chaks* in large towns and Kusbahs.

The Talukdars and Zemindars alike possess the full right of property in their estates; but they differ from each other in the degree of security on which their titles rest. Protected by Act I of 1859, the title of a Talukdar is unassailable, except upon a cause of action, which might arise subsequent to the settlement. The Zemindars on the other hand are liable at any moment to be called on by the courts to defend a suit, in which the cause of action may have arisen even before the annexation. The Talukdars have been also freed from the provisions of the ordinary Hindu *Shàstras* and Mahomedan *Shará*, which, except when over-ridden by a strongly defined family custom, usually regulate succession and inheritance among the *Mufrid* Zemindars. Of 250 Talukdars, a large number have adopted the law of primogeniture.

The Mufrid estates are generally the property of a whole community, being descendants of one ancestor, held partly in common and partly in severalty, through *Lumberdars*, headmen, who get 5 per cent. as their perquisite. *Fee-simple* estates are those, which have been sold and acquireed under the waste land rules. But these fee-simple and *Maafi* or rent-free holdings are very few in Oudh. The indirect holdings are otherwise called "sub-settled villages," which are, by Act 26 of 1866, defined, and are under Talukdars. The *tenants* are of two kinds, (1) tenants with a right of occupancy, and (2) tenants at will. The total villages of Oudh are thus distributed :—

	Villages. paying.	*Government revenue.* Rs.
1. Talukdari	23,157	65,64,959
2. Zemindari	7,201	28,45,183
3. Pottidari	4,539	18,19,214
Total,	34,897	112,29,356

The Sub-settlement Act of 1866 was otherwise called "the Oudh Compromise," to effect which there was tedious discussions and wranglings between Government and the Talukdars, who objected to the recognition of the sub-proprietory right in the manner the former wanted. The Oudh Rent Act of 1868 was passed with no less difficulty. "In return for curtailment of and restrictions on sub-suttlement, by which they as a body gained very largely, the Talukdars consented to the recognition of the rights of occupancy, one per cent. of their tenantry and yielded a very limited right to compensation for improvement. The main features of these measures have not been materially altered by the Oudh Land Revenue Act and the Oudh Laws' Act of 1876; and the different classes of the population have been left "free to work out their several good, to go forward in the bright career before them,"—and with what results it would be seen at no great lapse of time.*

Meantime we retrace our steps, and record the other important events after the final pacification of the province. After the summary settlement with the Taluqdars, the portion of the Terai, conquered from the Nepalese in the war of 1816, was restored to them as a reward for their alliance and aid. The English Boundary Commissioners proposed a slight exchange of territory, with a view to lesson the irregularities of the boundary lines; but the Goorkhas refused to any modification of their ancient limit. But the boundary-question, instead of being settled, became a vexed subject still more than it was before. The solution of 1860 was not satisfactory to the Katmandoo Durbar, who now began to clamour for more territories; and as Raptee generally changed its course, constant differences that were pending, grew great and were quite irritating. In November 1865, they complained of frequent aggressions upon their villages by brands of marauders from Oudh and other British possessions; and some correspondence took place between the two Governments, for the extradition of criminals. Much property was transferred by the river's vagaries. At last. in 1878, the boundary line was reconstructed, after a full local enquiry and discussion at a meeting held on the spot between the Durbar officials, the Nepal Resident, the Commissioner of Fyzabad and the Deputy Commissioner of Bahraitch. A straight line was drawn from the 13th, to a point between the 21st and 22nd pillars; the map was revised and corrected, and land was at once redistributed, being a slight advantage to Nepal.

"The Naipal Government thoroughly identifies itself with the welfare of its tenants, who hold lands at very easy terms, with perfect security of tenure and with no fear of being rack-rented in the interest of some needy landlord or greedy contractor, and in the name, falsely invoked, of political economy. The Naipal Terai has therefore become, what it would not have been under British Rule, a land of refuge for the cultivator, whom exaction in our territory has irritated to the bolting point." The Naipal Government moreover has placed some restrictions

*In a province, where occupancy rights are not encouraged by law, the sense of the landed proprietor is in favor of retaining upon the soil those cultivators, who have any sort of claim to consideration. That the primary object of the landholder has been that of bringing the tenants to terms rather than that of ousting him from his land, is shown by the fact that of 25,744 notices of ejectment served, only 4181 resulted in evictions. *General Barrow.*

upon local trade, by prohibiting its subjects from taking their goods into Oudh, in order to keep it in their own hand and to compell all British subjects to repair to Naipalgunge to purchase Naipalese products and to sell their own. The results of this restrictive or rather protective measure have been that the Bazars in our side of the country have been ruined. In 1864, the Chief Commissioner personally visited the spot and reported the matter to the Supreme Government. This prohibitory order, however, has not been extended to Debipatan fair, where the centre of pilgrimage and interest being in the British dominions, the Naipalese resort with their goods to sell and Oudh articles to buy.

After the settlement of the Naipal boundary, and the Revenue Department, the chief measure was the organization of the Judicial; and as the province was free from all disturbing causes, regularity and exactness in the procedure of the Courts and general business progressed satisfactorily. Litigation however increased, though still small in comparison to the older provinces, owing to the paucity of monetory transactions and the infancy of the English legislation. "The Talukdari settlement, moreover, obviates, by substituting a landed aristocracy for a number of petty landowners, the necessity for the constant recourse of the latter to the money lender, to meet the Government demand."

The want of a sufficient shifting and determination of the issues became a more constant ground of interference than difference of opinion on issues decided; so a tendency towards lodging appeals from even the decisions of the Judicial Commissioner already sprang up. The introduction of a new Act (XXXVI of 1860), which necessitates the use of stamps, has given a check to registration of all deeds; and the system of process-fees and institution-stamps, though financially favorable, proved that the people cannot get justice but with great cost and delay. For this reason, the people, not accustomed to English administration, did not, as long as they could help it, go to the new tribunals of justice, which departed from the old native system in every respect.

The regular progress of works was thus greatly impeded. Accordingly by the introduction of a new Act VIII of 1871 the system of registration was changed. and the supervision of this department was transferred from the Judicial Commissioner to the Superintendent of Excise and Stamps; and 121 offices for the registration of documents were opened. The result was that, "registration, as the income shows, is becoming more general, but not, it is feared, more popular; for some of the requirements of the Act, and notably that which makes the registration of certain leases compulsory are still looked on with disfavour." And so many tried to evade it; some succeeded, and some were caught and punished. English rulers forget, that when they create a new Law, they create a new source of crimes along with it; and thus instead of improving the moral *discipline* of the people, they make it worse than before. The rigorous enforcement of the stamp act brought on a full crop of conviction of crimes; while the breaches of the Salt and Saltpetre Laws increased with the separate organization of the Custom's Department.

The criminal administration of the province, however, showed favorable results; for many of the heinous crimes, which the old native Government could not cope with, were to a certain extent satisfactorily suppressed. Burglaries, violent assaults, affrays and other offences, though they occasionally increased in consequence of famine and other reasonable causes, on the whole diminished perceptibly. But there cannot be two opinions on the fact, that minor crimes increased greatly with the progress of legislation and civilization.

The arrangement of the offices under a Clerk of the Court in supercession of the Amlah system, the mode of recording evidence in English, and the statement of pleas and issues were the chief reforms of the year 1860, experimentally introduced with a view for the framing of the regular codes and procedures. Owing to the intricate legislation, all suits, original and secondary, as also thefts and other petty crimes increased at a rapid rate; the original suits for example of 1863 and 1864 rose to 11,199, from 8,432 of the previous year; and still more by 1983 the next year, chiefly owing to contracts and debts.

At this time, the people began to complain of the severity and summary character of their criminal trials, and of the abuse of the corporal punishments, resorted to by many officers, who, taking advantage of their discretionary powers, used to couple imprisonment with stripes. This was severely commented upon in the Administration Report of 1861. Accordingly corporal punishment and sentence to transportation for terms were greatly restricted.

After the re-occupation of the province, the number of prisoners increased with the introduction of new laws and Acts; and the want of sufficient accommodation for them was felt. Accordingly plans for the building of a Central and four Divisional Jails, on the radiating principle, were prepared and submitted by a Committee. The scheme was sanctioned in due course; and the construction was commenced and progressed in right earnest under a Superintendent. The prisoners were themselves employed in the works; thus a considerable saving to Government was effected.

Next in order of precedence comes the police. At first the department had quite a seperate organization, being independent of the Commissioners, Divisional and District. As a consequence, great distance, reserve, and punctilio frequently exhibited themselves in the relations of the officers of the two Departmants; and the progress of Government work was interrupted in no small degree. The constant changes and introduction of new and inexperienced European Officers acted prejudicially to the improvement of the police. The old Native Officers, promoted from the Sikh and Sepoy regiments for gallantry and fidelity were found wanting in their duties; and the low caste policemen, such as Kahars, Aheers, and Chamars, introduced with the new regimé after the mutiny, as a precautionary measure, proved inefficient to the highest degree.

Bad results followed from this incompetency of the Department. Many heinous crimes were committed with impunity in the province. Numerous mysterious murders occurred in Onao; but no official enquiry, held on the spot, by an able officer especially deputed, could detect a clue as to the perpetrators. At last, the policemen themselves were found to have been the criminals, who, in the hope of obtaining rewards, committed a murder and endeavoured to throw the blame on innocent persons. Considerable number of *sutties* occurred simultaneously, and the police could not prevent them. Of 173 dacoities and robberies, reported in 1863, only a very few were brought to trial. The same remark applies to ordinary thefts and crimes. The police were invariably found unsuccessful in dealing with these cases; and crimes, especially burglaries, increased with impunity; and the sophistry of the Department as to their causes knew no limit. "One reason has been assigned for the increase in the number of thefts, which is rather a matter for congratulation, *viz.* the great material prosperity of the province"!!!—material prosperity in what? the people did get but very little employment after the expiry of their kingdom; while at least two-thirds of the local revenue was taken out and spent in other provinces. In commerce? It is certain, that the indigenous manufactures and trade declined greatly with the advent of the new rule. In population? It was a well-known fact, that hundreds of thousands perished during the rebellion, while not a less number died during the subsequent famines; and this great loss could not possibly be replaced by the reproductive power of the underfed people in a few years (vide Sir H. Lawrence's Life.) In morals and civilization? then crimes could not possibly increase.

At last attention was drawn to the incompetency of the Department; and reformation was set on foot. The District Superintendents of Police were made completely subordinate to the District Officers, though its separate organization was maintained; considerable reductions and modifications were gradually effected in the force, which was now 8,523 of all grades in strength, costing about 11¼ lakhs; whereas it was formerly 14,760 costing 26 lakhs. More able Inspectors were appointed from the higher caste; and the policemen were recruited from the Brahmans and Rajpoots, in order to have a large amount of necessary intelligence in the Department. A new Act, being V. of 1861 was introduced, by which the respective duties of the police and the judiciary were defined, the procedure was simplified, and the change caused little interruption in the harmonious working of the Department. The Thuggi Department was abolished, as being no longer necessary. The military character also of the police was changed in conformity with that Act; and the Town and Cantonment Police was incorporated with the General Police force of the province. It was subsequently separated into armed and civil; and the employment of detectives was stringently interdicted. This new system was approved by the people; because it did not harass them like the old. "Not one per cent. of the population could personally feel the advantages of the increased detective skill on the part of the police; but 50 per cent. at least feel the relief from inquisitorial visits, sweeping summons to the Thannah and meddling interference." Beneficial measures followed from these measures; and the detection of crime improved a great deal. Several Sepoys, concerned in the Shahjehanpore massacre, were apprehended and brought to justice, though the hope of obtaining evidence was faint.

Many were punished for retention of arms; in fact, it was found that the disarming of the people was not complete, as was thought before. Many notorious dacoits and offenders, such as Koorban Ali, Ahmad Khan, Mehrban, and Ram Newaj Sing were captured and duly punished.

Village-police is as it were the eyes and feelers of the regular police. It is a relic of the old village republican community, wherein the Chowkidar was an indespensable member. The new English rule did not lose sight of his necessity and importance. The principle however of making the landholders, responsible for the efficiency of the indegenous watchmen, though undoubtedly correct, was not uniformly enforced. In fact, the Talukdars were bereft of all administrative powers; and hence the Chowkidars were dissatisfied. A special tax of 6 per cent. levied from the Talukdars, and appropriated to the payment of their salaries, was after a year found to be complete failure; and in December, 1859, Mr. Wingfield directed a return to the old system of remunerating them, by granting to each 5 *beegahs* of land, and this branch of detectives was reconstructed after that before the annexation.

With the introduction of English rule, self-governing institutions of the people, such as punchayets, arbitration, and the Talukdar's Kachahri were done away with; and the Judicial administration fell entirely into the hand of the foreigner. As a natural consequence, the results were not satisfactory, either to the people or to Government; and the officials were overworked. A return to the old system of self-government was thus but very tardily made; and so trial by jury in civil cases was a notable reform of 1861; for which the people were thankful to Mr. Wingfield, who strongly recommended it. The jury consisted of five members, the verdict of the majority being binding in all questions of facts. The people, however, at first did not like the manner of its procedure, being not in accordance with the notion of their old *punchayets.* The tribunal of commerce, otherwise called Chamber of Commerce, was now being used as a sort of standing jury on commercial subjects. And last but not the least of all was, that civil, criminal, and Revenue powers were granted to certain deserving great Talukdars, some of whom were made Honorary Assistant Commissioners. One of its main objects was to remove them from the affronts and interference from Tehsildars, which was an odious feature of our administration, and also to legitimise and regulate the authority they had always exercised over their tenants, of which it would have been impolitic to deprive them. In this duty Maharajah Man Singh shone greatly. In fact, the paucity of appeals from the orders of Talukdars, and the few instances, in which their orders have been reversed or modified by the superior courts, may be accepted as conclusive proofs that their decisions are just and give satisfaction.

A general scheme for making Talukdars and citizens Honorary Magistrates and Assistant Commissioners, was drawn and submitted for the approval of the Supreme Government for its introduction throughout the province and in all the cities. But many District Officers were against the measure; they could not brook to see the Rajahs and citizens to be empowered in what they considered their exclusive rights. And so they raised many futile objections; which were well met by facts and figures, as furnished by the superior officers. Both the Judicial Commissioner and Civil Judge were satisfied with the results of this measure; for the arbitration statement was very favorable; even though the proceedings of the Honorary Assistants were most jealously watched, and their irregularities commented on, which would generally escape notice, if committed by salaried officers.

The Chief Commissioner recorded in 1865, to what he had already written in former Reports, that " it is a milder measure of the Talukdar's agent to bring a suit for arrears of rent against a defaulting tenant in his Court, whose decision is open to appeal, than for the Talukdar, in his capacity of landlord, to destrain the defaulter's crops, which it is his undoubted right to do." Besides his processes as Honorary Assistants are served through Tehsildars. The general and imperative use of the popular institution of compromise and arbitration gave indeed very good results. The Chief Commissioner also in 1868, remarked, that he " does not desire the supercession of arbitration, which not only relieves the Courts but accustoms the people to the transaction of affairs apart from their domestic or individual interest." And so instead of the self-government system being suppressed, as many officials advocated, it was introduced more and more; assesors were increased; and at last in 1879, a bench of six Honorary Magistrates was constituted for the city of Lucknow for the trial of Police and Municipal offences. As early as in 1860, Lord Canning, while here, was so much satisfied with the success of this measure, that His Excellency received in audience the

Honorary Assistant Commissioners, and expressed his gratification at the good results, that attended the experiment of associating them with Government Officers in the administration of the province.

Finance is divided into two heads,—income and expenditure. Income included revenue from land, which was in 1860 a little over a crore; Assessed Taxes being Trade and afterwards Income-tax, was about 13½; Customs and Excise=6 lakhs, stamp=2, and opium and Salt, 30; miscellaneous, consisting of proceeds from forests, postage, local rates, Octroi, ferry and other impositions 4½; so that the total receipts were about 150 lakhs. After the completion of the settlement operation, the land revenue was raised to 150 lakhs; Excise, 7; stamp, 9; Salt, 20; opium, 50, Licence, about 20, and miscellaneous, 43; total a little over 3 crores. Of this large sum Rs. 50 lakhs are expended for civil administration; the military force about 35½ lakhs; so that after defraying all costs, there was a surplus of over two crores. It is now considerably more. From the surplus 12 lakhs are given to the Ex-king as his pension.

English education was introduced under the grant-in-aid system. The Talukdars established primary schools on the Hulka-bundi plan, in their estates; and two classes were formed in each school, one for their sons and relatives; the other for lower classes. A general scheme for the promotion of education was promulgated; a large imperial grant was obtained; and a supervising staff of 1 Director, 2 Inspectors and 12 Deputy Inspectors was appointed. Ten Zillah, and 22 Tehsil Schools were established in the principal towns, which with the indegenous schools numbered 263; and students increased by 30 per cent. On the 1st of March, 1864, the Canning College, which was intended to be a first class institution, was opened in the palace of Amin-ud-doulah, in commemmoration of the late Earl Canning. The Talukdars pledged themselves to raise 25 lakhs a year for its support; and Government gives an equal sum. For the support of this Department, a special fund, called the *schoolcess*, of one per cent. is also levied from them. A regular scheme of studies was prepared and introduced. But the results were rather superficial. The people very tardily appreciated the benefits of the English education, which was not sufficiently high to be felt, practical to be useful, technical to be profitable, or moral to be religious.

Very few, if any, of the students, rose to fame in their after-career, either in learning, money, or influence. Accordingly English education did not flourish; while the old training system declined at a rapid rate. The fact is, that the system of educational course is superficial; it is not based on the national literature of the country; and so it cannot touch and influence the mental spring of the people.

Public Works are subdivided into (1) military and (2) civil; civil is branched into buildings, communications by road and railways, and irrigation. In the first few years of the English rule, the military engrossed almost the whole of the budget grant; of 25 lakhs, for instance, allotted in 1861, only $2\frac{3}{4}$ were devoted to works of internal improvement. The military works executed are chiefly barracks and subsidiary buildings in number about 50 and 240 respectively for European Troops at Lucknow and Fyzabad. Up to 1862, the cost of military works amounted to 67 lakhs.

Of civil buildings, there is nothing important to record; only a few jails, opium Godowns and Kacharies were erected; whereas the demolitions of the city of Lucknow, around the Stone bridge fort and Baillie Guard, were completed at great expense. Of roads, those from Lucknow to Cawnpore, Rai Barelli, Sultanpore, Fyzabad, Seetapore and Shahjehanpore, were gradually metalled; and all the small rivers and nullahs were bridged or covered with culverts.

With regard to the railway system of Oudh, the project began in 1862; and an Indian Branch Railway Company was formed. An Engineer was sent, who examined the proposed line from Cawnpore to Fyzabad. The work, however, progressed very slowly; and the Cawnpore Branch, 45 miles long, was opened on 23rd April, 1867. A contract was duly executed between the Secretary of State and the Company in August of the same year, for the construction and working of a light system of 36lbs rails at slow speed,—15 miles an hour, in N. W. P. and Oudh. The original lines proposed were from Lucknow to Byramghat, via Dilserai, and from Dilserai via Shahgunj and Jounpore to Benaras, with a branch from Shahgunj to Fyzabad.

The designation was now changed from Indian Branch to "Oudh and Rohilkund Railway." The management and supervision of the Company are done by a managing Director in London, and here by an Agent, who with his Deputy, is responsible for the general conduct of affairs, a Chief Engineer, who with his Residents, sees construction and maintenance of Railway Lines and buildings,—a Loco-Superintendent, who in his Workshop, looks to the Locomotive and Carriage Department; a Traffic manager, who with his two Superintendents, controls the traffic, stations and staff; an Auditor, who checks accounts and expenditure, and a Consulting Engineer, who supervises the whole staff and works. The latter two are the representatives of Government of India. The business of the railway is transacted by and recorded in official meetings, which are held periodically; while Government sanctions all expenditure; and the lines are inspected in half-yearly tours.

The railway system has been remodelled, and consists of one main line from Benares to Moradabad, to be ultimately extended in a North-Western direction, to Saharanpore on the Delhi and Punjab line, a total length of about 540 miles,— which was opened by the end of 1874. This line passes through the important towns of Benares, Jounpore, Fyzabad, Nawabgunge, Lucknow, Hardoi, Saharanpore, and Moradabad, and ultimately to Hurdwar and Roorki. There are also branches, those of Cawnpore, 45 miles, Byramghat from Nawabgunge, 22, and of Aligarh, 60 miles :—These branches were originally intended to be the feeders to the main lines; but practically the Cawnpore Branch is the most profitable; while the Aligurh serves the purposes of the main line, and the main line from Chundowsi to Moradabad is but a branch, until the Northern Extention is completed, which will be done in a year or two. There were two other proposed extensions, one from Roorki to Ramnagur, near Naini Tal, distance 47 miles; the other was called the Buxar Branch, via Azimgurh, 100 miles, with a feeder to Goruckpore. But the necessity of these two lines does not now exist; for a subsidiary system of light railways has been promulgated and projected, being feeders to the broad gauge system. And so on the one hand the Trans-Ghagra, called Patna-Bahraich Railway, has been commenced; and the Kumaun Railway is being pushed on in right earnest for the convenience of the periodical hill-exodus. There is another line between Seetapore through Lucknow to Rai Bareli under proposal, which will be begun when another famine looms in the horizon, or when a sufficient provincial surplus allows it to be taken in hand. In fact narrow gauge principle is a great improvement on our railway system; for the construction and maintenance of the broad gauge have not been economical enough to keep their continuance, much less extension. The narrow gauge system is susceptible of great development, and is suited to the requirements of the country for local purposes.

Another important branch of the public works is irrigation. In 1862, Sir A. Cotton visited the province with a view of ascertaining its capabilities with regard to canal. After local enquiry and preliminary survey, he proposed two canals,—one from Ghàgra, about 20 miles above Byramghat, running in a South-Easterly direction, between that river and Goomtee; and the other from the Sardah, to South of the Goomtee. Of these two contemplated canals, the Sardah one has always been a favourite scheme with the Government;—and preliminary operations began in right earnest. But the British Indian Association, on the part of the Talukdars, raised various objections as to its utility, they affirmed that much harm will be done, if a canal is constructed; for wherever its water is used, *Usar* and *Reh* are produced, and in a few years land detereorates considerably, if it does not become altogether barren, as is proved by the results of the Doab Canal. The Government accordingly stopped the operations after incurring great expenditure.

Of the miscellaneous section of our Government, there was nothing very important to record in detail. Attempts were made to open river communication by steam ships, between Fyzabad or Byramghat and Calcutta; but they failed completely. The postal department, at its first organization, was under the district authorities; officers were established at all the Tehsils and the most important Police Stations; and Dak-runners began to ply their business throughout the province. But the want of supervision and uniformity produced inconvenience and delay, not only to Government, but to the people. The district management was therefore amalgamated with the imperial office under one Chief Inspector. Telegraph wires were run between the chief towns of the province. Of ecclesiastical matters, no aid was given to the religious requirements of the people; but Christian Churches were built at Government expense, at Lucknow, Fyzabad, Gondah, Rai Bareli, Lukhimpore and a few important towns; and in 1861, "a grant from the penal fines levied on the city of Lucknow, has been made to the Roman

Catholic community to aid in the erection of a chapel in the Civil Lines."

The after-events are briefly noticed. In 1867, Lord Lawrence, the Saviour of the Punjab, came on a state-visit; a grand elephant procession was formed, and Lawrence-Cross was erected near the Residency as a monument to his brother. In January, 1870, the Duke of Edinbourgh saw how the neglected palaces were white-washed and illuminated. In December, 1873, Lord Northbrook made a state-entry, and, finding from the multitude of petitioners, how miserably the people are passing their days, ordered revised settlement. In January, 1876, the Prince of Wales visited the city; and the four days' *Tamasha* engrossed the attention of the people, police and all. The foundation stone of the Northbrook-liberality-column, in memory of the loyal Sepoys of 1857, was solemnly laid by the royal hand, amidst the tears of the old veterans, the cheers of the Baillie-Guardites, and the booming of the artillery; while Sir George Couper maintained his old reputation by an able address. The barons of Oudh salaamed their allegiance in the Kaisarbagh Baradari, amidst the usual paraphernalia of fireworks, banquet, illumination and presents. But the *Tamasha* was dissected, and old Russell discovered that Oudh was not as prosperous as it looked in 1858.

On the first day of the next year, the grand Delhi Durbar takes place in the ancient *Aswamedha* ground of Judhistheer of Mohabharat, at a time, when a great famine loomed in the horizon, and the *Empress* of India inaugurates her rule by subordinating Oudh to N. W. P., a misname of the first magnitude, both historically and geographically. Little shows and little durbars were locally held, while the high officials were away at the head *tamasha*. Promises were made to restore the Mutchhi-bhawan buildings to the city, and to open higher careers to the gentry;—though none yet knows when that is to be fulfilled. Subsequently Durbar lists, provincial and district, were prepared, and this vexed question was set at rest.

The seperate organization of the local administration ceased with a sigh and much discontent; especially because Lucknow was not selected as the capital seat of the United Provinces. For few of their hard-won rights, the barons of Oudh saw ghosts around; and a memorial, signed by thrice ten thousands, was submitted to the Secretary of State, praying for the separate administration of the province, or at least Lucknow be retained as the head-quarters of the province. In forwarding it, Sir George Couper recorded a minute on the document, pointing out how little foundation there was for the apprehension expressed; and in his reply the Secretary of State adhered to the policy he had sanctioned. A few months after, Lord Lytton visited the city, and, at a Durbar, delivered an admonitory speech. The head of the opposition-party to the amalgamation had to retreat with no good name or results.

Before the close of the year 1878, the amalgamation was completed. All the departments, such as Public Works, Police, Prison, Vaccination, Dispensaries, Sanitation, Registration, &c., were brought under one head, and "steps were taken to bring into unison the practice and procedure of the two provinces." For these purposes, no serious difficulties presented; for generally the departments in both provinces had been worked on much the same principles. With regard to Dispensary and Education, where the functions of local Committees were involved, matters were left in *statu quo.* The elaborate code of Police circulars, issued from time to time, in N. W. P., was found to be generally applicable to Oudh; and here the greatest numbers of changes took place; and the principles of police administration, recommended by the Civil Administration Committee, and sanctioned by Government, were brought into operation. Oudh Government Press was abolished as a separate institution, and merged in that of N. W. P. Measures were also taken for methodizing, on the basis of that in force in N. W. P., Oudh procedure, regarding Municipalities, *Nazul*, pound, mortuary registration, official libraries, procedure of suits, in which Government is concerned, and other measures of miscellaneous kinds.

The saving, effected by these reforms, was devoted to the strengthening of the judicial and subordinate revenue establishments in Oudh. A Committee of Oudh Officials was appointed to suggest and formulate a judicial scheme in order (1) To give relief to the under-handed and over-worked revenue staff, and (2) To provide a body of judicial officers, who might have the leisure and eventually the experience, requisite for the adjudication of important civil cases. The scheme, evolved by the Committee, was, after great modifications, submitted to the Supreme Government; and in August, 1877, a complete separation of the executive and judicial staff, from the office of Commissioner downwards, was effected, involving an increased expenditure of about 1,61000 Rs., the saving caused by the amalgamation. Thus the administrative staff consisted henceforth of 4 judges, each for a division, 12 subordinate judges, each for a district, and 22 Moonsifs on the one hand; and an Executive staff of 4 Commissioners, 12 Deputies, 24 Assistants, and 24 Extra Assistant Commissioners on the other. This scheme was put in force by Act XIII., in July, 1879.

In minor matters, the assimilation was supplemented. Allotments for assignments, annually made to district officers for local improvements, from surplus provincial funds—pound and Nazul, was introduced into Oudh; and administration of local funds was taken up anew and systimatised. The excise administration was assimilated with difficulty; for there was great diversity of practice. A committee of experienced officers was appointed, and the reforms resulted in the (1) abolition of Abkaree Daroghas, (excise sergeants), (2) equalization of the still-head duty, by a reduction in the N. W P., and an enhacement in Oudh; (3) complete separation of the money-taking and account-rendering establishments; (4) introduction of vessels of standard capacity for the removal of spirits from the distilleries; (5) substitution of English for country locks; and (6) entertainment of police guards in place of excise peons.

The financial reforms of 1878 were, that (1) contingent expenditure, though left to the discretion of disbursing officer, (Magistrate), was to be supervised and economised; (2) Other items were to be checked by the Commissioner, the controlling officer. Detail-auditing by the Account Department was retained. The second reform was that the realization of Public accounts, which were formerly classified as Imperial, Provincial, and Local, was now divided into (1) Imperial funds, (2) Provincial funds, (3) incorporated local funds, consisting of items primarily applicable to certain objects or localities, such as rate, road, school; and (4) excluded funds, being special deposit funds, administered by Government as trustee, as the Hosseinabad and other endowment funds.

A general code, for the administration of municipalities, was now passed, embodying directions as to public health, safety, convenience, and decency: the local committees were also allowed well-defined discretionary powers. A bench of Magistrates, consisting of six native gentlemen, was constituted for the city of Lucknow, for the trial of police and municipal offences. The important question of municipal taxation was reviewed and defended, on a reference from the Secretary of State as to the necessity of preventing Octroi duty from acting injuriously on transit trade, and of restricting it to its legitimate scope for local consumption only. Though the *Nazul* fund is classified as provincial, the surplus of that of Lucknow was declared to be local. The surplus, in the beginning of 1880, amounted to 2¼ lakhs.

A gigantic scheme of stamp-frauds was discovered at Lucknow in 1879; many persons were sent to penal settlements; reforms were instituted for the better administration of the department; and the rules, in force in N. W. P. and Oudh for sale of general and court fee stamps, were assimilated under a uniform code.

In 1878, the Arms Act and the Vernacular Press (otherwise called the Gagging) Act were put in force in Oudh, causing no little discontents to the people. "A circular was issued to all district officers, requesting them to invite the attention of editors, printers, and publishers to the provisions of the new law, accompanied by an expression of hope, on the part of the Lieutenant Governor, that it should not be found necessary to put it in force or to resort to authority." The result was that not only free criticison was put a stop to, but the supply of important local information ceased; and the local press was deprived of its healthy growth. In less than two years, the evils of the Act grew so intollerable, that, thanks to Lord Ripon and Sir Alfred Lyall, it was repealed; and the native journals are slowly recovering from the blight they had suffered.

Another great reform of the year was the establishment of an Agricultural Department. In former years, experimental cultivation of foreign cotton, hemp, and silk-worms did not succeed at all, though continually perservered; while that of indegenous products gradually and steadily declined, and fuel-supply yielded less and less. The rains began to fail, and Government revenue suffered in no small a degree. For these reasons, the attention of the people and Government was drawn to the subject; and the Department of Agriculture and Commerce was opened in co-operation with the people. The province of this department is to improve agriculture on a scientific basis, to extend arboriculture, or planting of trees along roads, to create markets for the country manufactures; to collect statistics of trade and to supervise the Patwaries and Qanungoes, who are scattered all around the united provinces to report on the progress of crops and to see village accounts. Under the Patwari section, the agricultural Officers are dependant and assistant to the Revenue department; and so for the solution of the rent-question at present in agitation, they are co-operating along with the Special Commissioner appointed for the purpose.

The agricultural improvements are effected by the scientific application of manures, sowing of better seeds, cultivation of foreign plants, supply of water without being dependent on rain, and the employment of improved cattle, implements, and machines. Wells are dug here and there; European implements are indented; many kinds of ploughs are invented and distributed by sale or loan; and complex manuring is done for the nourishment of young plants. The difficulty as to how to bring the improvements effected within the reach of the people was met by introducing them into the estates under the Court of Ward. But the real difficulty is the want of cheapness; and the improvements effected, are disproportionate to the cost incurred.

In order to create markets and to bring into public notice, all indigenous products and articles of local manufacture, exhibitions are held here and there, in conjunction with the gentries of the land. The principles, which guide these shows, are open to competition in cattle, implements, agricultural articles, arts and manufactures; and prizes are given to those, who exhibit the best productions. In December 1864, long before the Agricultural department was in contemplation, an exhibition was held at Lucknow, on the open "place" between Chhutter Munzil and Huzrutgunge. Temporary ornamental sheds, 27 in number, were erected, costing 25,000 Rs. 77 sheds were devoted to live stock, 5 to produce, 2 to machinery, 4 to arts and manufactures, and 1 to miscellaneous articles. The Taluqdars contributed about 4C,000 Rs. and the people appreciated the object of the exhibition, in so far as it was thoroughly understood that there was no ulterior or covert design in the movement. The show of country-bred horses and cattle, though susceptible of great Improvement, was still a fair one. Of produce, 1426 specimens were exhibited.

Arts and manufactures were fairly represented. But generally the European manufactures and machines pre-dominated. The exhibition was open for 8 days ; and the machines were purchased by native gentlemen. But no lasting good was shown by its after results,—beyond satisfying the curiosity of the people. Certain it was, that no other exhibition was held for a period of sixteen years.

In order to produce a lasting beneficial effect, exhibition should be open for more than a week, and be held annually and periodically. On this principle, the two exhibitions of 1881 were held in Kaisarbagh, under the auspices of the Talukdars, and were open for three and five days respectively. The various articles, under the usual classification, were exhibited; and were supplemented by wrestling contests, a flower show, illumination and a display of fire-works. The collection of articles, however, showed evident signs of inferiority and decline, in comparison to those of 1864 ; and many a thing exhibited was of the worthless kind. Common lithographs, toy-books and missionary tracts, were prominently shown ; while rewards were given to those, who did not deserve them. 60 Rs. were awarded to a prostitute, for her dogrel rhyming ; while the best artizans could not get more than Rs. 5. These extravagancies do a great deal of mischief, when associated with exhibition-schemes ; and the people simply lose their faith on the noble object, which engross a great deal of attention of government. The principles, which guide the Agricultural Department in the management of the district shows, are broader, and are producing beneficial results, surely though slowly ; and the Lucknow exhibitions, which should be yearly, in order to produce lasting effects, should be directed under the same lines.

In short, the Agricultural Department, though still on its experimental stage, and susceptible of great development, is doing good to the country in trying to restore,—at least to check the decline of local arts, to improve cultivation and productions and to create demand for their sale and supply.

On the night of 17th February, 1881, the census of Oudh, and of the whole of India was taken, yielding a total population of......millions. The last census, being first of its kind, was taken on the night of the 1st February, 1869, yielding a grand total of 11¼ millions.

The great reformation of 1882, and 1883, is the promulgation of the policy of self-government, as schemed by Lord Ripon, the most popular of the Viceroys of India, ever since the establishment of British rule. His Excellency, on his arrival here, found, that while the Indian Government is constituted for the people of the country, there is no co-operation between the rulers and the ruled. Antipathy reigned between the Europeans and natives; and instead of harmonious workings, there was undue criticism and opposition on the one side, and suppression by Press Act, &c. on the other. In fact, the Government, as Russell once said, is simply political and superficial; it is not social enough to reach to the people. Accordingly, out of the existing materials of village *punchayets,* and old Brahman *sabhas,* and with the experience of a western system, His Lordship envolved a self-government scheme, which, while eradicating the above-mentioned evils, should educate the people for administrative purposes, and to teach the Europeans the value of the people's co-operation.

Sir George Couper, who was Lieutenant Governor of the old antiquated school, could not enter into the spirit of the new policy; and the resolution he framed, did not receive the approval of the Supreme Government. On his retirement, Sir Alfred Lyall, who succeeded him, had to reconsider the whole question. His Honor appointed a committee, consisting of eleven European and four native members. Their report showed the desirability of the elective system; and His Honor sanctioned its introduction in all the municipal towns, except a few, where the circumstances are exceptional. With regard to the size of electoral wards, the number of members, that should represent each ward, the qualification of voters and candidates, the registration of voters, the nomination of candidates and the mode of recording votes, the Municipalities are invited to frame their own rules. The Municipal Boards will be at liberty to choose their own chairman, official or non-official, as they think proper; and the chairman, if non-official, will be appointed a Honorary Magistrate. Local Boards will be constituted for each Tehsil; and the District Boards will be an aggregate of the territorial ones. The Municipalities and Boards will be relieved of police charges, except those for watch and ward; for which purpose, local income, consisting of rates, pounds, ferries, &c., are to be placed entirely at their disposal. "The proportion of cost to be bourne by both Municipalities and District Boards for works and institutions, in which more than one are interested will be decided by mutual arrangement;" and their administration shall ordinarily be conducted by a joint committee of deligates. Copies of all proceedings of the boards shall be submitted to the chief District Officer, who will have power not only to make suggestions, and to call for information, but to provisionally suspend their actions.

In concluding this rough sketch of the present history of Oudh, we must not lose sight, in comparision to those of the past, the results of the British rule, with regard to (1) the morals and religious development, (2) education and ability, (3) openings and fields of workings, and (4) provision, comfort and security of the people. But before doing so, we should take note of Lord Stanley's review on the English administration of Oudh before the mutiny, and the lines of policy he sketched for the guidance of the Oudh Officers.

In his despatch dated 30th October, 1858, the then Secretary of State, while, considering the causes of the disastrous events of 1857, so far as they were attributable to failures in the administration, observed that "the tardiness with which your officers proceeded to afford relief to those whom the change of government had deprived of the means of subsistence, there is nothing to justify or to excuse." With regard to the three year's Summary Settlement, "it is impossible to resist the conviction that the intentions to conciliate all classes of the community were, especially in respect to the most influential classes, frustrated, partly by the circumstances of our positions in Oudh, partly by the insufficiency of the means prescribed for the settlement of the country, and partly by the remissness of the agents employed by you to give effect to your measures. ......In as much as the paramount motive for assuming the government of Oudh, was the promotion of the happiness of the people, it was especially the duty of the administration to recognise existing rights, to be tolerant of ancient usages, and to pay regard to the habits and feelings of all classes of the community, however greatly they might be at variance with our views......greater regard than heretofore ought to be paid to the expediency of employing the native of the province in all departments of the executive government. To provide these people (enemies) with profitable employment, would be to disarm them of their enmity towards us." Now let us see what results have followed these directions, or in what way were they carried out during the quarter century of British administration after the mutiny.

First with regard to religious development,.it is a matter of notoriety that the social checks and institutions being slackened, the people began to exhibit signs of moral deterioration in an eminent degree, as soon as English laws usurped the place of local customs and authorities. Formerly the men used to cultivate their national literature; and the boys, the vernacular versions of their scriptures, which were both their lessons and amusements. Accordingly the natives knew more of their creed, and so cultivated their national feelings, and lived a life of harmony with their neighbours. Now as great ignorance prevails about religeous matters, their creed is declining; and there is less harmony and union among the people,—as is proved by the annual increase of crimes and offences.

Secondly, the education of the people is not founded on a national basis; and, while indigenous literature is ignored and local lore is forgotten, there cannot possibly be any healthy growth of intelligence, where higher instruction is imparted in a foreign tongue and view. It takes quadruple time more than you require in mastering your mother tongue in order to get a little command of a foreign tongue; so that many years are taken up for simply learning the English language, which ought to be devoted for acquiring a knowledge of practical art. Besides the present system of education imparted in colleges and schools are superficial to a high degree; what are learned there is foregoten, as soon as the students come out of schools. There is nothing practical in it. That education does not fit one for worldly, much less religious life.

Accordingly the qualification of the people are pitiable to the last degree. With all their vast bookish knowledge, the so-called educated are helpless to the last degree. Not susceptible of enterprise, originality, or any independent career they look around for support from others. They may talk and speechify well,— but cannot show much matter. The fault is not theirs,—but in the circumstances. Though there was no systematic education—in fact much ignorance prevailed under the late kingdom, still able men occasionally appeared on the field of worldly life; for it is the circumstance, that is the great educator of mankind.

With regard to the third head, there cannot possibly be any doubt that the field of higher career has been almost closed to the natives of the land. No longer can any able minister, Nazim or Chuckledar, come out; nor is there any possibility of meeting another Hakim Mehdi and Sital Persad or Dursan Sing in the field of official life. All the high official positions have been occupied by foreigners. The openings and fields of workings are therefore contracted to an alarming degree. Land is overloaded with sharers and cultivators; the few rich are encumbered with hangers-on and idlers; the law is suffocated with its practitioners; and evils increase in a geometrical scale. No one can be found to chalk out an original career for himself, much less for others; there is no inducement or encouragement for that. The utmost ambition of the so-called educated natives is to be enrolled among successful clerks and copyists, and stagnancy of energy accumulates to overflowing into some dire misery in no distant future. Poor pigmies, they cannot soar to see above the nether world, in which they grope and grovel!

It is natural, therefore, that the condition of the people is not as it ought to be. Luxurious existence is gone with the kingdom; comfortable life is few and far between; the majority—high, middle, and low, is drowned in debt and misery. Evils accumulate; immoralities increase; quarrels, litigation, and scrambling of ancestral property, and clashing of interests, are phenomena of daily and hourly occurence. This is undoubtedly a sad picture of the whole. This is not the way to restore prosperity and regeneration to the country.

Turning aside from this sad view of the case, we come to the bright point. The present Government is a system, of which the parts are so combined as to produce a harmonious whole. Every member is so situated with regard to others, that while he has discretionary powers in a limited scale, to use for good purposes, his misdeeds and extravagancies are rooted out as soon as they are reported; whereas in the former regime, there was no good name for an able officer; nor infamy attended those, who could do nothing but cruelty and bad actions. The Government then was weak to helplessness; the members had no organization or united action among themselves; and the king, if incapable, was a mere hump of precious flesh for luxurious living. In the mutiny, Khan Bahadur of Bareli and Rana Beni Madho of Shunkurpore, lamented want of

Bundobust in the rebel Government;—which *Bundobust* they found to their cost in their enemy. The specimen of royal diary given in Sleeman's journals, though too colored, still shows the want of vital power in the main body.

The next point of excellence in the English Government, is the rapid application of united energy in cases of emergency. It is true, dilatoriness is patent in the Law-courts, Accounts department, Commissariat and minor branches; but when true occasions require, conferences are convened at railway speed; deliberations are conducted by telegraphs; grand projects are settled by demi-official letters; and important decisions are arrived at in social gatherings.

But the chief beauty of the English system of Government is its comprehensiveness. Important Departments have their Secretaries, with Assistants; sanitation is looked after by a Commissioner; forest is protected by a Conservator; and education, agriculture and commerce are presided over by Directors; while science is not without its reporter: and so on the intricacy of the system is covered by its catholicity. It is easy therefore, to effect grand achievements in an incredible short time, as is sometimes done by such an establishment. Famine languishes by our relief-works; census is taken in one night; no Indian reign did such before!

It will be said, perhaps, that results do not follow proportionately to the vast machine; the reason of which may be the want of co-operation by the people. But this now no longer exists; for self-governing bodies have been established every where. And with such a people's friend as Lord Ripon, and our equally popular Lieutenant-Governor, Sir Alfred Lyall, there cannot be any doubt that a bright future is in store for us. And this hope increases, when we find that His Honor, who is a poet, historian, and scholar, sees with his own eyes the welfare of his subjects, walks about here and there like a private gentleman to observe the condition of his charge, and calls out able men from their obscurity. Every one feels the atmostphere of a new healthy influence, and so confidence breeds a happy future.

History finis.

PART II.—ETHNOLOGY.

CHAPTER.—I. *A brief history of the people, their caste, religion, and character.*

Oudh was at first peopled by an aboriginal tribe, known as the Rákshashas, Daityas, or Barbars (barbarians) in the Vedas, the oldest book in the world. Then the Aryas came, and colonized the land; and the *Surya banshies* of Aujodhya flourished in all their glory, as detailed in the *Ramayana.* * Latterly they declined; and Buddhism supplanted Brahmanism. But Buddhism too, with its empire of Magadha, evaporated in time; and the caste-system with all the Hindu gods revived with greater splendour. Sankáráchárya, known to fame as an incarnation of the deity, swept away the so-called atheists of the period. The poor Buddhists fled to Naipal, yielded to reconversion, or took refuge in Jainism. Bikramáditya, by astronomical calculations, restored the sanctity and temples of Aujodhyá to the number of 360, according to the days of the lunar year; and pilgrims from all parts of the Hindu world paid homage as now to what the great archiologist of the period had decided. In course of time, the province was split up into petty kingdoms of the *Bhars*, *Tahurs*, *Aheers*, and other low castes, at Srábasti, Aujodhyá, Manikpore, Koushambhi, and Baree, till they in their turn were all eaten up by the growing empire of the *Kanaugiá.*

* In this city of well-fed and happy people, no one practised a calling not his own; none were without relations; the men loved their wives; the women were faithful and obedient to their husbands; no one was without earrings; no one went unperfumed; no Brahman was without the constant fire; and no man gave less than Rs. 1,000 to the Brahmans. This city was guarded by warriors, as a mountain-den by lions, filled with horses from Cambodoyia and other places; and elephants from the Vindyachal and Himalaya mountains, and governed as India governs his city, by Dasaratha, chief of the Ikshaku.

This king was perfectly skilled in the Vedas and Vedangas, beloved by the people, a great charioteer and constant in sacrifice. His courtiers were wise, capable of understanding a nod (hint), and constantly devoted to him. Eight Brahmans are mentioned as Chief Councillors, two as chosen priests; six others were also in office. "Surrounded by all these councillors, learned, faithful, and eminent, seeking by wise councils the good of his kingdom, Dasaratha shone resplendent as the sun irradiating the world." *Ramayan.*

In the kingdom of Magadha, (in which Koshal—ancient Oudh—was incorporated), the towns and villages are large; the people rich and fond of discussion, but compassionate and just in action, and the Sramans grave and sedate; the paintings and sculptures are such as this age cannot produce. On grand annual festivals, the streets were crowded; and the people entertained with towers of lances, on cars, theatrical and gymnastic representations; flowers and perfumes are scattered in profusion; and when night falls, the whole scene is illuminated by lanterns. *Fa Hian*, Spier's *Life in Ancient India.*

Jey Chandra, the last Hindu king, allied himself with the professors of the new religion (Mahomedanism) then known as Turks. He was engulphed as a reward of his friendship; and Hindustan was Mohamedanized as a natural result. Syed Salar crossed the Gangá to spread Gazeeism, and the seeds of his true faith. But before he could properly settle at and colonize Satrikh, Manikpore, and other places, his invasion collapsed, and he was killed at the battle of Bahraich; and Sohildeo of Asokpore, the victor, rose to fame.

But meantime the foreign empire at Delhi was firmly established; and Bukhtiar Khilgi finished what the nephew of Mahmood of Guznee had begun. The last king of Aujodhya took refuge in the Naipal Tarai, and founded Semraon. The people were massacred or converted by the sword, or were maltreated, and paid heavily for a passport to their idol-faith, and the greater part of Oudh relapsed into a forest region.

But, by the wear and tear of time, the fanatical foreign government was toned down, and got naturalized in the soil. The Hindus regained their importance in financial and other matters; while many were sent as Jageerdars, and Fouzdars into Oudh to recolonize the land, and re-establish order as before. The principal elements of modern Oudh society were now laid. "The country was divided into a number of Chieftainships, ruled over by clans, such as the Kahnpuriahs of Pratapgarh, the Gourhs of Hurdoi, and their offshoots, Ametheas of Rai Bareilly, the Bisens of Gonda and Pratapgarh, the Bais of Baiswarha, the Bachgoti Chauhans of Sultanpur, the Sombansies of Pratapgurh, and the Kulhans of Gonda;" while the Moslem colonies prospered at Bahraitch, Manikpore, Bilgram, Mulliabad, Kakori, Lucknow, Rudouli, and other places. Somutimes they had feuds with one another, more on boundary than on religious questions.

Latterly Oudh was subjected to the neighbouring kingdom of Jounpore. But Rajah Tilok Chand headed a successful rebellion; and for a century the local autonomy was maintained. Civil wars, however, brought on a general weakness, and the whirl-wind of Baber's invasion swept away the existing order, and the sacred Aujodhya of the Hindus was Moslemized, and a mosque was built. But Akbar restored every thing to harmony and organization; and the Hindus were as happy as ever. The Delhi administration over Oudh was perfected with the *pargana* as the territorial unit of administration, with a system of double checks over all officials, and with imperial and local influences well balanced together. *

Alamgeer's fanaticism, however, sowed the seed of ruin in the empire; and the chieftains of Oudh at once acquired an almost complete independence. The Hindus then again broke out into internal war; and the Kahnpuriahs of Tiloi and the Bais of Dundia Kherha, both cadet families of the Bisens of Gonda, increased their territories at their neighbours' expense.

When Saádat Ali came into Oudh, his entry was opposed by the refractory local chieftains. The Bais seem to have yielded after a parley, and the Kahnpuriahs, with only a sham resistance; but the Kichars of Futtehpore were only quelled after a doubtful battle, while the Rajah of Gonda actually defeated the Nawab's lieutenant, and made his own terms, by which he retained an ancestral estate as a separate fief, paying only a moderate tribute. To this period belong two of the most spirited of the national ballads, the sword-songs of Araru Kichar and Dutt Bisen Singh. This Nawab and his two successors conciliated their hard-won subjects; and the Hindus rose to the highest offices. It was the golden period of modern Oudh, a happy result produced by the nature of the strong central government, which preserved, while keeping under subjection, all the elements of society. W. C. Benett.—*Oudh Gazetteer.* †

---

* We see the *Perganah* used as the territorial unit in arranging the jurisdiction of local officials. We see the pairs of officials, acting as checks on each other, the two judicial and two revenue officers chosen from the resident magnates of the district, but devoid of all executive power. Above them are the direct nominees of the government, strangers to the country, constantly changed, the *Amil* acting as chief district officer with his little force to put down disturbances; and his two subordinates, the *Crorie* and *Jagirdar*, one employed in the revenue, and the other in the Military work. Over a number of *Perganahs*, varying from 5 to 40, and called a *Sircar*, was the *Fowzdar*, who like the Commissioner of a Division, united all authority in his hands, and heard all appeals. Over the five *Sircars* were the officials of the *Soubah*, and the Governor (*Soubadar*) of Oudh, who was subordinate only to the Great Mogul. Elliot's *Chronicles of Unao.*

† The Dehli administration, admirable in its system of gradation and counterchecks, had failed for want of vital power at the heart to carry its authority over such vast distances. But Fyzabad and Lucknow being nearer than Dehli, the province of Oudh was of a manageable size, and such that one strong hand could control it unaided. By a slight modification of Akbar's plan, (*i. e.* the province was divided into large tracts, governed by *Nizams*, not by Fouzdars, and the *Jagirdars* and *Crorie* were abolished; and the *Perganah Amil* was henceforth called a *Tehsildar*) Sufder Jung introduced a system, which under his rule and that of his successor, Shujah-ud-dowlah, secured such prosperity to the country as any native government has ever done. *Elliot's Chronicles of Unao.*

But with the defeat at Buxar, this state of things changed, and British interference produced intolerable evils, with which the native government could not cope. The relation between the *ryot* and *Sircar* scillated between the Ijáráh and the Amáni, the contract and the trust; and there was no fixity of purpose or permanency of details. The middlemen, the *Rajwarha* waxed into big Talukdars; and the Government officials waxed weak in helplessness, unless they secured the intervention of some local chieftains or influential capitalists. "The more thoughtful and large-hearted among the Company's superior servants now saw here what they had seen elsewhere, that when the Company virtually took possession of a native state, and pensioned off the Chief and his family, a moral deterioration followed; he was not allowed to exercise real sovereignty; he became more intensely selfish, because he had nothing to be proud of, even if he wished to govern well, and he took refuge in the only oriental substitute, sensual enjoyment." Chamber's *Sepoy Revolt.* Hence the chronic misrule of Oudh was produced, and the unavoidable annexation was brought about.

The revolution of 1857 annihilated whatever local vitality was left, and the subsequent Christain Administration comes and flourishes "with solvents, strong enough to disintegrate the compact organization" of Oudh. The life-blood being extinct, society lives and lingers as if in venerable old age. That great spirit, reared with so much care by Manu and Vyás, Akbar and Oudh Nawabs, which subdued Buddhism, even after its own annihilation, and which considerably toned down Islam, the greatest of fanatical religions, is at last to be dried up under the cold blasts of the northern wind; and as an empty stomach and uneasy mind can never breed a solid good brain, Oudh's future is gloomy to the last degree.

Thus historically we find the people professing three religions,—Hindu, Mohamedan, and Christian. Of Christians, Europeans, Eurasians, and Natives, there needs no particular account, as their society is not yet naturalized or developed, nor has its influence yet been felt outside their own sphere. Nay, while it can destroy every structure, it can not, like the Vandals of old, build any, but foppish Babus and mechanical clerks.

The Hindus are divided into castes, so are the Moslems to a certain degree. The prime principle, upon which this caste system is instituted, is, that every member of the society follows a certain hereditary profession, so as to serve one another, reciprocally and individually, as framed by the original law-givers of the nation. Thus the Brahmans were to see about religious and intellectual matter ; the Khetrias about the executive, chiefly the military power of the nation, the Baisyas, trades, as of supplying the wants of the society ; while the Sudras represented the labour-power of the whole, as servants and cultivators. In course of time, the castes began to cross and usurp one another's place, till the climax of an undistinguishable mass-society was reached under Buddhism. But Hinduism, like a cat after its apparent death, revived ; and the caste system was regenerated on a purer basis and more exhaustive and extended scale.

The fanatic Moslem coming, the Hindus had an awful time of it. Many frail-minded embraced the fashionable court-creed ; and not a few conducted themselves in a half yielding way, by adding some Mohomedan terms to their family titles. But in the meantime, the rulers themselves submitted to the influence of the so-called idol-worshippers, and their marriage and other semi-religious ceremonies partook as now of those of the superstituous Hindus. They lived on terms of perfect fraternity and friendship. Umjud Ali Shah, the reformer, tried in vain to resist the current of imitation and accomodation. Human society, as well as nature, is not even and stationary ; they rise and fall and are influenced by external circumstances, as are all things in this ever-changing world. That is a current, which can never be made stagnant, much less to be restored to its primitive orthodoxy.

The British came with all their foreign ideas, and hitherto yield not to the social rules and standard of the people. And the means of subsistence being greatly diminished, the caste-system vanishes in substance. The name only remains, showing that such a man belongs to such a class, which professed such an art or branch before. Now the Brahman, for instance, is a cook, soldier, peon, water-carrier, priest, clerk, shop-keeper, and beggar. In this manner, the other castes supplement their means of existence, and deviate considerably from the original tribal professions.

The many-godded religion, as Hinduism is, limits superstition as also progress, and maintains the conservative and national power of greatness for a longer period than the one-godded. The latter gets cosmopolitan and loses its local tone in its temporary progress. Hence it is superficial, and has not depth of feelings and virtue. One God means an universal and unlimited idea, which vulgar men, nay even the adepts, comprehend not as a whole, but only in parts. Hence monotheism gets into a pantheon of incarnations, prophets, saints, and hermits, and the original deity is lost sight of, and religion becomes a formality. Such is the monotonous history of the Aryanism, Buddhism, Christianity, Mohamedanism, and all other religions. Thus all tend to conservatism and national contraction, which at its culminating point bursts into a temporary revolution and reformation, and thus on to the end of the world.

The religion of the Hindus is both simple and complex, and is well-graduated and adapted to every one's capacity. It ranges from the most abstract of monotheism to the grossest of superstitions imaginable. So that its effect on the people is of mixed nature ;—one is a godly *yogee* by the superlative negation, the other is a satanic Thug, by his abuse of idolatry ; one is a saintly Paramhansha, the other is an ugly Aghorpanthee; one is self-denying after the example of Ramchandra, the other is a debauchee after the manner of Kanahia, (Krishna corrupted.)*

The Arab after throwing away his gross idolatry, found himself a new man. He thinks himself the first to discover truth, like Christ of old. He became proud and fanatic, and was mad to regenerate the old-fashioned world. The upstart is swelled by his egotism ; he cannot see out and knows not higher sentiments or extended experience. So the follower of Mohammad goes out and propagates his system, till his sword is broken up and yields to the soft influence of the superior intellectual creed of Hindustan. He becomes more tolerant and less fanatic, and like Hindu *yogees* and *Babajees*, tends to Fakirism and Shahism. And both were happy, compact, and strong under Akbar the Great. And the Nawabs of Oudh upheld the policy.

* The first principles of the Hindu religion are (1) to abstract the mind from the concrete, (2) to fix it on an idea, spiritual or material, (3) to prolong it, (4) to intensify it, (5) to extend it, and (6) lastly to be absorbed in it. Thus given goddess Kali, a material idea, as a starting point, you are to fix the whole mind on it, to exclude all other ideas, and to look every thing as Kali. The highest point is reached when the individuality ceases, and the *ego* is lost in the universal, omnipresent Kali, who is no other than the great Power which destroys, reproduces and sustains (Siva, Bramha and Vishnu—the Hindu trinity) all we see in nature. But now these objects have been lost sight of; and the allegory of the pantheon is taken for reality. So Kali is understood to be a substantial living goddess.

The effects of the three religions, Hindu, Mohamedan, and Christianity, at home and abroad, are, that the Arya emerged from darkness, was a self-made man, and spread his civilizing agency, east and west, in an humble spirit of naturaligation. The Mohamedan, coming on the same mission, was ennobled by him and got additional strength. The Christian ruler, however, does not mix with his subject ; nor does he allow his energy to be expended in the Society of the natives of the country. He grows weaker; and the local interests are jarring to an unpleasant future. But mankind, as in duty bound, much more, when a sovereign-race, should fashion and correct one another reciprocally. But alas ! the Englishman aims not more than to divide and rule.*

---

* Duties of Sovereign :—Let the king prepare a just compensation for the good, and a just punishment for the bad; the rule of strict justice let him not transgress ... Holy sages consider as a fit dispencer of criminal justice that king, who invariably speaks truth, who duly considers all cases, who understands the sacred books, who knows the distinctions of virtue pleasure and riches......Let him continually learn habits of modesty and composure, constantly must he show respect to Brahmans (intellectual and spiritual men), who have grown old *both in years and in piety,* who know the scriptures, and who in body and mind are pure. From them, let him learn the triple doctrine of criminal justice and sound policy. From the people must he learn the theory of Agriculture, Commerce, and other practical arts......With extreme care let him shun the eighteen vices, ten proceeding from love of pleasure, eight from wrath, and all ending in misery......since he may lose even his life from public resentment. Hunting, gaming, sleeping by day, censuring rivals, excess with women, intoxication, singing. instrumental music, dancing, and useless travel, are the tenfold vices produced by love of pleasure. Tale-hearing, violence, insidious wounding (spleen-bursting from mental abberation for example), envy, detraction, unjust seizure of property, reviling, and open assault are in like manner the eightfold vices, to which anger gives birth. A selfish inclination, which wise men know to be the root of those two sets, let him suppress with diligence.

Let him act as a father to his subjects. Here and there he must appoint many sorts of intelligent supervisors, who may inspect all the acts of the officers engaged in his business......what the king has not gained, let him strive to gain by military strengths ; what he has acquired, let him preserve by careful inspection ; what he has preserved let him augment by legal modes cf increase ; and what he has augmented, let him dispense with just liberality and bestow on the deserving. This is the fourfold rule; which he must consider as the sure means attaining the great object of man, *happiness.*

After full consideration, let a king so levy taxes continually in his dominions, that both he and the merchants (and subjects) may receive a just compensation for their several acts. Let him, considering the diversity of cases, be occasionally sharp and occasionally mild. Sir W. Jone's *Manu's Code.*

Duties of a Sovereign from the Mohamedan point of view :—I command thee to fear God, and observe his ordnances, propagate true religion, restrain their passion......the people will judge thee according to thy merits ; love thy subjects and have affection for them in the same way as a father has for his son ; overlook thou their offences in the same way as thou expectest forgiveness from thy master. Thou shouldst mend the manners of those placed under thee. Be polite in thy manners, so that thou shouldst win the confidence of thy subjects ; be not hasty in thy punishment, lest the man whom thou punishest *may not merit thy award.* Never oppress the creatures of God ; for the cries of the poor soon

The two former epochs formed conjointly the national character into a happy cast, as now may be seen, but which is rapidly disappearing from the land. Honesty and integrity still form the chief features of the character of the peeple.*

---

reach the ears of the Almighty, and he is sure to punish tyrants. Follow such a system of Government as may be just and equitable. Do not act in haste. Take such men for thy ministers, who may be of acute understanding, who would not abet any one to acts of oppression or persuade thee to violate the dictates of religion. Never depart from that system, which may have been prescribed by thy predecessors in accordance with the wishes of thy subjects and on which the management of the kingdom depends. Assess the cultivators of land so as the payment of Government demand may not be a source of ruin to them, and thus put a stop to Agriculture ; for on the contentment of the peasant depends the prosperity of the kingdom and the happiness of the people. Warn thy door-keepers and warders to allow access to all the public audience, and let them speak freely, so that none for fear of being molested be afraid to speak to thee, and thus be deprived of their rights......... *Ally's Epistle* to Ushter, the Ruler of Egypt, translated by S. A. Akbar of Oudh.

† Character of the people :—from Greek testimony (B. C. 400 to 300). The justice of the Indians, their devotion to their king, and their contempt of death are themes, on which Ktesias loves to enpatiate, *Photias.* They live happily enough, being simple in their manners and frugal. Theft is of rare occurrence. They never drink wine except at sacrifices. The simplicity of their laws and their contracts is proved by the fact that they seldom go to law. Their houses and property they generally leave unguarded. Truth and virtue they hold alike in esteem. None of the Indians employ slaves ; for all are free. *Strab's Megasthenes' Indica.* They neither put out money at usury, nor know how to borrow. *Ælian.* No Indian is accused of lying. *Arrian.* But further there are usages observed by the Indians, which contribute to prevent the occurrence of famine among them ; for whereas, among other nations, it is usual, in the contests of war, to ravage the soil, and thus to reduce it to an uncultivated state, among the Indians, on the contrary, by whom husbandmen are regarded as a class that is sacred and inviolable, the tillers of the soil, even when battle is raging in their neighbourhood, are undisturbed by any sense of danger ; for the combatants, on either side, in waging the conflict, make carnage of each other, but allow those engaged in husbandry to remain unmolested. Besides they neither ravage an enemy's land with fire, nor cut down its trees. *Diodorus,* McCrindle's translation

Chinese testimony ;—" The people are rich and fond of discussion, but compassionate and just in action ;" while " the grave and sedate department of the Sramans" are noted by Fa Hian and the other traveller.

Mohamedan testimony :—The Hindus are religious, affable, courtious to strangers, prone to inflict austerities on themselves, lovers of justice, given to retirement, able in business, grateful, admirers of truth, and of unbounded fidelity. Their character shines brightest in adversity. Their soldiers know not what it is to fly from the field of battle. When the success of the combat becomes doubtful, they dismount from their horses and throw away their lives in payment of the debt of valour. They have great respect for their tutors ; and make no account of their lives, when they can devote them to the service of their God. They believe in the unity of God ; and although they hold image in great veneration, yet they are, by no means, idolators, as the ignorants suppose. *Abul Fazl's Ain Akbari.*

English testimony :—The limited amount of crime attributable to private and individual motive that occurs in this country (Oudh) must be considered as highly creditable to the natural humanity, love of justice, and forbearance of its inhabitants. Dr. Buttler, 1830.

But now alas, all is metamorphosed for the worse. Subjection to unsympathetic foreign masters breeds defects and deformity Constant failures produce want of steadiness, "an absolute incapacity to maintain resolution, on most subjects in the face of what would seem to us the most trifling discouragements." Open dealings and plain speaking not meeting success, chicanery and intrigue are the fashion of the day. Writing was invented to conceal, not to express one's thoughts; and the so-called civilization goes obliquely and zigzagly to its selfishness. Diminished subsistence has concentrated one's attention from neighbourly feelings to selfshness. Straitened enjoyment impels all to break the law and social delicacy. Want of employment and income has made the people quarrel and scramble and litigate about the little remains of their ancestral property. Higher walks of life are closed, and they are bereft of noble feelings and purpose. Scarcity of exercise, mental and physical, tends all to sloth and melancholy, laziness and vice. Their learning is bookish, education is cramming, its results are hollow; intelligence is dried up, and the future of Oudh is gloomy.

The moral atmosphere is charged with evil influences. It cannot be denied that society, as formerly circumstanced, was purer in its tone, surrounded as it was, with many checks from neighbours, friends, elders and all. They were fault-finders; and each took care to please all. There was abundance, and none wished for more. With all its noted debauchery, Lucknow was more free from the general and spreading vice.

Even among our servants, no one can fail to be astonished at the absolute safety, with which large sums of money may be intrusted to their keeping, when theft will be almost impossible of detection, and would secure them comfort for the remainder of their lives. In the higher ranks, the office clerks are faithful and trustworthy beyond any class of men, who can be procured for their responsible duties. Trade-transactions involving enormous sums are carried through with a want of precaution, which we should consider idiotic, but which is justified by the rarities of the breaches of faith. In a country, where writing is an art as common as it is with us, large debts are contracted every day on nothing but the verbal security of the borrower......In such cases, limitation is never thought of, and families, who have emerged from poverty, will discharge debts, contracted by their ancestors—a century back, of which no other records exist, but an entry in the money-lender's private ledger. Their whole social system postulates an exceptional integrity. and would collapse at once, if any suspicion of dishonesty attaches itself to the decisions of the caste *punchayets.* This point is worth insisting on, as on it depends the whole of their future as a self governing nation......The courage and high sense of honor of the Brahmans and the Rajputs, the thrift and industry of the Kurmi, are patent to the shallowest observer, and all perhaps may claim a natural aversion to cruelty, a gay and buoyant disposition of mind, and an imagination easily impressed by beauty and humour. W. C. Benett, *Oudh Gazetteer* 1877.

The people now, with their poverty, licentious liberty, selfishness and want of shame, are more open and less scrupulous in their social conduct. The only check is the British Courts of law, which, however, are often slippery, and cannot catch the breakers of public morality, if not peace.

The relation between the ruler and the ruled is wholly artificial and superficial. Now loyalty means empty *saláming*. It is shown in illuminations, explodes amidst fireworks, and is eaten up at state-banquets. It just filters in subscription-lists; and its visible manifestation is a congratulatory address, when a big man comes, or a success is secured, and empty condolence, when a disaster is met. Active loyalty is gone with the local prosperity; and hollow deeds are followed by hollow effects. Service now means servility as loyalty, flattery; for that loyalty is a huge sham, which is not grounded on patriotism. Loyalty now is nothing but indirect selfishness. Active loyalty loves not paraphernalia, but rests on a well-fed stomach. Still water runs deep. Hindu Oudh was loyal to the Mohomedan rebellion, and thousands died for their king. British Government should secure the thorough affection of all; and thousands of loyal swords will leap from the scabbard, and many more volunteers will come forward to sacrifice their lives, to avenge the least insult offered it, and to preserve the honor of the empire.

But there is hope yet, and the unfavourable comparison may disappear in time. "It is the stability, which his caste system has given to his own society, which the Hindu has to thank, that the disease has not penetrated deeper, and as yet remains a mere surface ulcer, dangerous but curable." *Benett.* And the eyes of the Government are opened. "In this (Fine Arts) as in all things in India, it is our duty not to stifle or overpower the national life of the country, but to develope and uphold it.........It is upon the ancient foundation of that civilization alone, that we can hope to erect, firm and enduring, the superstructure of that wider and higher life, which it should be the aim of our Government to foster and advance." (Lord Ripon's speech in opening the Simla Fine Arts Exhibition.) And the results of the reformation will be golden and harmonious. It is not yet too late to retrace the false steps of former rulers.

CHAPTER II.—*Citizens of Lucknow.*

As the residents of an old city are short in stature and have less of virtue but more of intellect, the Lucknow-man is not generally tall, brave, handsome and generous, as the Dahatee, the countryman. But he balances his defects by a superior knowledge of the evils of life, civilized manners, and talkativeness.

SEC. I. THE HINDUS.

The physical features of the Hindus are a round face with a peculiar ruddiness in their brown colour. Their forehead is broader and eyes larger than those of the Mohamedans. Their nose is not long. They keep clean by constant bathing and washing. They have sandal wood-paste mark on their forehead and arms. Their *Sikha* or lock of long hair, shows itself on their head prominently, when their cap or *pagri* is taken off. Their *chapkan*, a kind of tunic, is buttoned on the right side.

They can think well, though unmethodically yet practically. They have a good memory. Their grasp of a subject is not far-reaching. They have got a practical mathematical head. Of a temperament, half sanguine and full phlegmatic, their feelings are of the gentle kind. The mild Hindu is well-known for his resignation to whatever hard lot befalls him. He does not feel deadened in adversity, nor puffed up at a sudden turn of fortune. He has a great deal of patience and perseverence, is industrious and engages in all sorts of work, except those forbidden by his scriptures. He is never prodigal in expenditure, except on marriage occasions. His proneness to vice is of the mild type. Morally he is superior to his Moslem brother, as he has less civilization, as compared with him.

The Hindu women generally have well-proportioned face, rounded limbs and body. They are not educated, or but very little. Their disposition partakes of simplicity and purity. Though their manners are not refined, yet they have nothing mean or vulgar in them. They have something of innate dignity in their outward deportment, and mental development.* They are not so much confined in the Zenana, as their Mohamedan sisters are, and have more liberty in their movements and life. They generally perform all their household duties; for as the Hindus do not eat things cooked by other than their own clan, the women themselves cook and do all such works. But this holds good with the middle class. The rich families employ Brahman cooks, male or female.

The family government of a Hindu, which is on a joint system, composed of dependent relatives, brothers, father, sons, and others, may seem peculiar to a European. The eldest lady of the house, generally mother, or the grandmother, or the eldest *Bhawaj*, the wife of the first brother, is the stewardess, and has general management and superintendence over all the other women and children. The other fair members have their respective duties. One is to prepare and arrange flowers and other things for the family-god, who is worshipped by a priest of long standing. A second cooks and a third assists her. A fourth is to look after the babes and children, and so on according to the necessities of the house. In some of the latter duties, a maid-servant or two sometimes assist, if the master of the house can afford to keep one or more.

The period of their recreation lasts from noon till evening. The elderly ladies, then go out to a friend to hear recitations from the Ramayana, Mahabharat, or some Poorans, or any religious legends, or to a distant temple, Bhaironji or Kalkaji, to adore the deity therein confined. The younger ladies employ this period in singing, in gay topics, and in ornamenting themselves to captivate their respective husbands at night. Some, more business-like, may be seen sewing their old clothes or embroidering the new.

---

* If the females of India excel in any species of physical beauty, it is particularly in the fine mould of their limbs. A statuary might have taken those delicately-shaped arms and hands as models for his Venus. *Private Life of an Eastern King.*

The Hindostanee women (Hindu and Mohamedan) ... are in general exquisitely formed after the truest models of symmetry and beauty. Their countenances, more pleasant than handsome, are very expressive, their large black eyes in particular, full of the softest fire, convey volumes, and almost supercede the necessity of speech, ... (They) are so alluring in their manners, are ever so solicitous to preserve (the) affection (of their husbands), and again in a short time, get so wonderful an ascendancy on the most determined, that a separation becomes impossible. *Sketches of India*, 1814.

Truly, if Hindostan is to be saved, it will be by the virtue of its women; for more honorable, more honest-minded, more nobly endowed female humanity is not to be found in the most highly civilized regions of the earth, than among the Zenanas of India. *Private Life of an Eastern King.*

Of the male members of the family, the eldest one, generally the father, grandfather, or the first brother, who may have retired from the business world, has the management of the internal affairs of the house, such as buying necessaries of life, and keeping accounts of expenditure. The other members rise and bathe early in the morning, and after taking breakfast, go out to their respective employments. In the evening they return, hand over to the chief of the house, whatever they have earned, and after taking supper, retire about 10 p. m. to their respective private rooms, when only they can see and talk to their wives, for it is contrary to custom to hold conversation between the husband and wife before others, especially elders. The children sleep with their mother. The wives of the house always keep themselves veiled before elderly people, and hence are called *Bahoos*.

A particular account of each Hindu tribe may be briefly stated.—

The *Brahmans* are few in number in this city. They have got good features, large and prominent foreheads. Being generally poor, they have a beggarly appearance about them. The indispensable holy thread hangs from their left shoulder to the right side. The priests are of this class; but their run in Hindu Shashtras and lore is limited. Most of them are astrologers. Many are seen strolling about, generally on Saturday, in the streets and lanes, with a manuscript almanac under their arm, bawling out, "Pundit Brahman, Sanichar Dewta." occasionally some women call one in, and ask about their wished-for fortune, dear ones who are away and of whom no news has come for a long time, or about some valuable things lost or stolen. They are satisfied with the Brahman's answers, true or false; and he goes out, being well-pleased with a few pice (copper pieces) in his pocket, or a *Sidha*, composed of rice, floor, ghee (clarified butter), oil, sweetmeat, and salt so as to complete a meal when cooked.

Historically, Maharajah Beni Bahadur, a Brahman by caste, was minister to Shujah-ud-dowlah. Rajah Darsan Singh, his brother and sons, were able Nazims and officers. The Brahmans were astrologers to the Mohamedan Kings, without whose advice no important business was undertaken. Newly appointed Resident had to wait for days together at Dilkusha before the soothsayers of Lucknow could select an auspicious day, on which the king was to meet and conduct him to his palace.

The *Kashmiri* Brahmans or Pundits, as they are called, have fair complexion, large eyes, long nose, short and thin stature, small mouth and head. They are nervous in temperament. Their mental capacities are rather intensive than extensive; and they can apprehend well. They are generally educated in English; and many succeed well in law. Nothing is definitely known of the time and reason of their emigration into the plains from Kashmir. But it may be safely presumed, that about three or four centuries ago, when the Happy Valley was under Mohamedan rulers, the Hindu subjects were greatly oppressed. Hence many left the mother country and settled among the inhabitants of the great cities of Hindustan proper. They have great adaptability to naturalize themselves among foreigners. The Cashmeeree Pundits had no importance under the native rule. Only one is known as the author of *Indra-sabha*, the first and only local Drama, composed in *Urdoo*. Rai Dilaram was a well known *Chakládar* of Tandiaon; he was of this tribe.

The *Chhatris* are the military class properly so called, of which the *Rajput* tribe is a branch. Pure Khatrias are scarce. Hence the military recruits are taken from the country *Chhatrias*, mixed class and Brahmans, the latter having got the fighting propensity from the boundary disputes regarding their ancestral lands, opposition to Government exactions or any other kinds of affrays, that used to occur often in the olden time. The Chhatris of this city do not enter the military line, but engage in the peaceful calling of shop-keeping. They are generally Jewellers, *Jowhuris*, and money-lenders *Mahajans*. Their physiognomical features partake of those of the Kashmiri Pundits and the Baniahs. They have the large eyes and fair complexion,—though a little darker—of the former, while their nose, chin and mouth resemble those of the latter.

The *Kaiths* (Kayastha) are the race of writers. They are of short and thin stature, their faces neither broad nor long, eyes not large, and nose of middle length. Their mental capacities are contracted, because of the present contracted field of their career. Their ideas circle within their limited local sphere. They are generally *Munshees* or vernacular clerks. They earn their bread in judicial places or courts. Some *Lalas*, for Lalas they are called, are also traders, though they consider shop-keeping as beneath their dignity. Necessity, hard as it is, compels every body to get his means of existence by other than tribal professions.

Many get educated in English and with difficulty enter office-life as clerks. About one-fourth of the Extra Assistant Commissioners, *Munsarims*, *Tehsildars* and legal practioners belong to this class. They also serve exclusively as *qanungoes* and as *Dewans* to the native Nawabs; "while an inferior class of them carries on the business of village accountants or *Patwaris*." The Lalas were before the annexation an important class; they were largely employed under the native regime. Maharajah Newal Rai was an able lieutenant to Sufdar Jung. Maharajahs Tikait Rai and Jhaoo Lal were ministers to Asuf-ud-dowlah. Maharajah Balkishen and Rajah Kundan Lal were respectively financial minister and *Meer Munshi* to Wajid Ali Shah.

The *Marhwaris* are the people of Marhwarh or Jodhpore in Rajasthan. Their features are like the Kaisths, only not so dark-complexioned. They have a small red turban on their head, two rings on their ears, and the invariable paste-mark on their forehead. Their business life is quite monotonous, and seldom falls into ill-success. They are a fair type of the orthodox Hindu. They have no historical importance here. They are an enterprising race, and go even beyond the forbidden Indus to trade, as in to Cabul, Bokhara, and some Russian cities. With this instinct, they came here and prospered under the native regimé, till Umjad Ali Shah impeded their progress, in his orthodox frenzy. Now they are well off, and carry on their trade successfully.

The *Baniah* is an offshoot of the Baisya class of old Manu's four division of caste. He is a shop-keeper in every shape, but chiefly in grain-dealing. He is like the Marhwari in every respect; his stature and features are however, like those of the Kaith, and his business ebbs and flows. He is generally a fat man. He never appears in the higher circles of society. Jagannath Baniah, however, became great by embracing the Mohamedan creed, was honored with the title of Shurf-ud-dowlah by Amjad Ali Shah, and though illiterate and unable to write, yet by the strength of his natural talents, raised himself to the position of the able Assistant Minister to Wajid Ali Shah.*

The lower classes of the Hindus need not be detailed. Gálib Jung was a very talented Kurmi by caste. It was Gazee-ud-deen Hyder, who raised him from his humble situation. His son Maharajah Jeya Lal was a great leader of the rebellion. Thus at a cursory glance on the local inhabitants, it will be seen, that there is a fair sprinkling of great men in all the castes; who raised themselves according to circumstances, for it is the circumstance that makes a man. If you close the door of circumstance, no great man rises, as is the case in this English rule.

Of foreigners, the *Bengalees* were then known only as a race of magicians, now the inflated educated Babus. Their *Jadu* was celebrated throughout Hindustan, in the age of the Mohamedan supremacy. Even Jehangeer particularly described in his autobiography their wonderful exploits in the black art. Now the same race is more sceptical about it than any other. In the old Oudh kingdom, they were very few as clerks to the Residents or artizans to the Kings.

There was a Bengalee watch-maker to Gazee-ud-din-Hyder. He had two wives, one of his own race, the other a local Mohamedan. The Hindu wife could not produce any sons, while the Mohamedan did; and hence the husband was partial to the latter. A jealousy was the consequence, and the women quarrelled all their days and nights. The king after his wont, one night while strolling in the streets and lanes, in the garb of a *fakir* begging alms, in order personally to examine the success of his reign, came to the door of the Bengalee's house in Ismilegunge, now demolished. His Majesty heard the quarrelling of the wives, stayed for a while, and after some local enquiry went away.

---

* He had great influence, and by his increasing diligence, combined with great natural talents, though he could neither read or write Persian, contrived to unite in himself a very numerous string of offices, of which the following were not the least profitable; the *Hazur Tehsil*, or office, into which more specially direct revenue payments were made by those, who held that privilege; the payments of all Begums and wives of sorts; the supplying of all *khilats* or presents, ordered by the king for presentation; the contract of all city-bazaars; town-duties, prostitutes, and public buildings. Hutchinson's *Oudh Mutiny*.

Next morning, the king sent for the Babu, and pretending to be in great wrath, demanded of him, the reason how was it that he failed in his duty now, in which he had before succeeded so well. The trembling Babu knows not what to answer and is afraid that his end is near. His Majesty then asks why he has married two wives. The Bengalee, with folded arms, submits that when sovereigns are not content, unless they have filled their harems with hundreds, their subjects cannot but follow their example by taking only a couple. The King smiles and sends for the two quarrelsome wives. They are introduced under the cover of the *purdah*, in the hall of justice; and each pleads her cause with abundant tears and cries, after the manner of women.

The king, after patient hearing, decides in favour of the Bengalee wife, and out of five children, undoubtedly the property of her husband, two are decreed to her, with a royal pension and favour; while the husband is strictly enjoined to equalize his affection impartially between the two. Such is one of the many anecdotes of royal favours, shown to the people—which attract their affection more than anything else, and for which they lovingly remember the old dynasty.

The Lucknow people are still inclined to caricature the Bengalee as a fool. " A gang of buffoons was introduced, who began by imitating the cries of different animals; they then took off the singing and airs of the most distinguished *natch*-girls; but what seemed to give the greatest delight to the company, was a man who represented a Bengalee, and got a prodigious number of slaps in the face for various acts of stupidity. The caricaturing the poor inhabitant of Bengal as a fool seemed to tickle the fancy of the Nawab-Wazir and all his kinsmen, no less than it excited the glee of all the up-country servants, who were attending us behind our chairs." *Marquis of Hastings.*

Lord Canning introduced a Bengalee Talukdar, who did some good here. But the Bengalees in general are locally known as clerks and railway Babus. They are now looked on in the light of the Jews in the middle ages; and *demi-official* edicts were often sent-forth to expel them from the offices. Poor Babus! they know not how to assert their claims. In the mutiny they suffered equally with the Europeans, and yet no compensation, much less reward was given to them. While the *Poorbias* engross *lakhs* of Bengal money as sepoys and policemen, it does not look well, that the local administrators cannot brook the Babus to compete for, or take away a few hundreds.

Section II.—Mohamedans.

The distinguishing features of the Mohamedans are long face, long nose, a little arched, small and sunken eyes, short yet heavy chin, sunken low cheeks and temples, the forehead not prominent, lips thick and of the African type, and cheek-bones broad. They have a beard, though the Shias cut it short. Their *chapkan* is buttoned on the left side. The higher class has a fair skin with a general cleanliness. It is very difficult to know anatomically those Mohamedans, whose ancestors were converts from Hinduism. You will be able to distinguish them only by the outer signs, *viz.*, the *chapkan*, beard and the exterior deportment.

Mentally they have no power of patient thinking. Their memory and penetrative perception are generally less than those of the Hindus. They were never good mathematicians or metaphysicians. No Mohamedan was ever a Dewan; very seldom he was an able financial minister. But these short-comings are balanced by a great deal of imagination and power of intrigue, strength of feelings, and refinement of manners.

Morally, their feelings are those of the fanatic kind. They are easily excited and moved. They are generally lazy, and hence they are much prone to vice. When excited they can do more work than the Hindus. But then their busy life does not last long;—they soon relapse into inaction. For they have less patience and perseverance. Hence they are poor generally, and having no resignation, are more discontented than the Hindus, under the British rule. They have great taste for fine arts. They are generally ignorant. They have not yet forgotten, that they, a few years since, were a race of rulers. But the possibility of a second rebellion is far remote, for though they brag of their soldierly-qualities, the present generation is greatly deteriorated in body and mind; nor is a nation ever emancipated from its bondage by *Shodahs*, *Badmashes*, and bad characters.

Socially, they have more civilized manners than the Hindus can pretend to. "There is an innate gentlemanliness in the manners and address of the Musulman, which, taken as a national characteristic, exceeds that of more civilized countries. He has a dignified composure of countenance, gracefulness of action, and tact, in the use of the delicate instrument,—flattery—peculiar to himself." G. C. Mundy, 1827.

His mode of conversation is more conventional and less business-like. The style of his colloquial language is formal and high-sounding. When the Musulmans quarrel, they do so smoothly and ironically; after half an hour they separate, keeping in their minds vindictive feelings to be indulged in on a more favorable occasion, either by the employment of *Shodahs* or some other unfair means. The Hindus, on the other hand, would quarrel plainly, abuse each other furiously and come to blows. After a few minutes, they are separated by the bystanders or relatives, and a few days or weeks after, they are friends again.

There are two classes of Mahomedans, the higher and the lower, the middle being very few. The higher class are a few hundreds in number, who are known as Nawabs. Their appearance is generally well proportioned; and their behaviour towards others is apparently gentlemanly. Pride and presumption are however their reigning principle, being descendants of, or connected with the royal family of Oudh. Their education, which is quite superficial, consists of a little smattering of Urdu and Persian verses. They generally live on political pensions and *wasikas* or interests of the debts contracted by the old Company.

There are very few Moslems in the middle class; for even those, who are in it, show and conduct themselves in such a manner, that the outsider can not easily judge of them. They may be however known by some old carriages, ragged shawls and dilapidated houses, in which they live. Not unfrequently many of their family starve.

The others of this class are not exactly of this city. They are Rohillas, Dehatees and Kashmiris. They are not idle and live in some sort of business. The Kashmiri *Agas* subsist on shawl-manufacture. Their mind is of the business stamp, and is not wrought up with the dreams of some fairy land. Truth, however, is not a favourite goddess with them; they consider dissimulation to be a great diplomacy of life. "The old colonists as of Bilgram, Malihabad and Rudowli (and now Kakori) sent out a number of men distinguished in science, administration and war, and still provide the English Government, with a number of its ablest servants, especially at the bar."

The lower class is promiscuously composed of the refuse from the higher and the middle classes, of Syuds or religious mendicants, the *Shodahs* or rogues, beggars of all description, menial servants and those, who are of low professions. This class numbers more than three-fourths of the entire Mahomedan population of the city, of which nearly one-third are beggars. So that their features, mental and physical, can not be easily generalized. They are usually dirty and ignorant, and have less understanding than presumption.

The Syuds are the so-called decendants from their prophet, Mohamed, and hence are more respected for their higher and purer blood. Nawab Ali Naki Khan, the last Prime Minister of Oudh, was a Syud. It is generally considered below the dignity of the Syuds to serve or work for any body. Religion is their only profession; hence they are prone to idleness and beggary, which they do in the streets in the name of their saints. Though they are of the religious order, they understand very little the original Koran, which is never allowed to be translated. Their women also go about to exhibit the relics of the mortal remains of Huzrat Ali and his two sons, and pictures of the tragic events of Moharrum.

The higher class reduced have all the features, mental and physical, of their original class. They are now beggars, because of their own or their ancestor's extravagance in living, want of employment, consequences of the great rebellion, or the change of Government. They lead a very miserable life, as they can not adapt themselves to present circumstances. Instead of men supporting the women, here the women support and provide for their males by means of their relationship to the rich, sewing and embroidering. They are a perfect personification of vice and misery.

The *Shodas* are a mixed people. All the bad characters of the city are included in the term. They are thieves, gamblers, pickpockets, brigands of the streets, and rogue-beggars. They may be divided into two sections——the decent, and the dirty looking. The decent-looking have a polished exterior, good clothing, rose-watered, and hairs with *atar*. They are thieves, gamblers, and pick-pockets.

The pick-pockets are generally seen strolling in the Bazars and crowded streets, though it is very difficult to recognize them. The gamblers or their agents skilfully make friendship with strangers, and frequent their houses on some pretext for business. Their victim is thus secured. He is led one day to a distant garden, or an old palace-looking house in a mazy lane.

There he is ushered into the presence of a grand looking Rajah, Nawab or Begum. Congenial conversation is indulged in, till a game is proposed. The victim readily accedes to it, money being freely supplied to him. The play is begun and won; and he returns home joyously with a heavy purse. He then thinks in his mind, that "with a loan of Rs. 25 only, I have gained five times that amount; so it is natural that I should win more, if I hazard a larger sum. Moreover his Highness seems of the golden and liberal age of our *Shahi* period." So collecting a few thousands, by mortgaging some of his property, he with the agent, his now constant companion, walks fast towards the quarter of his impending ruin.

He is well received, and after formal enquiry as to health, the real transaction is begun in right earnest. At first he wins a little according to his wish; but then the ebb-tide flows in steadily, till a few hundreds remain, when a ray of hope again appears. But the last wheel of fortune is irrevocably turned, and he finds himselt bereft of every thing, even his finger-ring and costly shawl, borrowed from a friend for the occasion.

Now his eyes are opened, though too late. Repentance did not restore Paradise to Adam and Eve. At once the electric truth flashes across his mind. He casts a piteous glance around, and is horrified to see in the distant corridors many unceremonious men with clubs and daggers. He holds his peace and returns home. The police are informed; but the men, as usual, take hours to prepare and appear on the scene, where, now no soul is to be found or traced. The policemen lose temper and pour their wrath on the poor fellow on a charge of falsehood, unless timely satisfaction is given.

Then our scene shifts into the streets, where the rogues of the second type are begging or exacting *pice*, (copper coins) from the travellers with plenty of abuse. It is their business to insult gentlemen and unguarded women, to oppress the weak, and to make a noise throughout the day. They are also hired for beating one, who has fallen under the wrath of somebody. The present police system can not check them.

Of the remainder of this class, who are employed in menial service or low professions, it will be sufficient to observe, that they are generally industrious and lead a contented life like their Hindu brethern. Many of them are good cultivators. They are not so immoral as others of the Mahomedans. They are by profession tailors, bakers, embroiderers, dyers &c. The servants of the Europeans are mostly of this class.

CHAPTER III.

Section I.—*General Society.*

In spite of the many changes, that are taking place, the local society is still a harmonious whole, of which the component parts are the Mardana, Zenana, relation to neighbours, amusements, festivals, religious observations, and variety of living.

The Mardana is the male society, literally the front division of the family-house of one of middle or higher class. It consists of servant's quarters, religious service room, pigeons and other establishments, the Moulvi's room, where the children are taught, and drawing room, in which the head of the family sits with his friends and relatives, and talks and attends to the affairs of life.

The Zenana means the female society, in its widest sense. Literally it is the back or inner division of the house, where admittance is denied to all men, but the nearest relatives. There is an open Courtyard in the middle, surrounded on four sides by rooms, of which some are

Opium-smoking at different stages.

Justice in olden days.

devoted to the kitchen, some are set apart for stores for maid servants, for sleeping, &c., one for prayer, and the largest room or hall serves as a drawing room. Here in the Zenana, the ladies of the house, live in perfect confinement and contentment, having no concern with the male part Here they talk, eat, bathe, and do whatever they like, uninterrupted by the men of the house.

Their connection and intercourse with neighbours and distant relatives are maintained for gossiping purposes, assisting one another on festive occasions, or when misery befalls a house, and other affairs of life. Thus in marriage festivals, they are invited to the house, the men to Mardana and the women into the Zenana; and all join and assist in the ceremony and heighten one another's joy. Occasionally enquiries after some distant friend's or relative's health are made through servants, male or female, and good wishes are interchanged with fruits, presents, and music.

In case a difference of opinion or conduct occurs between two families, it is usual to have the matter settled in a *punchayat* or by arbitration, board of the village, mohulla or district of the city. *Punchayat* is an old system, by which the harmony of society is restored. All the elders and hoary heads of the locality assemble in a convenient place, and discuss the unpleasant matter at issue and come to a satisfactory conclusion. The opposite parties are reconciled, and the temporary complaints are forgotten. Mediation is another means of pacifying discordant families, in which a few friends are the peace-makers, and as the natives are not vindictive, but forgiving, old friendship is easily restored. But now the English system changes everything; it can not, the law courts do not, restore social harmony, but break it, breed and prolong a full crop of discord, disunion and disorganization, even among the family members.

The general nature of the amusments of the people of the present generation is rather childish and sloth-indulging. Cards, paper-kites, pigeons quails, and dancing women, are chiefly the pastimes and pleasures of the citizens. The men of the past age, however, had nobler pursuits and better exercises. Now all is showy, that simply kills time. The festivals are more for display than for religion's sake, at least the inmost heart is very seldom, even temporarily, affected by them. Thus the noisiness of life is maintained, not for a purpose, but for the empty parade, from an idle pride of ancient greatness.

The manner of living of the people varies according to season, family-occasions and pleasure. In winter the cold is avoided and air is expelled by sticking covering sheets into ill-ventilated closed rooms, sitting or sleeping round fires and stories. In summer the day-heat and the *loo* (hot winds) are avoided by retiring to the *Tykhana* (under-ground rooms), shade, *Khas-Tattees* (cooling apparatus) and fans or *punkhas*; and the night air is enjoyed and the breath of life is maintained by lying or sleeping in the exposed places and on the flat roofs, with music and shampooing. In autumn many of the rich go to their gardens and contemplate virgin nature, now growing luxuriant and refreshing green, while the Begum, pendulum-like, oscillating in her swinging frame, between singing and laughter, enhances the beauty of the scene of Zenana life.

When a change is required, or when a damaged constitution is to be restored, or a distant estate is to be inspected. the family migrates from the town to the country; and village life is enjoyed in the fields and among mango-topes. The women are of course, well-protected from the rude gaze of men. There "in the village squares or *choupals*, in front of the house of the leading Zamindar," (the migrated family being one) "under the shadow of the spreading tamarinds or banians, the people collect after the labours of the day, with *hookka* in their hands, to discuss the local news, the last action of the magistrate, the rent demanded by the landlord, rumours of new taxes, or intentions of a distant government, the price of grain, the weather, and the health of the neighbourhood. It is there that the collective conduct of the little society (village community) whether to resist or yield to fresh demand, is determined on, and the judgment of tribunals of their caste fellows is pronounced on offender against the caste rules."—*Oudh Gazetteer*.

In this period of transition, let us compare the two societies, native and foreign, of the ruled and ruler, the latter of which is influencing the former; so that their merits and defects may be roughly estimated. The European lives singly, his wife and children are his utmost cares. The native lives on a joint family system, with brothers, parents and relatives, and with his short earnings, provides for more stomachs than the foreigner does with his princely income. Hence he is less selfish and more self-sacrificing, at least he was. He has more cares to attend to than his white brother. But he has no joint worship; all are to pray separately and singly; while the Europeans do so in an assembly, at the same time, at the bidding of a superintendent—the Reverend priest. So that the results of the two systems are, that the native becomes more kind-hearted and religious; but withal mentally fettered and physically weak : while the foreigner gets more selfish, independent, less encumbered with cares, capable of devoting his mind to thoughts, worldly improvements and aggrandisements. The inevitable results are that the native has only what satisfies his wants, poverty, duty, resignation and subjection, and the ruler has liberty, over-flowing luxury, and dissatisfaction with at his present condition. "This organization (joint family) is not without certain advantages. It is this that has rendered possible that calm, happy, tranquil life......to which they are so strongly attached. But it has also banished from the hearts of these men the sentiments of national ambition. If the present masters were consigned to destruction, these nations would remain at the disposal of the first conqueror." Rousselot.

Section II.—Mardana or male society.

The dress of the people consists of a loose *paijama* (pantaloon) *kurta* (small coat) *chapkan* (tunic) over or under it, and a *choga* or *Labada* (gown) over the whole, while the *Kamarband* (waste hand) ties the upper piece externally with a silver band ; an embroidered *chadar* covers the whole dress, hanging folded from the shoulder. Tight *paijamas*, called *churhidar*, (entwined at the lower part), are not in fashion here. The head-piece is a skull-cap of different embroidered designs or a *paghri* (turban), a long sheet folded round the skull-cap, and its ornamental adjuncts.

The dress differs in form and matter according to rank and class. The *Dhoti* (an unsewed cloth) serves the purpose of the lower garment with the orthodox Hindu; a *lungi* (half pantaloon) with the poorest Mosulmans. The Moulvi or Mulla never wears a *chapkan*, but a long loose *Kurta*. The *Kurta* is of two sorts, tight and loose, which are preferred and worn according to fancy and fashion.

The general effect is tasteful and picturesque. In this hot climate, loose dress is the best that can be used, for by it convenience is secured, and at the same-time airiness to the limbs is given, and the evaporation from the body is not impeded. The blind apers and imitators of the ruler's fashions and whims should remember, that the foreign style is almost a geometrical figure, which tightens the body to inconvenience and ugliness.

The home dress is the *lungi, payjama* or *dhoti*, and the upper half of the body is exposed or covered with a *Kurta* or *chapkan*, and a common skull-cap. Full dress is worn by the master of the house, when a gentleman, not familiar to him, is received, or when going out for a walk, on business, or to visit friends and relatives. But the Choga, Labada and Kamarband and turban are now falling out of use, as either the people can not afford to keep them, or they are thought unnecessary, the people seeing that the rulers of the land have not more than four pieces in their dress, pantaloon, two coats, inner and outer, and the hat. The decline of the full dress of the natives dates from the fall of the local dynasty.

The dress varies with the season. In summer it is composed of thin, very thin cloths; in winter shawls, woolen and cotton drapery. The cotton dress is cheap, convenient, and not bad looking. The cotton is skilfully laid between two colored cloths, sewed separately and then together. But danger lies in this kind of drapery, for it catches fire easily, when it is very difficult to extinguish it, thus jeopardizing the life of the wearer to the highest degree. Many a Sepoy died in this manner in the wars of the attempted revolution.

Thus clothed according to his convenience, the master of the house sits in his drawing room, the dead walls of which are relieved and adorned by prints, photographs, native pictures, lanterns and large mirrors. The floor is matted and carpetted; and he reclines on a big *Takia* (pillow), chewing *pan* (betle) and smoking the *Hookka*, which is ready-prepared placed before him. His friends or flatterers squat around. His relatives, say younger brothers, are in an adjoining room, conversing in a subdued tone; while in a third, the Moulvi or tutor with the boys are chattering their tasks and lessons. If the house belongs to a Hindu, there is a worship-room with a stone-god in it, also a cow, which serves the double purpose of nourishing the children of her master, and keeping the family-luck in her presence; so that the evils of misfortune enter not, which, however, when they do, are explained otherwise.

If the house belongs to a Mohamedan, there are numerous appendages. The cow and the stone-god are not kept, but to eat away the family-luck, fighting cocks and quails, flying pigeons and kites are carefully located in wooden frame-works. In the morning the lord of the house, as if in duty bound, superintends their feeding and exercises, and thus misspends much time, which might be better employed on his more important affairs. Then he goes to his drawing room, *Hookka* in hand, and sits and talks according to his taste and fancy. His companion dittoes his conversation, or varies the gossip according to his pleasure.

The general topics of conversation are the fighting and flying powers of his birds, review of a previous proceeding of matches, scandals of the neighbourhood, law-suits in the local Courts, comparison between the former rule and the present, stories and other light talk, the idlers are known to indulge in. If however strangers, equals not familiar, or elders are present in the company, the conversation becomes more general or personal, serious and learned-looking; and the Hookka and Pan are handed round to all, amidst mutual *saláamings* (salutations) between the giver and receiver. Personal matters are not generally talked of, much less looked after, which is the business of the family Dewan, Munshi, or Darogah. Newspaper-reading is not yet in vogue. But the Hindu is more personal, and settles his business first before he squanders his time in idle tales.

When a gentleman wants to see the houselord, a servant announces his arrival. No card is sent in. He is received in due courtesy. If he is equal to him in social position or rank, the host rises from his seat, advances a few steps, embraces the guest, and salutes him, with the right hand thrice raising and touching the forehead. If the new-comer is his inferior, he rises not but simply saláams to him by the hand once raised. One, who is superior to him, very seldom pays him a visit; but sometimes honors him in marriage and other important festive occassions. The host then advances to the gate, salams him thrice in a bending posture, and leads him respectfully to the prominent seat in the hall. "I had received my lesson as to this ceremonial, in which a most pointed difference is made, according to the rank of the individual, some being met by rising and embracing them, others being suffered to put their foreheads to your knee as you continue sitting, and to be only marked by putting the hand on their shoulder, as a kind of inferior embrace, while another class is to make their obeisance at a distance." Marquis of Hastings.

The preliminary salutations over, Hookka and Pan are given and received with salaams. Then mutual health and those of the family are enquired into, and answered not with thanks, but with Salams. The usual reply is thus given, "I, he, they, my children are all right, by the favour of God, by your good wishes and blessing." Wife is never directly mentioned, but is meant and understood by the term, 'Mahal,' that is, house. Then different topics are talked about at random. Meals and dishes, covered with cloth, are sent from the Zenana in proper time; and all present, both the invited and the uninvited, share in the eating with, "bismillah," in the name of God. The Hindu, however, can not take food conjointly, but separately, and on the floor, washing his face and hands with clean water. He must also bathe and worship before doing so.

Etiquette is strictly adhered to, and the men of different positions conduct themselves accordingly. In case any one offends the established rules of society, a great outcry is raised against him; and he is expelled from the orthodox company, unless he apologizes in time. Poor educated natives and men of the new lights, they can not impress the people with the superiority of western civilization and manners; they become laughing stocks in consequence of their idiosyncrasies and attemped reformations.

At noon, the masters of the house, takes a nap, and his companions go to their respective houses. Those who are employed in offices or in other out-door work, can not sleep during the day time. In the afternoon and evening, all go out and the affectionate father drives or walks with his children, or wends his way to a neighbouring assembly or some *Tamasha* At night he returns, and after eating enters the Zenana, and takes to his bed after the manner of common men.

This monotonous life is varied. Sometimes a dancing girl with a party of musicians and fidlers is introduced to enliven the dull spirit of the company. A perfect decorum and stillness are preserved. Though she is known to be an abandoned character, yet no indelicacy is allowed. The girl is fully dressed, and no part of her body is exposed except her half bashful half smiling face. And the hearers attend more to her singing and dancing than to her beauty. A most ugly woman would be most industriously courted, if she has inner parts of attractiveness. Hyder Jan is a famous courtizan, because of her musical power, though she is as well known for her deformity among her class. Thus the audience thinks on her fine performance, and their imagination is excited, and all are pleased.

The general conduct of the men towards the fair sex is dignified. They treat their wives and female relatives most affectionately, Divorce is never heard of. The wife never quarrels with her husband, nor does the husband ever beat his wife. When one falls sick, all the women of the house and distant relatives attend him ; one constantly fans him, a second gently rubs his limbs or flaps the flies, a third prepares medicine, a fourth cheers him with sweet words, and so on ; while the *Hakim* (Mohamedan physician) or *Baid* (Hindu) after duly feeling the pulse of his patient, writes down a *Nuskha* (prescription) in due form. And the *Najoomies* (astrologers) to drive away the evil spirits and influence of the stars, pens in a chit choice mystic verses from the *Koran* or *Mantras*; the chit is folded into a little metallic or cloth-cover, and is hung down on the breast or bound on the arm of the sufferer.

The influence of these *Najoomies* (Mohamedan) and *Jotishi Pundits* (Hindu) is thorough and permeates the whole native system. Without their advice, no new work is undertaken, no new place or high person is visited. They must be consulted, of course with a fee, when no news is got from a relative in a foreign land, and when things are stolen or otherwise lost. They must be refered to, when an examination is to be passed, or a case is to be fought. The people must ease their minds of fear and anxiety, when one falls seriously ill, by their prophecy ; and when the physicians fail to cure a case, astrologers are requested to determine the nature of the disease and remedy. When a birth takes place in a family, it is their business and profession to make a horoscope and drive away evil influence from the house.

Section III.—*Female Dress.*

The Mahomedan women are dressed with a *Paijama*, very loose, and trailing at the lower part, but closely fitting at the upper. It is generally folded in front, and the trail ebbs in. The breast is covered with a tight *ungia*, while the middle part has a *coorti* (bodice), the whole upper body is enveloped with a *Dopattah*, or a thin sheet of cloth hanging from the shoulder. The *borka*, a veiling garment, envelopes the whole person from the public gaze; but this is now seldom used. This is more in fashion in western Asia, where the system of female exclusion is not so strict. They have no cap on their heads, which are ornamented with jewels and gold. Their shoes are pointed slippers adorned with spangles, embroidery and bells, silvery and small, which ring pleasantly to the cadence of the footsteps of the wearer. The pieces of drapery are dyed differently, and the general effect is picturesque, and heightens the original beauty.

This loose dress is now falling out of fashion, and with the change of rulers, the tightening process has already begun. The *Ungia* is going off; the *Koorti* remains in a state of transition; while the *Achkan* (tunic buttoned in the middle) narrows the waist, if not the heightened bosom. The *Chudder* too is now looked upon as a piece of redundance; and handkerchiefs and caps are felt as necessities of fancy, while the oriental slipper slips its place, and the flowery shoe boots and noises its walk. And the *Paijama* loses its loose folds and tightens the knee and the leg to inconvenience and ugliness.

The Hindu ladies have, instead of *paijama* and *ungia*, *lehnga* (skirt) or *Dhoti* (an unsewed piece of cloth about five yards long,) a *coorti* longer and broader than that of the Moslem, and *chudder* (sheet), which is double, the underneath one is of red colour, the outer thin and white. When the *dhoti* is worn, half of it covers the lower body, the other half is folded on the upper part, and no sheet is then required. The milk-women and other low caste wear the *Dhoti.* This *Dhoti* and *Coorti* look picturesque, and the women, while pacing to a bathing ghat or a neighbouring temple, remind the classical reader of the picture of the ancient Grecian dames going to worship the goddess Minerva.

The ornaments as worn by the ladies, Hindu and Mahomedan, are too numerous to be detailed or illustrated. The feet have anklets, the fingers of both hands and feet many rings; the wrists have bangles; the arms have some plated jewel and gold ornaments, the neck and breast—neck-laces and other circlets, the nose—a big ring—too big with the Hindu married ladies; the ears, smaller ones but too many, and the forehead adorned with a fringe of pearls. The skirts of the whole garment are relieved by fringes of different sorts and patterns of jewels, gold and silver. But the mania for ornaments is now dying away, and the day is not far distant, when the goldsmith's art is to be replaced for that of the tailor, not for the adorning but for the tightening.*

---

* A friend of Mrs. Park who visited the seraglio of Nasir-ud-din on the morning of his coronation, on the 18th of October 1828, thus describes a *royal Begum* in her state-dress.

" The present King's wives were superbly dressed and looked like creatures in the Arabian tales. Indeed one, Taj Mahal, was so beautiful, that I could think of nothing but Lalla Rookh, in her bridal attire. I never saw one so lovely either black or white. Her features were perfect, and such eyes and eye-lashes I never beheld before. She is the favourite queen at present, and has only been married a month or two; her age about sixteen; and such a little creature with the smallest hands and feet, and the most timid look imaginable. You would have been charmed with her, she was so graceful and fawn-like."

"Her dress was of gold and scarlet brocade; and her hair was literally strewed with pearls, which hung down upon her neck in long single strings, terminating in large pearls, which mixed up with and hung as low as her hair which was curled on each side her head in long ringlets, like Charles the Second's beauties. In her head she wore a small gold circlet, from which depended and hung half way down large pearls interspersed with emeralds. Above this was a paradise plue, from which strings of pearls were carried over the head, as we turn our hair. Her earnings were immense gold rings, with pearls and emeralds suspended all round in large strings, the pearls increasing in size. She had also a nose ring with large round pearl and emerald, and her necklaces &c., were too numerous to be described.

" She wore long sleeves, open at the elbow, and her dress was a full petty-coat with a tight body attached, and open only at the throat. She had several persons to bear her train when she walked, and her women stood behind her coach to arrange her head dress, when in moving her pearls got entangled in the immense robe of scarlet and gold she had thrown around her. This beautiful creature is the envy of all the other wives, and the favourite at present of both the king and his adoptive mother, (Padshah Begum), both of whom had given her titles." Mrs. Park's Wanderings. Vol. 1, page 87.

The natural beauty of a person is heightened by the application of *Missi* (a preparation of antimony) to the lips, the gums, and "occassionally to the teeth of every married lady, who emulate each other in the rich black produced." The eyelid is penciled with a prepared black, called *Kájal,* and the large eyes look more beautiful by the contrast. The palms of the hand and the soles of the feet are reddened with a dye, called *Mehdi,* with designs varying according to taste. The native ladies have not yet learned powdering and white-washing their faces, or pomatoming their hair. Their *attar* is a scent congenial to their taste.

SECTION IV.—*The inner life and society.*

Thus dressed according to her taste, the mistress of the house, like her lord in the Mardana, sits reclining on a *musnud* on carpets spread on the floor, or on wooden seats or *charpies,* in the hall of the Zenana. The musnud is the seat of honor, and is not allowed to any other person than an equal who shares it, and to a superior guest, who temporarily occupies it, when the lady of the house takes her place most humbly on the very edge of her own carpet.

On this seat of honor, the first lady of the house sits almost throughout the day. Her companions squat around chatting all the time ; while the slave girls fan her, brush away flies, prepare *pawn* and the Hookka, and otherwise administer to her wishes and pleasure. The lady rarely stands, "but when distinguished guests or their elders among relatives are announced, this mark of respect is never omitted. It is an interesting sight, when they stand and walk as they have much ease and grace in their manner, which no tutoring could impart ; they rise and arrange their drapery, advance a few steps from their place in the hall, and embrace their visitor thrice in due form, ending by salaming with the head bowed very low towards the ground, and the open hand raised to the forehead, three times in succession, with solemnity and dignity."

The inmates of the Zenana are very fond of hearing stories. Story-telling is an art professed by many with success, in which their prolific imagination is brought into full play to the delight of their audience.

They bathe seldom, only once or twice a fortnight, and then it is a very laborious process. Water of different temperature is placed in cells and jars, generally two kinds, warm and cool, in the family bathroom (*hammam*) and the slaves are employed for hours together for rubbing the limbs of the bather with ground peas (*beson*), and water is applied little by little for washing.

Begum at her toilet.

Begum preparing Paun.

P.C.M. 23.12.82.

From sketches by Fuzlen Ali

The Zenana-women are called *pardah-nashins* or *Pardah-ke-logs*, which means ladies under *purdah*, a kind of waded curtain, constantly used to screen them from public view. Thus on going to a place full of men, or through a crowded street the *pardah-nashin* is secure, squatting comfortably within a *dooli* or *palki*, not more than three feet in length, two feet in breadth, and two and half in height; while the *Kahars* (bearers) make their way shoving, crying aloud all along "Dhakka-bacho" (take care of the stroke of the *Dooli*). By this means of covered conveyances, the Zenana-women maintain communication with their outside friends, or go out to see Melas and Tamashas. This covered conveyance varies with the rank of the occupant.

In the palaces, which were extensive, as may be easily seen from what remains of them, the princesses did not walk from one part to the other; but *Tanzans* (sedan chairs) of various designs were used, carried by female bearers, for, as has been said before, the men are not allowed entrance into the Zenana. Female or eunuch soldiers guarded the harems with pistols, sheilds, swords and all of the picturesquely dressed ancient Amazons. "There were eunuchs, woman soldiers also on guard in uniform and with musket, beyonet &c., at the entrances of the female apartments of the palace and in the corriders."

The manner of eating in the Zenana is also to be noted. The slave girls bring in well-filled dishes, covered with cloths, from the kitchen, and place them in order on the carpetted floor in the dining hall, if of a rich, or sitting room, if of the middle class. Ablution of hands and mouth is done, before eating is begun. With the word '*bismillah*' (in the name of God), the process of the hand to mouth goes on without much noise, according to their appetites. Spoons and other paraphernalia of western civilization are not yet in requisition. "Shukr-i-khoda" (thanks to God) is offerred, when eating is ended. The hands and mouths are again carefully washed before the indispensable Hookka is smoked and the favourite *Pan* is chewed, to excite digestive powers in their organs.

There are two meals in a day,—one at about noon, the other after evening. In the morning *Sharbat* (sugared water and other cooling draughts) is drunk and fruits are tasted; in the afternoon, refreshments of light edibles are partaken. After her morning slumber, the Bagum Saheb gets sore in temper, and abuses her domestics, unless toned down by a timely cooling draught.

The good lady of a house prays five times a day, as directed by the Koran. Extra prayers are offered on occassions of sickness or distress in a family. The Shia women then propitiate their saints by constant cries of "Hassain Hossain." Their time besides prayer is occupied with their household affairs, in sending words of enquiry after health and other matters to their neighbours or distant friends, with games of dice and cards, with hearing songs, and stories, and with naps. There are thorough idlers among them, and the existence of those, who have a more luxurious life to indulge, evaporates in unmeaning talks, tales, laughter, jokes, scandals, singing, swinging, sleeping, shampooning, playing and going out in covered conveyances, on pleasurable trips, &c.

The temporary migration of the ladies from their domicile is an event of great importance and interest to them ; and therefore the superior classes "make it a matter of necessity to move out in such a style as is most likely to proclaim their exalted station in life." But the low class and poor women can not provide for companions, and so while travelling in their *dooli*, they have no followers but the two *Kahars* (bearers.) If of middle class, the fair occupant has one or two maid-servants accompanying her; if rich, two favourite slave girls (*Kaharies*) on the immediate two sides of her Palki, with other women and men in front and back, followed by one or two beggars running after and clamouring for charity, and the good lady disappoints them not in their expectations. But with the Royal Begums of old, it was a regular equipage and procession.*

---

* Padshah Begum, the adoptive mother of Nasir-ud-din Hyder, once paid a visit of religious vow to the Shrine of Hazrut Abbas, and her procession is thus described by an eye witness :—

"First in the Badshah Begum's *Sawari*, I observed a guard of cavalry soldiers in full dress with their colours unfurled ; these were followed by two battalions of infantry, with their bands of music and colours. A company of spearmen on foot in neat white dresses and turbans, their spears of silver rich and massive. Thirty six men in white dresses and turbans, each having a small triangular flag of crimson silk, on which were embroidered the royal arms, (two fish and a disk of peculiar shape). The staffs of these flags are of silver, about three feet long ; in the lower part of the handle a small beyonet is secreted, which can be produced at will by pressure on a secret spring. Next followed a full band of music, drums fifes &c.; then the important Dunkah, which announces to the public the lady's rank : she is enclosed within the elevated towering *chandole* on each side of which the *aftaadah* (embroidered sun) and *chauries* (made of peacock's feathers) are carried by well dressed men generally confidential servants appointed to this service.

"The *Chandole* is surrounded by very powerful women bearers, whose business it is to convey the vehicle within the compound (court-yard) of the private apartments, or wherever men are not admitted at the same time with the females. *Chobdars* and *Sonta-bardars* walk near the *Chandole* carrying gold and silver staffs or wands and vociferating the ranks and honors of the lady they attend, with loud voices the whole way to and from the Durgah. These

When the ladies assemble, it is an interesting sight to see them talk and move, which they do in an animated yet dignified manner. The expression of their countenance varies according to the sentiment, that prevails in the topics. They, especially Mohomedans, are less reserved, but more excitable than the European ladies. They are as ready to shed tears as to laugh and smile. Their gestures too are to be noted. Generally native gestures are horizontal, while European vertical. In questioning the Begums or Bibies gently move their right hands horizontally. In using "what," when one fails to hear a thing mentioned or enquired, they raise their eye-brows slightly arched. Invoking blessing, they press and crack their fingers on their temples. Comparatively the Begums are more talkative, sprightly and witty than the Hindu ladies.

Let us now compare the four classes of women, and we will roughly understand all the different forces and influence, active and passive, progressive and conservative, in the body-society of the present Oudh. *Mem Saheb* is the European lady, who is to fashion native civilization after her mould. *Bahuji* or *Rani Saheb* is the Hindu house-wife, orthodox and conservative. Begum Saheb is the Mosulman Zenana lady of the town, and aspires to be progressive; though her country-sister *Bibi Saheb*, the *Dehatin*, clings to the old system, and sanctions not any improvement. The Bengalin is the Bengal lady, who has already become the imitating machine after the fair European's example. Some of them require a little explanation.

---

men likewise keep off the crowds of beggars attracted on such occasions by the known liberality of the ladies, who according to established custom, make distributions to a large amount, which are scattered amongst the populace by several of the queen's eunuchs, who walk near the *Chandole* for the purpose.

The chief of the eunuchs followed the queen's *Chandole* on an elephant, seated, in a gold howdah, the trapings of which were of velvet, richly embroidered in gold; the eunuch very elegantly dressed in a suit of gold cloth, a brilliant turban, and attired in expensive shawls. After the eunuchs follow the Padshah Begum's ladies of quality, in covered palanquins, each taking precedence according to the station or the favour she may enjoy; they were well-guarded by soldiers, spearmen and Chobdars. Next in the train, follow the several officers of the queen's household, on elephants richly caparisoned. And lastly the women of inferior rank, and female slaves in Raths (covered carriages) fifty in number; into each of which from four to six are crowded, comprising the house-hold establishment of the great lady—such as companions, readers of the Koran, Khawases (the higher classes of female slaves) Muglani (needdle women) &c. This will give you a tolerable idea of the number and variety of females attached to the suite of a lady of consequence in India. The procession, at a walking pace, occupied nearly half-an-hour in passing the road opposite to my house: it was well conducted, and the effect imposing, both from its novelty and splendour."—*Mrs. Hossein Ali.*

Bahuji is not a showy creature, but personally looks after and superintends her family duties;—suckles her children, cooks and otherwise serves her husband and family elders. She does not show out in ride or drive, but humbly walks with other females to a neighbouring temple or bathing *ghat*. She is not vain about her dress and ornaments, but is pleased if her husband approves, or her female friends admire them. She does not dance, but secretly sings sometimes with her companions in leisure hours, or festive occassions. She does not read novels but hear religious tales with a pious heart. Much time is not spent in her toilet; and her leisure-hours are occupied in sewing the torn garments of her children, or arranging the bedding. She does not command but obeys her husband and imperceptibly softens his temper, if wild.

But our Begum Saheb is a type of the Mem Saheb's kind. She too gets progressive and tightened in fancy fashions. Stories of love, fairies and oral novels, engage her attention mostly, and lounging luxuriously on a big pillow, hears singing from the *Domnies*. She does not look after her affairs, but chews *Pan* and smokes the *Hookka* all her days. She also loves airing; and scandal has it, that she more than once attended a Parsi theatre amid the rude gaze of the audience. But the orthodox lady like the Bibi Dehatin, never goes out of her Purdah, much less tries to break it; nor does she hanker after fancies and idle-dreams. She never seeks admirers, seldom sings; and it is a disgrace to her to dance. She cultivates female society to an unlimited extent, and all are impressed with her courtesy, hospitality and good wishes. She spends much time in her toilet, but not daily. She little influences her husband, who lives quite separately during the day. The Begum Saheb has generally more intelligence and activity than Nawab Saheb her husband.

As a contrast to these four classes of women, I will, in conclusion of this subject, introduce the village girl. Her figure is noble and her dress is made of thick and coarse country cloths, red and blue, the heavy folds of which remind one the severe beauty of a classic statue. Her movement is dignified, her mien full of rustic grace, and her countenance innocent and grave, mild and expressive. She draws water from well, and comes home well balanced with a pitcher on her head, and second on her waist, and a third in her right hand. She is a milk-maid and goes out to sell the precious fluid, *ghee*, butter, and other articles. She rises at 4 A. M.

After an old nati painting

P.C.M. M.I.S.
camp Beti

Life in Zenana.

Domnies singing before Begums.

and humbly grinds corn with a plaintive note, that sweetly rings in the expiring night's atmosphere and echoes through the then calm neighbourhood. In the rainy season, she with her female relatives and friends goes out to the fields, and sitting in a row and jointly chattering a pure rural music, roots out weeds from the corn, already sowed, and now watered by her brother, father and all. In short, she is humble industry itself, full of contentment and happiness; she is not yet fashioned into a fanciful being, toy or plaything, nor stereotyped by stories and idleness, civilization and vice.

A Mutahi (secondary) wife of the Ex-king was one of this low class. Her eyes were full of fire, while all the rest of her person looked like a marble statue. She had been betrothed to a village youth, before the king saw and took her into his seraglio. In spite of royal life and affection, the girl fervently loved her old poor friend, and in disguise one day fled from the palace. She was however caught and brought back, but not punished. On this his mother remonstrated with Wajid Ali Shah, who then exclaimed ;— "I grant her none of her desires, she will not express a wish for any thing. I can not make her out..............she interests me. I offer her jewels and ornaments ; she says, she does not want them. I get dancing girls for her amusements, she looks on and smiles not. A villager ! yes, she is a villager. But by the beard of the prophet, she knows how to act the queen."

Chapter IV.

Some sketches of local life.

To give an insight into local character, some specimens are necessary. So I record some of the extremes of native life, though I confess, it is very difficult to select the fittest person s, and exhaust the subject within a short compass. Of female life nothing is given, because it will take more space than I can allow.

General sketch of a life, Hindu or Mohamedan.

Ushered into existence from the womb of its mother, the child, if male, gladdens the whole family and a festive occassion takes place at the time of birth, and on the sixth day. Musical bands play, friends are invited, the poor receive alms, and all contribute to make the occassion auspicious by presents (ornaments, play-things &c.,) to the new born member of the family. Formerly the birth of a son was announced by the firing of cannons or pistols, according to the position of the family, so as to make the child familiar with military life from its very infancy. Now the custom is abolished.

A wet-nurse is engaged, and she with her children, is looked upon more as a member than a servant of the family. The child is carefully laid recliningly on cotton, is generally rubbed with oil, and is every morning basked in the sun. A grain of opium is occassionally administered to it for medicinal purposes, and its motions are thereby regulated.

On the fortieth day, it is thoroughly washed in a warm bath, and is ceremoniously with a procession taken to a religious shrine,—if Hindu, to *Kalkaji* or *Bhairoji*, and if Mohamedan, to *Hazrat Abbas ki Durgah*,—to ask a blessing from the spirit of the god or saint there presiding. And it is on this occassion, for the first time, that the baby is brought out of the room of delivery, to the public view.

The birth-day is observed with a religious ceremony, called *Salgirah*, when the mother ties a knot to a long sacred thread, kept for the purpose, by which means the number of one's years is counted. Meantime, the child moves, crawls, then walks; cries, smiles, then laughs; utters, pronounces, then speaks; learns, imitates, then plays, to the delight of all. He affects the man, and gives a forecast of his future.

In the fifth year, the commencement of education takes place with a festival; and all the friends are invited to the house, to witness, amidst dancing and singing, how the Moulvi (Mohamedan) or Gooroo (Hindu) teaches the little boy to hold the pen or pronounce the first letters in the alphabet.

In the seventh year, the boy, if Mohamedan, undergoes the rite of circumscision, and if Hindu, gets twice-born by the *Janau*, the holy thread being worn with a religious ceremony. The *Kaiths* and *Chattris*, however, deviate from this rule, and get the thread, when they are married.

At his marriageable age, that varies according to taste, custom or convenience, from ten to twenty, the youth gets wedded to one, whom he has not seen before, and whom the parents select with due regard to matching astrology and horoscope, more than the physical or mental conditions of the bridegroom and bride. Such however is the force of custom, that both approve each other, and abide by their parents' choice. The future happiness of the husband and wife seldom breaks.

A few years after, the father or rather his earning ability dies, and the married son's struggle for existence commences, for as the means of employment are now very limited, the young man begins to experience the hard side of the hitherto pleasurable world. He stumbles many times in the way before he succeeds in getting a living. He becomes a flatterer or dependent to a rich man by pandering to his vices, or gets a clerkship in any office, or a shop-keeper or any other low profession.

Thus with a bare subsistence he passes his days, and all his sanguine temperament and youthful hopes are gone and rapidly dissolved, and he becomes a melancholic and premature old man; while his fertile wife begets and increases additional mouths to eat, extra troubles to look to, and accidental mishaps to ward off; till a disease attacks the husband, and he leaves his mortal frame and cares on the shoulders of his inheritors, and all go on amourning for ten (Brahman), thirty (other Hindus), and forty (Mosulman) days. The widow leaves off her ornaments, wears plain clothing, and becomes quite religious by daily worship, prayer, periodical fasts and counting of beads.

PUNDITJI.

Punditji is a Brahman priest of Ranikatra, the oldest Hindu quarter of Lucknow. He is a perfect picture of humility, innocence and virtue. He is however not a very learned man, though now and then he composes pretty Sanskrit poems; nor is he always infallible in his calculations of astrology. He lives contentedly on his humble means, and his neighbours, in spite of his poverty, seek his advice both on social and on religious matters.

Just at dawn he goes to the Goomti river, for his morning bath, and after an hour, on his prayer being duly recited, returns home. He then goes to the houses of his *Jajmans* (parishioners), worships their family-gods, gives them his blessing with flowers, and returns to his house.

Repeating the noon-prayer and worshipping his own house-gods, he takes his meal and then sits in the Thakoordwara (temple-house), to teach Sanskrit gratis to the Brahman boys of the neighbourhood. He then counts his beads and repeats his *Mantras* (incantations) till late at night. He aims at holy living, for a holy dying (the third birth) to have a holy happy future.

He is never selfish; nor does he ever quarrel with any body for a transitory thing of this world. He never speaks out in a higher tone, but calmly conducts his discussions and conversations and impresses his views on those who determine to be never convinced.

He serves his parishioners spiritually, and gets a little rice and vegetables, and a few copper pieces as *Dakshina* (fee). He writes their horoscopes and receives a few silver pieces. He drives away their evil influence by the power of his *Mantra* and has a trifling reward. He foretells their future prosperity and is paid a few annas. Thus his means of livelihood are scanty. Yet Abundance, the daughter of his Economy, is wedded and smiles on the stern Poverty, the son of his hard circumstances. He has a heart of charity too, and exercises it according to his power, physically and mentally, if not pecuniarily. But rice, *cowrhies*, *pice*, a few worn clothes and necessaries of life, he fails not to give to the really needy and in proper time.

The high and low, the rich and poor, equally revere him, and ask his advice on many a point. Even the *shohdas* of the streets feel a veneration for his person, and never molest him, they, who are noted for ill-treating the travellers. His innocent smile reaches the heart of the sinner, and does the work of the bitterest satire and the sermon.

He has a very old mother, whom he reveres as though a goddess. His wife is a true housewife,—industrious, economical, and cleanly in her works. His sons are promising and obedient lads; and his daughters imitate their mother in womanly duties, and learn, from their brothers, the purport of the *Shástras.* When in the evening the father sits with the children all around him, and examines the boys about their past lessons, the sisters sometimes join and successfully compete with the brothers in their answer.

The Punditji never thinks for the morrow, nor ever squanders time in idle talk or musings. But once he often held fruitlessly some hour's consultations with his mother and wife, as to how to match suitably his girl. Now, however, he never does so; for unforeseen and unprepared, his eldest daughter got married to one, satisfying all his conditions. So now he leaves that matter as every thing else to God. Thus he leads unostentatiously a virtuous and happy life.

A SUDRA.

Ramdin is a fuel-seller by profession, Hindu by religion, and oilman by caste. He is a god-fearing man, and lives according to the tenets of his Shastras. He is a strict man of integrity, and his neighbours have more faith in him than their relatives. Those who go to a foreign country for a living, send him whatever they earn; and he distributes the money to them, for whom it is intended; and he will not take anything out of the sum, even though the sender is largely indebted to him.

He never goes to the Court to recover his little loans, when not to be got by gentle means; nor does he ever keep any stamped agreement for whatever is contracted. His simple word is more permanent and trustworthy than any written parchment. If he ever knows, which God forbid, the value of stamped agreement and the word of *honor*, possibly he will be otherwise than he is. To aid his memory, he just jots down his money transactions in his book. He never quarrels with anybody for any disagreement, for recovery of debts, or any personal loss, that occurs for another's fault. He contentedly resigns to fate and points to God as the immutable ordainer of whatever befalls him; and it is useless to quarrel with or appeal to men for the decrees of a superior being.

He has six brothers, professing different lines of earning their bread, in as many towns. All their families are here, and live jointly. The brothers send to Ramdin whatever they save; and he spends impartially and equally amongst the members for the necessities and luxuries of life, in making ornaments &c. for the childern and the *Babus*. No regard is paid, that because one brother earns more than the others, therefore his wife and children will be supplied accordingly.

There is a strict discipline kept in the family, and each fails not to do his or her duty. Truant boy or naughty girl is unknown in the family. If one woman gets quarrelsome and disobedient, she is separated from the family with a bare subsistence, which she is herself to cook in a distant corner room of the house, and is not allowed to mix with or talk to any body, even to her husband or children; till she repents and begs forgiveness from all. Thus the family live happily in the ways of God and virtuous men.

NAWAB SAHEB.

Nawab Sahib was a noted gentleman of the neighbourhood. He was known all over the city for extravagance, foppishness and vice. His father, who was rather miserly in his habits, died while he was quite a young and unformed man, and he inherited his ancestral property only to squander it recklessly and to bring himself to ruin, without a check to his abandoned career. No elderly woman, not even his mother, could venture to remonstrate with him, and he would not listen to anybody, but his flatterers. His daily life is thus detailed.

Very late in the day, the Nawab Sahib rises from his bed, and with the mouth-piece of the Hookka on his lips, amuses himself for half an hour with pigeon or paper kite-flying ; he then goes to and superintends the fighting cock and quail department, and has his meal at one o'clock. He then takes a nap with the usual shampooing, and with the smoking pipe ever in his mouth, till evening, when he orders his buggy, and drives with great ostentation with Mosahebs (flatterers) to some *mujlis* or assembly to attend the great fight between cocks or quails.

No sooner the Nawab Sahib enters the hall, than every one rises and respectfully salams him. He is led to a prominent place, and is seated comfortably on a big pillow, the spectators moving away to make room for his august person. He then casts his eyes around to observe how his presence is appreciated by all, returning at the same time salutations to all salaming him. When the preliminary business of salaming is over, the Nawab-Saheb looks seriously to the match, gets excited, lays down wager of a few hundreds, and waits uncomfortably for the defeat of the cock or quail of the opposite party, when lo! his own defeat is proclaimed; and he dignifiedly loses his wager, amidst the condolence of all.

Of course, he has his dissatisfaction, which he hides with a smiling face, amidst a gang of flatterers. After a few minutes, however, he slips away from the scene, to save his pockets from further deductions ;—for our hero is a frugal person ; he always affects to act on the saving principle, though it is always of the penny-wise and pound-foolish kind.

To console his mind, he then attends a Salaming party, at the door of a *Burrah Saheb* (the Highest Local Government official) ; but finding in his rigid look no hope of increase of pension *(Wasika)*, or grant of land, he respectfully turns away towards the river side, to regale himself on the refreshing air of the strand *(Thandee Sarhak*, cool-watered road).

There he happens to see a *Palki-garhi* (carriage) with some charming Begums peeping through the open venetions,—a most important opportunity, which is by no means to be neglected. He however does not stop but drives onward, and then as if on recollection of a forgotten business, returns and overtakes the Begum's carriage, and marches off triumphantly ahead. The Begums are awfully pleased and raise a loud laugh which sweetly ring in the ears of our hero. Then again he turns or lags behind, followed by another roar. This way of turning and returning, going ahead or lagging behind, victory or defeat in the pleasant race-course, occupies a quarter of an hour, when the Buggy and *Palki-garri* reach a lonely shady place near a ghat. Presently formal negotiation for some sort of business, say, concerning a distant nephew's marriage, is set afoot through the Mogalanee or Kaharee (maid servant), who finds a favourable opportunity for filling her pockets.

This woman is a peculiar animal, ugly and black, with a blacker mind, who, though a slave, manages to reign over her mistress. Now she is the mistress of the situation ; sometimes she turns towards the Nawab Saheb, sometimes towards the Begum ; and though they are anxious for direct talking, she protracts it to extract her own advantage. In the meantime, the night gets advanced, and the moon peeps over the horizon, and dispels darkness to expose the unlawful meeting of the momentary lovers. So they reluctantly part, wishing for a future engagement, no one being the gainer, but the go-between.

The disconsolate Nawab Saheb then turns towards *Chouk*, where the sons of fashion and daughters of debauchery congregate after dark. There he attends a natch-party, who gets wonderfully pleased to have such a victim of wealth. Immediately he is surrounded by an army of flatterers, who praise his liberality to the sky, of course for a consideration. Then as a special business-transaction, the favourite song of "Wajid Ali Shah, Subeh Oudh ká Kanhayia," is sung by the dancing girl, who means to be understood, that the Nawab Saheb is the one; whereupon he hands over *Pawn* (betle leaf prepared with lime nut and spices), filled with a gold mohur, amidst the charms of "wah, wah.!" He gets immesurably pleased, and rolls on the big pillow (*takia,*) with waving head, occassionally giving more *pawns* with gold mohurs. The night grows late; and the hero finds his pockets empty. His Highness, then feigning sleepiness, straightway flies homeward, more disconsolate than before.

Returning home, he loses his temper, and pours his angry passion on the head of the lazy, sleepy, opium-eating, though otherwise innocent servants. His Mosahebs intercede in their behalf. After this feat, his wrath subsides; and then he has a chat with his companions, reviewing the proceedings of the day, the latter seasoning the conversation with praise at every turn.

After 12 p. m. he retires into his harem, where he attends, if his fancy has it, every one of his numerous ladies (married wives and concubines), till dawn, when he ends his busy daily life in sleep, for to him the night is day, and day is night.

This way the Nawab Saheb passes his days. Meantime his expense increases at a rapid rate, till he becomes a bankrupt, and his whole property is mortgaged. His income is then farmed out among the Mahájans (creditors) with enormous interest. His large establishment vanishes by degrees. Even his married Begums imperceptibly withdraw from the scene. His mortgaged property is sold by auction. At last the creditors, those vultures, who would not be satisfied while the last blood remains, drag him to jail.

After a period he comes out of that life of confinement, and finds himself an altered man. At least the ungrateful world does not recognize him as the same person, in whom a few years before the goddess of wealth and luxury was tenanting. After great thinking, he at last relieves himself by betaking to beggar's or fakir's life, or by going on pilgrimage to Macca and Karbala.

CLAUDE MARTIN.

Claude Martin was born at Lyons on 5th January 1735. He came to India with Count Laly's army. In 1758 he landed at Pondichery, and with great bravery fought as a common soldier in many a battle, till his Chief being defeated, he deserted to the English who were then beseizing the French capital. That time was on the eve of the great revolution; the consevative inertia blunted the national and religious feeling; and the heart of the Frenchman repented not for the treason to his nation. His conscience was sugared by the prospect of reward. Shortly after he was appointed as Captain of all the other deserters; he then came to Calcutta, and was sent up by the Company to Behar for surveying and mapping.

While Martin was engaged in this work, Shuja-ud-dowlah noticed his talents, and requested the loan of his services. The Company gladly parted with him, especially as it was its policy to get its work done at others' expense. The Colonel was for this reason retained nominally in the military department with prospect of promotion and claims of seniority. So he came to Fyzabad and Lucknow, and served his new master with zeal and success. From this place he again went down in 1790 to assist with horses in the Mysore War, and was promoted to the rank of Major-General in 1794.

While here, he established a gun-foundry and manufactured cannons of different calibres. He also opened new lines of business, as glass-work, statuery, banking, indigo and other works. And thus he amassed great wealth. He taught the natives new arts and professions, and to him is due what remains of the celebrated toy and glass works and other finery of Lucknow.

He was Chief Engineer to Asuf-ud-dowlah, and was in charge of his arsenels. "He built two houses, both of them complete fortifications and capable of holding out against any sudden commotion. He lent money to the rich natives taking their own or their wives' trinkets on pledge. He was besides very extensively concerned in trade to every part of India. He built several ships, and was on the whole a very useful man".—*Wilson's Wonderful Charactor.*

Lord Teignmonth, while here in February 1797, dined one evening with "this extraordinary character." He says "the old General is a Swiss, and talks English about a degree better than Tiretta, interlading every sentence with 'what do you call it,' 'do you see.'............... He is however a man of great penetration and observation. His singularities are amusing, not ridiculous."

He used to buy girls and bring them up to youth when the affection of the father was changed for the love of the husband; for they, as he confesses in his will shared his bed,—Bholan willingly, Sally reluctantly. He also got some slaves married and had them well provided for. His adopted son was James Martin or Zulfiikar, an illiterate man in spite of his father's cares in his education;—he was great grand father by his daughters's side to Khas Mahal, first queen of Wajid Ali Shah.

Though addicted to sensual enjoyment, he was otherwise a kind hearted man, and remembered all his relatives, dependants, poor, and prisoners, in his Will and Testament, which he made on the first day of the first year of the present century. To extenuate the frailties of life, he requested all, Mohamedans and Christians, of course with a consideration, to pray, after his death, for his soul. For this reason, he amply provided for his dependants; and the remainder of his vast property he devoted to charitable purposes, such as opening schools at Lyons, Calcutta, and Lucknow, releasing prisoners confined for small debts, giving alms to the poor, &c. The Lucknow school was to have both Mohamedan and Christian masters, and to teach the boys and girls of the respective religions, who were to be equally and impartially provided with clothing, food, &c. When out of their scholastic career, the students and girls should be assisted in marriage and in the commencement of their future life. The General perfectly remembered that he got all his wealth from the people of Oudh; to them he must give something in return. But now on the plea of bad English and bad Law, all the different items have been curtailed or allowed to lapse, and monopolized for the fattening of the European teachers and children only; and the people fail not to charge the English Government with bad faith and bad policy.

On the 13th of September 1800, Martin died unconfessed, for Padre Banton, the Roman Catholic Priest of that time, did not go to him, when he called him in his last moments. This priest was a plain-hearted and simple-clothed man; he with his umbrella and sandals, but without stocking, used to go every where, to the Resident and men of the highest circles. This the General did not like; he according to his ideas of respectablity, wanted pomp of conveyance and every thing to match his exalted rank. Hence he refused to see the Padre unless better clothed and conveyed. The priest felt insulted and never went to see him again, even at the request of the Resident, when the coffin was laid in the tomb. Though near forty years in the Company's service, Martin progressed very little in the English language as well as in Law, he himself priding on being his own lawyer; so his will abounded with manifold contradictions and equivocal expressions. The consequence was, that the whole estate was thrown into Chancery, whence it was with difficulty extricated, after a full period of forty years. His costly furniture were bought at almost nominal prices by the Company for the use of the Governor-General.

JOHN MORDAUNT.

LIEUTENANT-Colonel John Mordaunt was another specimen of the eccentric Eurasians of the period. He is known to the present generation only by the celebrated picture of the cock-fight by Zoffani, in which he stands opposite to Asuf-ud-dowlah. Let us snatch his short biography from oblivion. It is compiled from Wilson's wonderful characters, published in 1841.

John, a natural son of the Earl of Peterborough, was a most truant boy in his school, where he was flogged one half of his days for the faults, as he said, of the other half. He was then sent to Madras as a servant of the "Company," which could not get better men. Being fit for nothing, General Clavering made him an aide-de-camp, and he came to Calcutta. There, however he attended more to his gains than his duties.

The Commander-in-Chief, to test his qualifications a few days after, ordered him to write a letter to a colonel commanding at an upper station. " John very readily undertook the office, and in a short time returned to the General's apartment with the letter written according to the *data*. Sir John did all he could to unravel the various pot hook combinations, and to arrange them into any thing like penmanship, but in vain. The orthography was not a whit better." The General being amazed asked him to read out what he had written or meant. His *protegi* deliberately said, "that was no part of his duty; he had obeyed the General's orders by writing the letter; it was the business of the Colonel to whom it was addressed to read it."

A specimen of his diction is given. "A person once had occasion to borrow a horse from him for a day or two, and received the following note from him with the animal, "you may kip the hos as long as you lick."

When he came up with a party of pleasure to Oude, Asuf-ud-dowlah was impressed with his figure, his manners and qualifications for different games. His Excellency took him into his service, and Mordaunt became a great favorite with the Nawab-Vazir, who employed him as an aid-de-camp, " though he never attended him but according to his own fancy, and then generally either to shoot or gamble with him. The various applications and sarcasms directed against Mordaunt, as an absentee from his corps for so many years, and at the distance of full two thousand miles, were alike disregarded by himself and by the supreme Government, of which all individuals were personally attached to him. Some persons did not hesitate to assert, that he was kept by Mr. Hastings, as a spy over the Vizier, in consequence of the high favour and confidence the latter reposed in him."

In the use of pistols, playing of cards, and racket, his performances were wonderful. In the last game, he could and did beat most people, even with a common ruler. Poor Taylor, deputy to Colonel, afterwards Major-General, Palmer, the Private Agent, often received some smart tokens of his remembrance; and once Mordaunt was so terribly severe, that his antagonist lost his temper, and the metaphysical duel would have been enacted in all its reality, but for his witty remarks.

The Nawab-Vazier used to refer all Europeans to Colonel Mordaunt on occasions requiring his advice. His Excellency gave him a handsome salary and many distinguished privileges. But the Colonel knew nothing of even the ordinary points of arithmetic; so "he kept no books, but all his money concerns were on scarps and under terms and figures intelligible only to himself. He had many extensive claims on the Nawab, and he had immence losses and gains to register in the I. O. U. way. Yet even the most intricate cases never puzzled him; and at settling times, he was rarely, if ever, found to be in error."

Marquis Cornwallis, when in Lucknow, "one day seeing Mordaunt at his levee, asked him, if he did not long to join his regiment? "No my Lord," answered Mordaunt, 'not in the least.' 'But,' resumed the Marquis 'your services may be wanted, perhaps.' 'Indeed my Lord,' replied Mordaunt, 'I cannot do you half the service there, that I can in keeping the Vazier amused, while you ease him of his money."

Thus revelling his whole life in games and feasts, Mordaunt died an unnoticed and untimely death of a liver-attack, that orginated from a pistol shot, lodged in his breast, some years previously in a quarrel. He was buried at Cawnpore, in the old cemetry.

Chapter V.—*Education.*

Section I —*Mohamedan Education.*

As the road to a high career is closed, education, especially English, the state language, is not popular among the Mahomedans, who adhere to the old orthodox system. The sons of the aristocracy and generally of the lower classes are bred under the Moulvis, half fanatic, half illiterate fellows. They teach only some old antiquated books, which treat more of love stories than anything else, moral or scientific. Hence their training is as defective as possible..

The sons of the Nawabs are brought up in the Zenana, where superstition and prejudices reign supreme. It is below their dignity to be sent to school. The family Moulvi Saheb is employed more for show than for use; he yields to Zenana influence or else he will be turned out.

The boys are rolled over some high sounding Persian books. Their attention is not drawn to the sense and general idea of what they read, but to the meaning of detached words. The most easy way to master the language is to learn its dictionary by heart ; sometimes grammar is introduced for fashion or fancy, not for its use and advantage. Then the standard of perfection is reached,—though very seldom,—when the learned scholar uses bombastic words in conversation, quotes untimely and unmeaning verses at every turn and composes poems at leisure.

This way the sons of the higher class are educated with more of effiminacy in them than of manliness. As they grow, their occupations become the plays and amusements of boys. Long before they reach the age of youth, their moral atmosphere gets contaminated, surrounded as they are with the daughters of the slave-women, and sons of the servants, whose sole business it is to administer to their youthful pleasures. Consequently when they grow to manhood, they become thin and weak both in body and mind ; their constitution withers in its blooming. Their forefathers were more robust, manly and business-fitted men.

Their literary clubs are peculiar. They are held for the purpose of exhibiting each member's versifying power. The subjects, generally chosen for the poems, are love to women, very seldom to God. Sometimes a beauty is described :—the eye is the morning star, so dimly pleasant ; the eye-brow, the rainbow ; pupil, a dot of the Arabic alphabet ; the face, the moon ; (why not crescent, for the mouth ?), the hand some unmeaning resemblance ; and so on, every limb of the body is pourtrayed, until the hyperbolical metaphor soars to such a climax, that the composition loses its ground, and begins to fall to pieces in nonsense, when the already thrilled and excited assembly relieves the exhausted and perspiring poet with a blaze of applause and gusts of "wah ! wah !"

Sometimes the poems treat of sentimentality ; and pathetic and tragic scenes are introduced, such as the *Mersias* or funeral dirges, in honor of the martyrs, Ali and his two sons, Hossain and Hussan, and their persecuted family. These are generally indulged in during the Mohurrum, the mourning festival and the month of the Mohamedans. An example of such a production is given :—"The ocean sheds tears for them in its froathy waves, the wind sighs in its gusts, the sky weeps in its morning dews, the world is moved by earthquakes, the vegetable kingdom sympathizes by its stirring leaves, the night cries by its howling jackals, the mountains vouch vengeance for them by its volcanic irruptions;—when inanimate nature thus feels for the saints, will ye, true Musalmans, remain silent spectators in the field ? I say do it like true Shias." Immediately the whole assembly is electrified;—sobs, sighs and screams make an awful hum, while the hired mourners carry it to exaggeration. The stanger, who is not used to it, flies from the scene.

Section II.—*Educated Natives.—Results of the English system.*

With regard to the education of the Hindus, the boys, as their parents have less prejudice and dread for the loss of family dignity, are sent to the public schools, where they lead life of learning as students always do; which need not be detailed. Suffice it to say that the pupils are crammed in their class-books after the manner of the Moulvies. The teachers can not understand the innate parts of those, who are placed under their charge. But the principal defect is at the bottom of the system. Supposing a student with an aptitude for thinking, and nothing for the calculating, his career is practically closed in the University, which requires an equal capacity in all the subjects of examination; while the moderate and adaptive intellect, I mean memory, shines in the list of M. A's. and B. A's. Hence the result is superficial, and originality and genius are phenomena so scarce among the educated. Language and education, foreign and formal, cannot naturalize; nor can they touch, much less stimulate, the national feelings. And a nervous nation can never adapt itself to or have any congeniality with a phlegmatic tongue and system.

The so-called educated native is a little big fellow with hollowness within. His original powers are buried under a heavy crust, or get rusty by the cramming system. As an empty jar sounds much, his speech and verbosity are patent, and are intolerable bores to the sedate tempered orthodox society. He can not see but through spectactles; he can not speak but in the foreign tongue or rather a mixed jargon. He is a heterogenous phenomenon for self-glorification and congratulation of the panegyrists of the educational system. He is a gentleman with pomatomed hair on his head, and a denational beard under his chin. The looseness of the original dress is gone; he is tightened in a prison-garb; his cap is Turkish or so, his coat is angular or shortened, and his pantaloons are length without breadth. His walk is oblique, his movement is zigzag, his deportment foreign, his conduct conceited; his religion is no binding back to his soul; his conception is almost denational, his production is abortive.—He vomits forth undigested matter. Ego and mother-country he knows not, nor cares much for them; whatever concerns non-ego and foreign country he is quite conversant. There is no healthy glow in him; so he suffers in constitution and is dwarfed in stature and contracted in mind. Sick man as he is, he is thinned in a consumptive chest; his brain is spent up to giddiness or head-ache; and he prematurely ends his miserable career. The crow assumed the peacock's feathers amidst the laughter of all; his own class excommunicated him; the other shunned him as unworthy of the honor of their society: so our friend is in a dilemma; he is a social outlaw, while the Englishman hates him as an aping machine of his baser parts. This educated native is one of the chief ephemeral products of British rule. Of course there are honorable exceptions. As a last solace, giving him credit for his performance in the foreign tongue, let us proceed with his and his humbler friends' career.

When they come out of schools and colleges, their run of life begins most unpleasantly. Work they find very seldom. Those, whose parents are rich, do not care for employment, and so spend their time lazily in reading the fashionbble novels of the day, or in immoral pleasure, theatring &c., of the half-educated. But those, whom their fathers have reared with difficulty and debts, and consequently on whom they wholly depend, are compelled to seek earnings. Alas! all the fine results (whatever those may be) of the University are engrossed by a sickly craving after no higher position than an humble place in the envied kingdom of clerks and candidates. Such are hard circumstances, and the necessity-bound nation can not speculate and advance. No breathing time between college and career; and the brain crammed by one, gets crazy and care-worn by the other!

So, early one fine morning of an auspicious day, they rise, bathe and take breakfast. The mother invokes all the gods and goddesses in aid to bless her son, for it is a great day for his future life. She then with tears again blesses him,—"Mayst thou, my dear son, prosper in the world; and remember we have suffered much for thee." The father gravely advices him, "try to please your superior in every way. To say "yes sir, your honor" at every word of an officer, goes a great deal in the success of life. Humility and *salaming* are royal roads in heaven and earth." The wife, before handing over the prepared *pawn*, whispers to his ear "my love, do not forget to bring that ornament I told you last night."

Thus half-a-dozen friends go out for employment, full of hope and ardour. Little do they dream that their end will be quite different. First they go one by one to the different offices. They send in application every where, to which the invariable answer "no vacancy" is given, even when there is real need of new hands. Then they experience that their beginning of life is not so smooth as they thought before, and that the official world is full of interest and selfishness. A man, however qualified, is rejected in preference to one, who, though he knows much less, has recommendation and other influence to back him. The claims and qualifications are overlooked, and favoritism rules the day.

At last the six friends get disappointed. Their misery knows no bound. One however, more patient than others, frequents the Bungalow of an officer, whom he daily *salaams* and to whose children he presents fruits and playthings *(Dali)*. The officer at last takes notice of the *Umedwar*, (candidate). He smiles, jokes, and then after some days being pleased with his humility gives him a recommendatory letter, or provides a place in his own office.

The other friends, who are less fortunate, try their utmost to get some place, even in the most humble situations. But every sort of work is filled up to suffocation. Of manufacture and enterprize there is almost nothing. So the year closes with one as apprentice, the second in service, while four others are still unemployed, and their families almost starving.

Then they renew their exertions. One begs subscribers and becoms editor of a vernacular newspaper with anti-government feelings as a natural consequence of his and his friends' sufferings. The remaining three, finding all hopes gone and every attempt failing, respectively proceed to the Punjab frontier, Central Provinces, and to Hyderabad, Deccan.

The first person gets a little employment in some military work, which being finished, he is dismissed. He tries for other places, but succeeds not. In this way some long years pass away, and his days are most miserable. At last he has acquaintance with some *fakeers*, who smooth his troubled soul ; and he renounces the secular world, which has no attractions for him ; whereupon his dependants are in dispair and lead a wretched life.

The one, who goes to Hyderabad, gets some situation after much difficulty and delay. From this time fortune begins to smile on him ; and he forgets Lucknow, British *raj*, and perhaps loyalty.

The person, who is in the Central Provinces, has hopes. A great officer has made some vague promises. But times roll on rapidly, and yet no fulfilment appears, while want and necessity do pinch, and are felt in geometrical ratio. At last hunger rebels against his patience ;—he is compelled to get a definite answer from his patron. So he waits on his pleasure. The Hazur Sahib comes out in the verandah. The Umedwar humbly salams him, and reminds him of his promises. On this the Sahib gets angry and roars, "go away to your country, I cant do anything for you."

The disappointed young man, being penniless, begs some Rupees from railway Babus, and returns home by rail or foot. Here he finds his parents and family almost starving. All their ancestral property is mortgaged or sold, and the proceeds have been eaten up in anticipation of their son's employment. But he is now poorer than ever ; moreover he is reduced to a skeleton. Tears flow from every one's eyes,—these tears are not tears of joy at their son's return, but at the sight of the dread future. Meanwhile the son stands pale and speechless ; he can not comfort the elders. His already weak and care-worn brain gets confused. He faints and falls. The mother fans him, the father feels his pulse, the wife supplies cold water, and the other relatives make useless noise. Night at last comes and relieves the pathetic scene.

As crying and sighing can not fill their empty stomach, the mother tries to get some sort of work. She grinds flour from wheat, and does other menial work for some neighbours, though secretly, that others may not know about it, thereby keeping her family respect as much as possible. By this means, she gets half an *anna* a day, but not always. The father earns a few *pie* by writing accounts for an illiterate Buniah. The young wife (Bahu) leaving off her veil and Purdah, goes out to cook, and serve in a gentleman's house, her youthful beauty being much exposed to temptations and allurements. The other female relatives shift for themselves.

The son sees everything,—his noble ideas vanish away,—his mind breaks his system. "What were we intended to be, and what are we now reduced to!" His sufferings get unbearable. At last he procures opium secretly, and goes out to a retired place in the Baillie Guard. "To be or not to be is the question." Thus he makes long soliloquies, for the quality and quantity of which any secondary poet might have been proud. In the evening after oiling the opium he eats it up. He writes in pencil much of his dying thoughts. Then feeling bad, he wends his way back miserably along to expire at home. And all are in despair.

The one, who was apprentice here, is dismissed. He has nothing to depend upon. He tries everywhere but in vain. A private tutorship once relieved him. That gone, he is again surrounded with all kinds of difficulties. In his moments of misery, he applies to the Chief Commissioners, Viceroys, and Secretaries of State, but to no effect. His stomach burns his body ; his brain gets dried up ; while the world or rather the society, which cannot see his qualifications, that have no moneyed back-ground to help them to bold relief, hates him. Now despair and melancholy seize him, and he cannot eat, even when he gets proper food. As days pass on, his melancholia increases, till he is a regular lunatic.

So that of the six friends, who began life cheerfully, one is well off here by salaming and presents, the second is better in Hydrabad, the third is a racy editor, the fourth is an ascetic, the fifth committed suicide, and the sixth is a declared lunatic. I have digressed to show that the faults and discontents of the English-educated lie more in circumstances than in intentions. Hence the English education does not attract the people, who say that because it fails in monetary advantages, the first condition of man's existence, it is not worth the trouble of acquiring.

Chapter VI.—*Festivals of the People.*

Section I.—*Semi-social.*

On these heads, I will largely quote from the different eye-witnesses, who came to Lucknow in the days of its glory, now gone and extinguished for ever. Their impressions being taken from a foreign stand-point are more valuable and expressive.

The festivals of the people are both social and religious in their character ; of these there are two classes, (1) personal as those concerning birth, marriage, mourning, and such matters, and (2) impersonal by which I mean those professed or observed by the whole community of one creed at the same time, as *Mohurrum*, *Eed*, *Bukreed*, and *Nowroze*, of the Mohomedans, and *Basant*, *Holee*, *Ramlila*, *Dewalee* of the Hindus. The local *melas* are also to be included in the latter class.

Of birth and birth-day a rough idea has already been given, while the ceremonies observed on one's death are too general and uninteresting, to be here particularly described, more so, as they have no special local tone in them. When a Hindu dies, his corpse is taken by friends and relatives, borne on their shoulders to the river side to be burnt to ashes with a little ceremony of Mantras, followed by that of *Srádha* and *Pinda*. And all eat of the feast of woe, with an increased appetite.

A *Musulman* dying, the relatives and friends leave the room. The dead body is then washed by the Syeds, the descendants of *Mohamed*. Some ornament is usually left on the person, that the deceased may not enter paradise empty-handed. The corpse being wrapped in a piece of white cloth is placed in a coffin. It is then taken to the grave, with a funeral procession. A pall or canopy of rich cloth supported on the ends of four poles, carried by four hired mourners, shades the coffin, while it is taken to the place of burial, which is done amidst the reading of the Koran. Fires are lit for three consecutive nights, at the head and foot of the grave, to keep off evil spirits, while at dawn, the relatives daily pray. A feast of mourning follows on the fortieth day ofter death. On the night of the *Shabbarat*, all the dead relatives are honored with a feast. And one by one, their respective names being repeated, cakes (made of flour, ghee, (clarrified butler), sugar, almonds and raisins) are offered into a holy fire kindled for the purpose in the grave-yard, to appease their periodical hunger, while fireworks are brought into requisition in the house to drive away the evil spirits, who might be excited from their normal condition by such a display.

How the bond of holy matrimony is tied, is a subject interesting to all. Among Mohamedans marriages are of two kinds—Nikah and Mutah.

Nikah is permanent and holy and contracted between equals. But *Mutah* is a civil contract, temporarily binding for three hours, three days or three years. It is done between a superior and inferior, where the bridegroom never personally attends, but is represented by his sword, belt, turban, or any other ornaments of his person. A *Mutahi* wife may, as usually happens, becomes a Nikahi one, when she gives birth to a son. A *Musulman* cannot marry by Nikah, more than four, while there is no limit, theoretically to the number of *Mutahi* wives. The Hindus have no *Muta* system, and are therefore less licentious than the Mohamedans, with whom "it is esteemed a mark of gentility to have several wives."

The marriage (Nikah) ceremonies of the Mohamedans resemble, and are copied from those of the Hindus. The ceremonies are principally four in number namely, *Mangnee* (asking of the betrothed) *Sachak* (registering by eating) *Mehdi* (coloring red dye, a kind of herb) and *Barat* (*fate* of marriage.) The *mangnee* is the first contract by which the marriage parties are bound to fulfil their engagement at an appointed time. Now the dowry and other matters are settled, and arranged, and for the first time the bride-groom and bride elect or rather their parents send each other dresses, rings, ornaments and fine fruits and things too numerous to be detailed, to be worn, enjoyed and eaten, as a preliminary profession of affection for the future connection. Presents are also exchanged, during the intervening time, between the betrothed families, on occassions of *Bakreed* and other festivals. For a month before the marriage, the bride is fed exclusively on milk, unleavened bread and sweetmeats.

The three other ceremonies are held on three consecutive days or nights of the marriage proper. On the *Sachak* day, the friends and relatives, male and female, are cordially invited to the house, or trays of ready cooked dinner, especially made for the purpose, are sent around, that the forthcoming nuptials may be registered in the minds of those, who partake of the food. A wedding is a perfect peacemaker; it is the medium of reconciling long standing estrangements between friends, and the two contracting families forget not to remember their enemies in the feasting. The mother and relatives of the bride (Dulhan) employ the intervening time in finishing the preparations for the young lady's departure from the parental roof, on the day after marriage, with a more ostentatious provision of worldly necessaries and luxuries, than she may require for an independent living in her husband's house. " Many parents incur heavy debts to enable them to make a parade at their children's wedding, which proves a source of misery to themselves as long as they live."

During the three days merriment, the *Dulhan* is kept in strict confinement in a dark room or closet, " whilst the bridegroom (Dulha) is the most prominent person in the assembly of the males (in his house), where amusements are contrived to please and divert him, the party vieing in personal attention to him. The ladies in the Zenana are occupied in conversation, and merriment, and are amused with the native songs, and music of the *Domnies*, smoking the Hookka, eating *pawn*, dinner &c. Company is their delight."

On the second day, Mehdi is sent to the bridegroom with a procession and trays of presents ; and the male and female friends and relatives of the bride go in suitable conveyances to the other house. " The gentlemen are introduced to the father's hall, the ladies to the youth's mother," in the Zenana, which they enter under purdah (screen). " Bustle and excitement pervade every department of the mansion." The fair guests then crowd the central hall to perform and witness " through the blinds of bamboo chicks or thick cloths, the important process of dressing the young bridegroom in his bride's presents." The *Mehdi* is rubbed on the hands and feet, with great laughter and jokes, and the time of its adhering is considered the lasting character of the affection and union of the couple. These done the friends of the bride return home, amidst dancing, singing, illumination, fireworks and dinner, " to detail the whole business of their mission " to the expectant dames and mother, who do not join the party.

The third day is that of Barat (fate, that may give a good or bad husband or wife). The *Dulha* (bridegroom), with a grand procession of friends, innumerable torches, bands of music, sepoys or policemen, and servants, goes to the other house to fetch his betrothed. " The marriage ceremony is performed in the Zenana, by an old *mulla* (priest) who, after respectively asking the bridegroom and bride certain formal questions, reads that part of the Koran, which binds the parties in holy wedlock." And the new husband and wife are led to a retired place, to see each other for the first time, under a screen, and through a mirror, while the holy Koran sanctifies the interview. After this many absurd customs follow.

The *Dulhan* is now taken, with all her things given by her parents, to the house of her husband. Here she is called the *Bahu Begum*, and every one pays her regard, affection, and attention. After a short stay of a day or two, she returns to her father's house, and lives there for a month or so before she finally settles in the other. The husband occasionally or regularly once a day, pays her a visit, remaining in the night and departing in the morning. After this period, she goes to her father-in-law's house ; but until the birth of a son, the *Bahu Begum* is not allowed liberty of action except in the privacy of her own apartment.

SECTION II.— *The Religious Festivals.*

Under this head the important ones are noted, such as Ramzan, Eed, Bakrid, Nowroze and Mohurrum (Mohamedan), and Basant, Holi, Ramlila, Dewali, and Bathing (Hindus).

Ramzan is a holy month for fasting. The Mohamedans are enjoined to spend the whole day time solely in the service of God, and not of men or in any worldly pursuit. But few now pray, and almost every body sleeps over the fast as much as one can, and is relieved by stories, and other light amusements. After evening the fast is broken by a cooling draught, called *Sherbat* or *Thandái*, followed by a sumptuous supper. "The *Thandai* is composed of the seeds of lettuce cucumber and melon with coriander, pounded and diluted with cold water, and then strained through muslin, to which is added rose water, sugar, syrup of pomegranate and *keorha* (a pleasant flavoured distilled water from the blossom of a species of aloe)." During the night, eating, drinking and merriment go on, and very little sleep is indulged in. In the third quarter, beggars or *fakeers* stroll in the lanes or streets, to awake those who might sleep, and breakfast is eaten and finished before dawn. The day fast commences with sleep or any other help.

On the thirty-first day, or the first appearance of the moon, after the Ramzan, the feast of *Eed* commences. It is a day of joy, visiting of friends, and mutual congratulation, amidst dancing, singing, eating and other amusements. A grand service is held at about 9 A. M. in the great Jumma Musjid, to which the Mohamedan nobles and Begums, and formerly kings and queens attended with all their paraphernalia of glory.

Bukrid (Eed of the goat) is celebrated some days after the above festival. It is held in remembrance of Abraham having been about to sacrifice his son Ishmael (not Isaac, as the Jews and Christian believe), when the angel stopped him, and threw down a goat from heaven," to be offered to God in his place. "When the goat fell, it so happened that it fell on a fish and locust, and killed them both, and hence the fish and locust are the animals a good Mohamedan can eat, without having them first killed by cutting their throats. On this day every good Musulman must eat the flesh of a goat, if he wishes to get into Paradise. Besides goats, the queen (mother of Wajid Ali Shah) had two camels killed, so that every servant of the household might have a small portion of their flesh to eat, for those who sacrifice and eat camels on this day will enter Paradise riding on a camel (so as to be able to) pluck the luxurious fruits from the trees therein, as they go along, while those riding on the goat cannot (have the advantage of) reaching them."—*The Eastern Queen.*

Nowroze (Mohamedan new year's day) is a great day of family reunion, feasting, mirth, fun, and jollity. New clothes are worn on this day, presents are given and favours are shown. Both in the Mardana and Zenana, but more in the latter, the inmates of the house and friends visiting sprinkle one another with a red fluid, made by boiling the flower called *Har Singhar.* "Mobarak Nowroz!" (may the new year be fortunate) are the terms of salutation now exchanged by all classes of society. The *Nowroze* teems with friendly tokens between the two families of a bride and bride-groom elect, who interchange presents with each other. The children receive gifts from their elders; their nurses reap a harvest from them; the tutor (Moulvi) writes an ode in praise of his pupil, and receives gifts from the child's parents, the servants and slaves are regaled with dainties, and with presents from the superiors of the establishment; the poor are remembered with clothes, money and food; the ladies make and receive visits, and the *Domnies* attend to play and sing in the Zenana. In short the whole day is passed in cheerful amusements, suited to the retirement of a Zenana and the habits of the people." *Mrs. Hossain Ali.*

In the palace, the last king used to pay, with the usual Nazzar, a complimentary visit to his mother. With him came a stream of the royal Begums of his Majesty, whom the Queen would not receive at other times. They were a hundred or hundred and twenty of them salaming and presenting Nazars. "Some of them mere children, many of them very pretty; some old, one a negress—all in their best clothes, to the great amusement of the Queen, who never looked upon them without laughing." Then the red dye was sprinkled into one another's clothes; and hand-fans, large and small, being trimmed with red cloth, were handed from one to the other with a slight waving. But it was in the evening that the greatest hilarity prevailed in the palace."

Mohurrum is the Mohamedan month for mourning, which the Shiahs observe with due show and ceremony, for ten or forty days according to their taste, means, and convenience. The Sunnies observe it for ten days only, but without images, parade, models or acting. During this festival of woe, no luxury is indulged in, or pleasure is partaken, but all ought to lament and mourn with body and soul. The devout men and women especially do not for forty days change their clothes, do not use oil or any sweet scents or put *missee* to their teeth, nor rub *mehdi* on their hands and feet; all leave off their ornaments and fine dress but simply wear black or blue clothes. No marriage is now contracted, much less celebrated; and in properly conducted families, men and women live separately. *Mujlises* or mourning assemblies are daily held, at the conclusion of which the poor are given bread.

The origin of this annual manifestation of woe is thus briefly told. Hazrat Ali, Yazeed (the usurping Caliph), Abbas Alam, and Ameen Alam, leaders and brothers, disagreed among themselves on points of faith, policy and interest. Abbas sided with Ali, while Ameen with Yuzeed. The Commander-in-Chief of Ali's army was Syed Salar, who after a short time deserted with all his forces to the enemy. A civil war was the consequence. Ali having a few followers was shut up, beseiged, and was in want of every thing—water, provision, aud amunition. Surrounded with these odds, Ali still maintained his position, till at last he was assassinated, while praying in the Musjid, by one bribed so to do by the beautiful daughter of the Caliph (King of Sham), already betrothed to Hossein. The two sons of Ali, Hussan and Hossein, carried on the war, and once attempted to bring back the dead body of their father in the Musjid, guarded by tigers! but they failed. One of the daughters of Ali, beautiful as a *peri* (fairy), was in torture for want of water; so her uncle Abbas Alam, cut his way out to a well, filled the skin (Mashak) with water, and though wounded and pierced with arrows in every part of his body and Mashak (both of his hands were cut off) he still brought with the help of his teeth a little of the precious fluid for her; and died soon after. The two brothers were also killed in the fight at Karbala. Their mother, Fatima with her four daughters, weeping and throwing ashes on their faces, went forth, bare-footed, to seek for the dead, but not succeeding took refuge, tired and weary, in a tent, whence, however they were betrayed and turned out with blows. Thus with exposed faces and in miserable plight, they were conducted by a loyal slave to the forest, where they lived for a month or so. Collecting and sewing together 180 pieces of rags, they made a sheet or veil (Borka) which they wore in turn when they went out. There however they were found out, and murdered or led in captivity to Mecca, by the wicked hand of the enemy.

This story is often recited in pathetic verses, called *Marcia*, and sung in the mourning assemblies both in the Mardana and Zenana, and is heard with tears and sighs, loud lamentations and beating of hearts. Professional mourners are also hired, who with cries of "Hussan ! and Hossain !!" beating of wooden bits and a whirling waving dance in a circle heighten the effect of the display of grief and holy sympathy. This is called Matam (weeping).

During these anniversary days of woe, representations of the tombs of of the martyrs at Karbala, called *Tazia* (literally meaning grief) are bought in the bazars and after being duly consecrated in the *Huzrat Abbas ki Dargah*, are brought with due tomtoming, trumpeting and dirges and flags, to the house, and ceremoniously kept on the elevated places in the family-Emambarah (house of the Emams—saint). There the altars are covered with black cloth, and votive offerings are given. There also Alams (silver or tin hands) daggers, swords, turbans &c., are displayed. On the floor between the Taziahs are curiously shaped lanterns with colored wax-candle, which are in the night lit. For nine consecutive nights the house is illuminated, and friends and strangers, male and female, come on *Ziarat* (pilgrimage). On these occassions the illuminations of Husainabad and Shah Najaf are grand and worth-seeing.

On the seventh day, after evening a procession takes place in honor of *Kasim*, the cousin of *Hossain*, who lost his life on his wedding day ;

and trays of *Mehdi* are carried about from house to house, with weeping and lamentation, for *Mehdi* being used in marriage, is significant of *Kasim's* untimely and tragic end. On the eighth, ceremonies are performed in honor of *Abbas Alam*, and *Sherbat* is given to appease the thirst of the poor and the invited. But the ninth is the great day for illumination and mourning ; *Mersias* and *Soz* are heard and sung with beating of breasts and noisy cries are raised throughout the night, when no sleep is allowed.

On the tenth or the fortieth day *(Chehlum)* after the 10th, the *Taziahs* are taken with the *Duldul* (favourite horse of Hossain) and with pomp ; according to the means of each, to be buried at Karbala of Talkatora, and a grand Mela takes place, where the people from miles around, congregate. Lucknow then seems to be the city of the dead or deserted, where such a perfect calm prevails in the lanes and streets, that no soul is to be seen, but the myriads of flies that are buzzing in the air, and the street dogs barking here and there; while as you approach Victoria street, your attention is attracted and absorbed on the house-tops, right and left, where fair Begums of green or blue robes, and pretty Bibies of picturesque attire, are sitting or standing in a row, to see whatever procession of woe passes the road. There as you near the Karbalâ, the vivacity of life increases in intensity and extension ; till the whole scene is presented to the view, as a promiscuous crowd of men and women, noisiness and cloudiness, a wavy stream that disolves into nothing. Here in this garden the whole city is concentrated, and all is animation and dustiness. Here a Nawab may be seen relieving himself, after the delivery of his burdensome woe and lamentation, with a chatty talk to a damsel of the verandah, who in a little tent attracts the passers-by by her manifestation. Here the mystery of love and crime reigns supreme, while the policemen float about as though wooden statues in a vast machine, and the breakers of the moral law and right dive, steal and laugh at the unsuccessful endeavours of the poor. detectives, who, perhaps taken by a sight, stand or move absent-minded. Here a youth, on an aerial pleasure-voyage in the whirling frame, accidentally loses his life from the folds of his cloth being rolled in the beam ; while his fair partner of enjoyment, after a formal cry and display of tears, consoles herself in the company of another paramour.

Of the Hindu festivals, the important ones are Basant (spring), Holi (carnival), Ramlila, and Asnán (bathing.)

Basant is a festival, in which the Mohammedans also partake. It occurs when the winter season changes for that of spring. Now new clothes are worn, and friends meet one another for merry-making. Dancing is seen, choice-songs are heard, and nice meals are eaten with a glad heart and increased appetite. On this day of festival, the Kings of Oudh used to indulge in all sorts of royal display, and amusements. All the fancy boats were adorned with fantastic forms, and paraded in rows on the Goomti. Dancing girls, *Bhards* (commedians), musicians, and fiddlers, all performed their vocations to the delight of the spectators, who stood or sat on both banks of the river, lined with picturesque palaces and mosques; while the sovereign, Resident, and nobles, with Begums and Princesses on silver or gold bedecked peacock or fish-like boats, encouraged and enlivened the scene, which concluded after nightfall, with a grand illumination and fireworks.

"No description can do justice to the scene presented on some fine, dark, clear night, when the Goomti is covered with boats, of those, long canœ-shaped graceful forms belonging to the King, some resembling alligators, others swans, peacocks, or dolphins, enamelled in various colors, intermingled with gold, and filled with a splendid company of natch-girls, glittering in gem and tissues. Blue lights, so artfully disposed, as not to be visible, while they clothe the whole pageant with their unearthly gleams, render every adjacent object distinct; and as the blaze of ten thousand rockets burst forth, palaces, mosques and temples seem to rise majestically during the brief illumination. In the next moment all is dark, save the pageant on the Goomti, and again minarets and domes, cupolas and spires spring up, and spouts of fires ascending to the skies"—*Mrs. Roberts.*

'*Holi*' is also an occasion of festivity. The people observe it in commemoration of their beloved Kanhaya's (Krishna) once playing with his wives, with a red dye called *Rang.* This festival of carnival is very ancient; it was almost universal in some form or other, in old Egypt, Greece, Rome, and Europe of the middle ages. Here the Hindu citizens celebrate it with red dye and powder, which are at first consecrated to the god. This dye is applied to one another's clothes, amidst laughter and songs. Many practical jokes, sometimes not decent, are also indulged in. In the Zenana, the woman have a most pleasant time of it; the sisters-in-law get greatly pleased to sprinkle their brothers-in-law, who, not undaunted by a blaze of laughter, raised at their expense, reply to every charge, with pitchers of the colored-water or globules of the powder. The boys and adults are seen to run from room to room, neighbourhood to neighbourhood, and from lanes to lanes, after their grand-parents, friends and travellers, with large syringes in their hands. All is noise and excitement, amusement and delight. The festival concludes with *natches*, eating of nice sweet-meats and display of pretty clothes.

Dewali is a festival of lamps, of which millions are brought into requisition, and lighted on the roofs, Verandahs, doors and every part of one's house, on the night of the Kartik Amabashya. Offerings are given to the goddess Luchmi (wealth), who is invoked with due ceremony and worship; evil spirits are driven away that are dreaded; and a sumptuous supper is eaten. The boys, with lighted torches or bundles of reeds, play with one another in the streets; while the shop-keepers congregate and ignite great fires in the cross-roads to extinguish the contagious bad air (*bhoot*-ghost), that might infest or attack the neighbourhood. Thus the dark night passes pleasantly, while within the house of the gamblers, all the Banias and Mahajans go in to see, experiment, and calculate how the goddess Luchmi will show her favours during the ensuing year.

Rámlílá is a religious dramatic display observed for half a month, in commemoration of Ramchandra of Ajodhyá with his monkey-hordes conquering Ravana, the King of Lanká. With great devotion and ardour the people congregate at Aishbagh, Goornarain bagh, Chouk and Sadar, and with no less pleasure and agility assume and act the holy and unholy heroes and heroines of *Ramayana*. Homer's Illiad is dead, and is only a reference or amusement-book to the antiquarian and the literati, while Valmiki's great epic is a living one, and is yearly reproduced and played in characters, bold and pathetic, in which even the non-Hindu takes great delight and interest. Seeta is represented by a beautiful boy, attired in choicest female-garb, while her husband is done by a youth with bows and arrows, quiver and crown, and so on. Thousands of people go to witness the scenes. The lazy Nawab attends in his buggy; the Begum of the progressive school drives in a screened carriage, the unsympathetic European with an eye-glass looks obliquely from his horse, the fat Mahajan squatting on his *palki* sees devoutly; the bad characters congregate for evil purposes; the Babus on elephants, borrowed for the purpose, make a prominent figure under a dusty tree or in open place of no cleaner atmosphere, while the pedestrians, sweet-meet sellers, stall-keepers, *Pawn-walies* (prostitutes selling betle-leaves and tobacco), the whirling frames with occupants, fair or foul, the doll-vendors &c.,—all around keep up a vivacity of life, not less in importance and interest than the performance within the inner arena, where the rows of devout and silent spectators, women and men squating on the ground, witness how the valiant combatants, men, monkeys, and demons are noisily and unsystematically rushing to the fight, which after many a charge and counter charge ends in a glorious victory to the sons of man and God. Seeta is delivered from her captivity, and Ravan, the typical vice, falls and explodes in fire. The whole proceeding ends in the hero becoming the king of Ajodhya and emperor of Hindustan.

The *Asnan*, or bathing festival takes place on the conjunction of some planets. This time of conjunction or *Yoge* is held peculiarly sacred all over India, as tending to restoration of health, both of body and mind. Now is the favourite occasion of washing off sins and propitiating gods. So, early in the morning as the day dawns, while the expiring night's darkness yet lingers, devout ladies issue forth from their Zenanas in doolies, palkies or on foot, and go as though in a constant stream of procession of Grecian dames of old to the temple of Minerva, to the several ghauts (of which the Kuria ghaut and those of the Iron bridge and Brick bridge are the principal). There they dive into, or sprinkle themselves, with the half-holy water of the Goomti and changing their clothing, rapidly return home, lest the profane eyes of the public may catch their ever-hidden charms. As the sun-god rises higher, the promiscuous crowd of bathers, men and women, chiefly the latter, thicken, and the hitherto pure water gets dirtier by the constant process of ablution ; while the poor Bramhans seated on mats spread for the purpose, invite them and apply *chandan* mark on their forehead, and get a little rice or a few pice in return. Now the idlers and Shohdas assemble, and if they can not ease the pockets of the bathers, they reconnoitre here and there, in reconnaisance parties, to view and take a glimse, from favourable points of observation, how the fair limbs of a beauty of fifteen are exposed and washed, who, however, baffles them by a skilful display of her then slender clothing, or a proportional diving in the water. But with the morning, the modest women have disappeared, and with the heat of the day, the heat of the Mela commences; and the holy bathing is changed for the exhibition of amusements. The boys are mad after kite-flying, the children cry for dolls, and the Shohdas keep up their mischievous noisiness. The fatigued dames with their daughters-in-fact, and veiled daughters-in-law sit in rows along the roadside, or in irregular groups under the shades of trees, and refresh themselves with the chewing of sugarcane, or eating of sweetmeats, of which the neighbouring shops tempt their tongue, and increase their appetite; while the tall policemen, those preservers of morality, if not decency, oscillating between duty and negligence, now drive away the crowds unnecessarily, now stand at a sight, now exchange a word of love with a little distant friend of his in reference to a passing or seated lady, doubly enveloped with dress and *dopattahs*. In the festivals of women or affairs concerning them, the guards should be of that sex. It was so under the old system; the men were not then allowed even the vicinity. Hence the morality of that time was better in effect as in appearance.

CHAPTER VII.—*Pageants of old Lucknow.*

The kings of Oudh, like the Moguls of Delhi, loved splendour and ostentation. Regal dignity can not be manifested otherwise than by extravagant displays and paraphernalia, and the people see and judge according to the oriental standard. The greatest show has the greatest impression on the mind of men. But in these hard days of calculators and accountants, the glories of Lucknow are gone; and the local citizens love to remember what happened and attracted their eyes and ears in the golden period of the *Shahi*.

State-entry of Governors-General, Residents and other high personages to the city, and their reception by the Kings of Oudh was a great occasion for display on the part of both the host and the guest. When the Marquis of Hastings came here on the 25th of October 1814, he thus records his entry :—" We moved early towards the city. The Nawab Wazier (Ghazee-ud-din) met me about two miles from it, and descended from his elephant. I quitted mine also, and after embracing him, I got with him upon another elephant, equipped with a magnificient howdah calculated to carry us both. Then we proceeded. The wealthier inhabitants were all in their holiday-clothes on the flat tops of their houses

.... I scattered Rs. 1,000. Natch-girls in their gaudiest habiliments sang congratulatory verses, from the tops of the houses, with which we were generally on a level. Persons every now and then ran to meet us, throwing up into the air a number of live-quails,—a pretty compliment, as it was understood to mean a liberation of prisoners on the joyful occasion,"

When Lord Cumbermere, then Commander-in-Chief, came here on 11th December 1827, there was also an occasion of pompous procession. "The two cavalcades approached, met and blended themselves into one, producing an impenetrable cloud of dust. The young prince (Khemajah) having quitted his own howdah for that of the Commander-in-Chief, the whole procession rushed on together in one compact mass of about forty elephants. The two escorts led the way, followed by a pedestrian crowd of *Chobdars* (mace bearers), standards, heralds calling the high-sounding titles of the boy-prince and led horses richly caparisoned. On the front, flank, and rear, we are surrounded by a crowd of picturesque-looking cavaliers, who are constantly employed in displaying their horsemanship and dexterity in the use of the spear and sword by curvetting and careering at each other in mimic jest, with the most noble disregard of bank, ditches and uneven ground.

"This day (11th December) having been declared auspicious by the soothsayers for the entry of the Commander-in-Chief into Lucknow, we mounted our elephants at an early hour and started our march towards the city. About two miles from the town, we encountered His Majesty of Oude (Nasir-ud din), accompanied by a numerous and splendid retinue. The king and the Commander-in-Chief after a fraternal embrace continued the march in the same howdah. Our cavalcade was formidably augmented by this last re-inforcement, and it must have presented an imposing spectacle to the myriads of lookers-on as we entered the city...............The houses, from the windows of which were displayed silk and draperies, were as well as the streets thickly crowded with spectators; some of them employed in greeting their sovereign with profound *salam*. The greater proportion however consisted of wretched-looking beggars, who followed the cavalcade vociferating for charity and greedily scrambling for the handful of rupees, which were from time to time thrown by the king among the multitude. It was curious

to see with what care the elephan s avoided treading upon or injuring some of the paupers, who in eager pursuit of the scattered largesses fearlessly threw themselves under the feet of these animals, the slightest touch of which would have shattered a limb. A few coins, thrown on the roof of a house, sometimes caused the most amusing scramble, and I saw more than one of the gleaners roll into the streets on the heads of the gaping crowd below. In some of the narrow passes the crush was awful, the elephants trumpeting, jhools and ladders tearing and crashing, and now and then the projecting (thatched) roof verandahs (*chappars*) of a house pushed away by the resistless progress of these powerful animals."
Ch: Mundy's Pen and Ink sketches in India.

State-entries were followed by formal receptions, in Durbar, of the august guest in the palace, Moti Mahal or Farhat Buksh. "The Nawab-Vazir (Ghazi-ud-din) obliged me and Lady Lowdon" says Lord Hastings, "to occupy the central places (of a rich *Musnud*). On each side of us sat the two brothers of the King of Delhi, who reside at Lucknow. (They never enter the Vazier's palace, but now to honor the occasion). The Nawab-Vazier was at the extremity of the couch............ Mirza Sultan Mohamed, a Persian prince of royal lineage, now seated himself on the other extremity", but was obliged to retire in great indignation. Then the formal introduction of the Nobles of Oudh to the Governor-General took place.

Next came the State banquet in the order of the usual programme amidst illumination, fireworks and music. Saadat Ali Khan, Ghazi-ud-din Hyder, and Nasir-ud-din ate Kaffir food and wine with the English; but the latter kings, Mohammad Ali Shah, Umjad Ali Shah, and Wajid Ali Shah, never tasted wine and meals prepared by men of another creed. They merely sat with the English gentlemen, and sipped what was made and brought by their own men. And such a banquet is thus described. "At last the king (Wajid Ali Shah) made his appearance; and the guests all jostled into chairs as best as they might. My position, almost opposite his Majesty, afforded me ample opportunity of inspecting the quality and quantity of the jewels, with which his person was absolutely loaded, and which I have never seen equalled in magnificience: a rope of pearls passing over one shoulder to the other, was tied in a knot at his waist from which the costly ends negligently descended; his turban and breast were covered with diamonds and other precious stones; and it was a matter of wonder that he did not sink under the heat of the room, combined with the extent of mineral productions he carried on his person. But the jewels, though worthy of great attention, did not possess nearly so much interest, as did the mode by which he removed the burly person that they adorned. On one side of him stood the bearer of his magnificently jewelled hookah, on the other, the bearer of the royal spoon, the the contents of which he was already wistfully surveying, as it was mixed up by the skilful feeder into the form and consistency, that his Majesty loved, and put as a nurse would put the pap into his Majesty's mouth, which was then carefully wiped by another, who I presumed, is called the 'piper' and who was in his turn of duty succeeded by the hookah-bearer, who gently inserted the mouth-piece between the royal lips, in order that his Majesty might fill up, by a puff of the fragrant weed, the time required for the preparation of another spoonful. This routine of feeding, wiping, and smoking was only varied, when the king slowly licked his lips, which he did in a dignified manner, and with a reproachful look at the wiper, whereat the wiper might be observed to tremble." *Oliphant's Nepal.*

While on eating, I may also introduce a zenana royal banquet. "The longest room in the palace was the scene of festivity in the evening, and in this preparation was made for the family banquet. New carpets were spread, and over them two long cloths from end to end, on each side of which plates were arranged. At right angles to this, across the top of the room, was another cloth, supported by a carpet of the richest material, fringed with gold lace. The most splendid cushions were made ready, and massive gold and silver articles displayed on all sides. At the shorter table cloth, the seat of honor, at the upper end of the room, the queen-mother, king (Wajid Ali Shah), Khas Mahal, the heir apparent, the General Saheb, and his eldest son, took their places, amid the loud flourish of trumpets, the playing of bands and the roar of cannon. Then came the wives of the King, trooping in to take their places,—some tall, some short, dark and fair, young and old, beautiful and ugly, all in rich kinkhobs, and clothes of gold, wearing their finest jewellery.

"The chandeliers from the roof were all lit up, and the wall-shades by the side of the large mirrors on the walls; the room was a blaze of light, and the sparkling of gold and silver cups and plates, and jewellery and rich dresses, reflected by the large mirrors, made a gorgeous scene. It was as the court of Indra, the palace of the Peries(fairies). And soft silvery voices rang forth in laughter. And the sweet tones of girlhood were mingled with the roars of drums and trumpets, and all kinds of musical instruments without. Down the whole length of the room the chandeliers flashed upon rich garments and gems, and many beautiful faces, all reflected mirrors around, and as the music without ceased, and the banquet began, the hum of many voices rose from the long lines of sitting figures, subdued voices and whispering mingled with the soft laughter of girlhood, and happiness was over all." *Private life of an Eastern Queen.*

After the state banquet with Governors-General or other high officials, came the private conference in a retired room, where points of business and administrative advice were raised and given, discussed and settled to a satisfactory conclusion. This conference also used to take place biweekly between the king and the Resident at the Residency, and the palace alternately, after the tea party was dismissed or "chapani" was over. The charge of this "chapani," (literally tea-water) was 3,000 Rs. per month, paid from the Royal treasury.

The illuminations and fire works of Lucknow are noted throughout Upper India. Every year the Taluqdars of Oudh show their loyalty to the rulers by these displays; while the Nawabs of Lucknow do the same in Hossainabad and Shah-Najaff, of which the Mohurrum illuminations for consecutive nine nights are also important. But our business is with old Lucknow; so hear what the Marquis of Hastings saw and recorded. 'From one of the gates of Constantia, we saw the whole road towards the palace bordered with posts, on each of which many lights were fixed. As we approached it, triumphal arches of lamp, raised on bamboo frames, had an elegant and brilliant appearance. Proceeding further, we came to a place, where on each side, there were in transparencies, the representation of a bazar or market. The costumes of the Hindus and Chinese were strikingly pourtrayed. Then we approached a kiosk or summer house, decorated in a manner extraordinarily tasteful. But all this splendour faded in comparison with what opened upon us, when we came to a sort of esplanade, before the windows of the banquetting hall. It was as large as a middle-sized field in England. The whole of it was laid out to imitate a *parterre* of flowers. The number of lamps, with which the ground was covered for this purpose, must have been immense, and the disposition of their various colours, to render the representation accurate, was very happy.........The illuminations were certainly beyond anything of the kind I have elsewhere witnessed."

Illumination of the Goomti. "The scene that here met our eyes was beautiful in the extreme and truly oriental. It appeared a realization of some of those splendid fictions in the "Arabian Nights". The night, though dark, was calm : the balcony where we stood overhang the river, which flowed deep beneath, and was thickly studded with many-shaped boats. In one of these, in the middle of the stream, a group of *natch*-girls and musicians were dancing and singing. The whole was made visible to us by blue lights, so placed under the verandah as to throw their cold mysterious lights over the scene, without annoying the eyes of the spectators. The fireworks, which were extremely well-managed and of great variety, were arranged along the opposite bank of the river and in the vessels on its surface. At intervals, fire-balloons were sent up, which as they majestically floated over the city, showed us alternately in the distance some elegant palace, temple or mosque, whose white and guilt minerets were for an instant brightly illuminated, and then left their original darkness"—*Mundy*.

Fireworks of Lucknow are too numerous to be detailed. These have quite a distinctive character ; no spasmodic flights or intermittent outbursts of rockets, but continued activity—Catherine wheels, fountains of fire, revolving wheels and balloons." *Russell's Prince of Wales' tour*. "The glare of the lamps lighted up a square, in which was a garden fitted with the grotesque frames of the fireworks of the evening. Birds and beasts of all description" (as also forts, battle-array, ram-fights &c.) were there, waiting to be set off............At length dinner was over, and inmediately there was a rush to the windows to see the fire-works, which seemed to be let off all at once, so that it was impossible to distinguish anything but a universal twisting and whirling, and fizzing and cracking, and an elephant looked very brilliant for a moment and went off through his eyes with a bang, and was no more;— sham men exploded; and real men jumped into sparkling flames; and rockets and fire-balloons went up; so that if the lessee of Vauxhall or Cremorne could let off, or send half as many thing as were let off, and went up on this occasion in the Courtyard of the Lucknow Durbar, he would make a fortune".— *Oliphant's Nepal.* There is still a Nawab in Muftigunge, who is famous for his pyrotechnic art.

Grand Durbar in the throne-room. The Kings of Oudh did not every day sit on their thrones. It was on occasions of display, festivals and ceremony. They used to take their royal seats about four or five times a year at the utmost. There was a rumour here, that a snake lay hidden in the throne, and its poison soon ended the sovereign's life. But this rumour was a moral allegory, which none understood at the time. The hidden snake was pride, which at its height snatches away one's life by its poisonous sting. Accordingly when Wajid Ali Shah was crowned, His Majesty did not sit on it but simply touched the *Guddee* seven times bowing, and then sat himself apart from it. The old Durbars are thus described, and an illustration of the scene is given, as sketched by a noted native artist, Mohammad Ali, at the time, when old Mohammad Ali Shah was on the throne:—

"Coronation-day is a great day at the court of Oudh. On each anniversary of that day, the King receives his crown afresh from the hands of the Envoy, in the throne-room. No one is allowed to be seated in his presence but the Resident. The crown was handed to the envoy by the Chief Mulla, and by him was placed on the head of the King. This was no sooner done, than the room rung with cheers and by the firing of royal salutes without. Many seed pearls and other small jewels were scattered abroad in abundance, among all the parties who were in the room. Then he proceeded to the verandah, where a similar scrambling for money was made among the populace generally, accompanied by the cheering fun and jollity, which is the usual attendant of such scenes." *Nott's Memoir.*

A better account of the Durbar is given:—"The throne is a square platform raised two feet from the ground, with a railing on three sides, and a canopy supported upon pillars; of these the frame-work is wood, but the casing pure gold, set with precious stones of great value; the canopy is of crimson velvet richly embroidered with gold, and finished with a deep fringe of pearls; the cushions, on which the King is seated, are also of embroidered velvet, and the emblems of royalty, *Chhattah*, is of the same, with a deep fringe of pearls. The King appears literally covered with jewels, the whole body down to the waist being decorated with strings of diamonds, rubies, emeralds &c. His crown is a perfect constellation of gems, overshadowed by the plumes of the bird of paradise. A native of rank stands on either side of the throne, waving *Chowries* of peacock's feathers set in gold handles. To the right of the throne are guilt chairs for the accommodation of the Resident and his wife, if he be a married man. The English-men attached to the Residency take up their position behind, and to the sides of these chairs standing, those in the service of the King wearing very handsome dresses of pure colored cloth, richly embroidered with gold. The left of the throne is occupied by natives of rank, holding high official situations, splendidly attired in the picturesque costume of the country.

"The prime-minister stands at the king's feet to receive and present *Nazars*. These consist of money from 21 gold mohurs down to a few Rupees in silver, according to the circumstances of the parties presenting. The person offering, advances to the throne with many Salâms" (by kneeling and touching in succession all the steps leading to it) "and having his gift placed upon a folded handkerchief, presents it to the King to touch in token of acceptance; it is then given to the minister, who adds it to the heap by his side. After this ceremony the King and the Resident rise; the former takes from the hands of a person in waiting, certain necklaces, composed of silver ribbon ingeniously plated, which offer a cheap mode of conferring distinction; the investiture is made by the King in person; and upon taking leave, the Resident is accompanied by the King to the entrance, where he salutes him with a short sentence, "God be with you" (Khoda Hafiz,) pouring *âttar*, on his hand. Should the ambassador happen to be in great favour, at the time, the compliment is extended to all the English visitants as they pass out.

"Titles of honor, Khilluts and their accompanying distinctions—such as elephants fully caparisoned, or a charger, or a palanquin are frequently conferred on these Court-days; the *nazar* is then of proportionate value, persons anxiously coveting some grant or distinction offering (sometimes) not less than a *lakh* of rupees; this sum is conveyed in 100 bags covered with crimson silk tied with a silver ribbon"—*Mrs. Robert's scenes and character*. For fuller description, see Mrs. Hossein Ali's Musulmans in India.

A specimen of a royal procession is given. Mrs. Roberts thus describes the scene, when Nasir-ud-din Hyder went to the Eedgah on the occasion of a Bakreed festival. "The van of the cavalcade is formed of 50 elephants, carrying suivels, each accompauied by a driver and two gunners in white uniform with turbans and Kamarbands of red and green, the colours of the cloth composing the housings of the camels. A party of artillery succeeds, the gunners being in blue uniform; next two troops of cavalry in the picturaque vests worn by *sawars*, of scarlet cloth, with painted caps of black-lamb skin. After this a regiment of foot, only half-clad, in wild barbaric costume, the trowsers scarcely extending midway down the thigh, where it is vandyked with black points; they have red jackets and small turbans of black leather; and the war-like but discordant music of the *Dankah* or kettle-drum assimilates well with the strange fantastic display made by the troops. The Najibs are closely followed by the most gorgious portion of the spectacle, the elephant carriage of the King and his court; the great satrap himself sits enthroned in a sort of triumphal car of silver, canopied and curtained with crimson velvet, embroidered and fringed with gold, and drawn by four elephants, exactly matched in colour, height and size. The others have two elephants each, but all glitter with gold and silver; and the gallant company so proudly borne along, shine from head to foot in gems and brocade. Their turbans are adorned with costly aigrettes of jewels; claps, studs, belts, rings, and bracelets, of the most precious treasures of the mine, appear in greatest profession, down to the gem-enamelled slipper; and these are set off by the graceful flow of drapery, composed of the most beautiful-woven tissues, and shawls of the finest fabric. Round these chariots, *Chobdars* (mace bearers) *Chaprasis*, *Harkaras*, and other state-servants, some brandishing sheathed scimitars, and others fanning the air with *Chowries*, shout out the titles of the illustrious and puissant personages, to whom they belong; while a cloud of irregular horse hovers on either side, tilting and curvetting apparently with disorderly recklessness, yet in reality conducting their evolutions with the most consummate skill.

" The King's led horses next appear to swell the pomp and parade ; they are all richly caparisoned and attended by grooms in handsome liveries. The royal Palki and palanquin next appear; these native vehicles are of the most splendid description, constructed entirely of wrought gold, each carried by bearers clad in long scarlet vests, embroidered with gold, their turbans ornamented with the emblem of royalty. The state carriage also forms a portion of this part of the show; it is of English make, drawn by black horses, driven in hand by a European coachman in scarlet livery or rather uniform. The English gentlemen composing the foreign portion of the King's suite appear in their court-dress, mounted upon elephants, and after them a long train of native nobility, also mounted in the same manner, the whole being closed by horse and foot-soldiers, those belonging to the India Company marching with their colors unfurled, and their bands playing, whilst hundreds of banneroles of gold and silver tissue, flow in the air in every direction.

" Notwithstanding the want of order and discipline, which seems essential to the movement of so large a body, the procession arrives at its place of destination, without being materially disarranged by the apparent confusion, which is considerably augmented by the clashing of instruments, those of Europe striving with hopeless efforts to vie with the clang and clamour of the native trumpet and drum. The cavalcade being drawn up at the place appointed, the superior priest or Mulla, after going through the usual religious ceremonies, presents a knife to the king, who repeating a prayer, plunges his weapon into the throat of a camel, the victim selected for the sacrifice. The artillery men are all in readiness, and when the signal is given of the completion of the ceremony by the King himself, a general discharge of the musketry and cannon announces the circumstance to the whole city."

In contrast to the above I will introduce a Hindu marriage-procession on the occasion of a rich merchant's (*jowhri's*) son's wedding. "First marched a body of drummers and pipers...ragged and dirty, followed by an elephant richly caparisoned, then hoary fathers, splendidly dressed in Lucknow turbans of brocade and cloth of gold with grand Cashmere shawls, with fine jackets and nether garments, shuffling along in gorgeous slippers on foot. Next in single file comes, in quite open palanquins, the children of the relations of the contracting parties, attired with a magnificence, which cannot be exaggerated by the use of any language,— and the notion of which can only be conveyed by the painter's brush. Some ponies with beautiful saddle cloths and tails dyed red; others were in silver *Chaisen á pourteur*, with ivory bearing poles, lined with purple velvet and cloth of gold. Inside one of these sat a child like a cabinet of gems crusted all over with diamonds, pearls and emeralds, and yet so tastefully dressed, that this weight of ornament was not at all vulgar. The boy was pretty. After him came more little ones, some two and two, in their palkies. They were flanked by guards and men with fly-dusters, who flapped and fanned the little fellows' faces.

"The defile lasted for half-an-hour. but at length the bridegroom made his appearance—a child of 5 or 6 years old, with demure round face, lighted by a pair of great round eyes, surrounded by painted eyelids, mounted on a milk-white pony, which was covered with rich broc des and gem-studded saddle-cloth. The little creature, who was a mere mummy swathed in sheets of gold and silver and weighted with precious stones, hid its features completely by a veil of pearls stung together, so as to form a sort of vizor hanging from the turban. The procession closed with a band of musicians, some mounted on horseback with Kettle-drums and trumpets, others on foot with drums and pipes, who wheeled round from time to time, and blew and beat their congratulations into the faces of two venerable parents, who in gala-dress brought up the rear." *Russel's Diary in India.* (1857-58)

While on marriage, we can not dismiss the subject, without referring to the wedding of Wazir Ali, which was celebrated by Asuf-ud-dowlah, with such pomp and magnificence, that India had not seen since the decline of the Mogul Empire. It is fully recorded in Forbes' Oriental Memoirs. "He (Asuf-ud-dow ah,) had his tents pitched on a plain near the city. Among these were two of great size, made of strong cotton, lined with different colored stripes of the finest English broad-cloth, with silken cords. Each of these pavilions cost about £.60,000 sterling. Their walls were ten feet high and latticed in part for the ladies of the seraglio to see through. On the marriage day Asuf wore jewels to the value of two millions sterling. The *Shameana* was illuminated by 200 magnificient European girandoles, 200 glass shades and many hundreds of flambeaux. There 100 dancing girls, richly dressed, danced and sang in Hindo-Persic. The bridegroom, then in his thirteenth year, so loaded with jewels that he could scarcely move, and the bride in her tenth year, were conveyed at 7 P. M. on elephants to a wonderful garden, a mile distant. The procession included 1200 richly caparisoned elephants; of these 100 bore silver castles or howdahs. In the centre was the Nawab in a jewelled howdah of gold, on one of uncommon size, caparisoned in cloth of gold. On his right, sat our Resident, Mr. George Johnstone and on his left the bridegroom.

"The ground from the tents to the garden, forming the road on which we moved, was inlaid with fire-works and at every step of the elephant the earth burst before us, and many hundred wooden shells burst in the air, and shot forth a thousand fiery serpents, these winding through the atmosphere, illuminated the sky, and aided by the light of the bamboo scenery, gave the dark night the appearance of a bright day. The whole of this grand scene was also lighted by 3000 flambeaux carried by men. In this manner we moved in stately pomp to the garden, which we entered after alighting from the elephant. It was illuminated by inmumerable transparent paper lanterns of various colors, suspended from the branches of the trees In the centre was a a large edifice, to which we ascended, and were introduced into a grand saloon adorned with girandoles and pendent lustres of English manufacture, lighted with wax-candles. Here we had an elegant collection of European and Indian dishes; at the same time, about a hundred dancing girls sang their lively airs and performed their native dances. Thus passed the time until dawn when we returned to our respective homes. The whole expense of this marriage feast, which was repeated for three successive nights cost upwards of £300,000,"

CHAPTER VIII.—*Arts.*

The arts of Lucknow, taken collectively, were celebrated throughout India, in the days of its glory. Even when the city was in its infancy, I mean, during the time of Asuf-ud-dowlah and Saadat-Ali Khan, the local arts and manufactures were in a high state of improvement. In 1814 an English writer says, that "at Lucknow are to be found the best artizans and mechanics of every kind, men little inferior in skill to our best workmen at home." But now, with the extinction of the native kingdoms, these arts have been ruined or have considerably declined. With an empty stomach and a care-worn head, it is next to impossible, that man's progress can be attained or retained in any art or work. "There are still a few of the artificers, who abounded here in the days of the native court,—when Lucknow was like Paris under the Empire—workers in gold and silver, makers of curious jewellery, enamellers and pipe stick embroiderers, workers of filigree ornaments, excelling in the inlaying of iron with silver. They admitted that they liked the good old days, and that they did not admire being improved off the face of the earth." *Russel's Prince of Wales' Tour in India.*

Critically speaking, the arts of Lucknow are generally beautiful in execution and possess great delicacy of detail. When the work is simple in design, it is good to perfection, leaving nothing more to be desired. But when the design gets extensive and complicated, the productions are crowded with too much ornamentation, that offend feelings of chaste taste. The artificers are perfect in small things; in grand designs or higher performances they are below higher standard. They have no originality, but generally follow one who becomes great in any art. Hence we do not find any individual peculiarity of style among them, but a sameness throughout the profession. These remarks particularly apply to the present deplorable state of the arts.

In the two late exhibitions, the specimen of works, though not the finest or advantageously or thoroughly shown, were after all creditable to the local manufacturers, and the visitors from different provinces were impressed with a high idea of Lucknow arts. If exhibitions of this kind be anunally held here, then some of the chief causes of the deterioration of the local works—namely want of appreciation and encouragement, will vanish by degrees. But then the danger is that, with the introduction of foreign taste, that will prevail, the artificers will conform to the ephemeral fashions of the day; and the original beauty of Lucknow arts will be neglected, forgotten and lost.

The Lucknow arts are these:—

Jewellery.—Jewels are employed in the ornaments and dress of the native nobility, in a variety of designs too numerous to be detailed. The arrangements of the jewels are generally circular and flowery, very seldom square and geometric like those of Europe. They are used as pendents and fringes, which beautifully heighten and relieve the effect of dress and ornaments. The cut of the diamonds, however, are not so good as to command the admiration of the Europeans. But taste differs, and the Lucknowites, as natives in general, will not conform to the dictates, or will not be corrected by the criticism of the foreigner. In the cutting of precious stones, human or animal figure is sometimes attempted; of these two illustrations from among many brought in the late exhibition were noticed viz, one of bracelet (*bazu*) having the face of Budha in the large central diamond, and another of saphire, showing Hanuman praying with hands clasped. Altogether the jewel work of Lucknow, though greatly declined, is still a high art.

Embroidery was a profitable profession here, when Oudh was a kingdom. It was an indispensable luxury of the local citizens; and with the large demand, there was an abundant supply. The art improved to the highest degree. There was a keen competition both among the manufacturers and the wearers. Even the poor people were anxious to make an impression on their humble friends, with a suitable ostentation of finery. The scull cap is a net-work of flowery thread; the turban is full of lacework, and with nobles a fringe of pearls ; in *Chadders*, *Chapkans*, *Payjamas*, shoes and all kinds of dress, both of men and women, the needle is handled to great perfection and delicacy.

The *Shawls* manufactured by the local Cashmirees, introduced by Hakim Mehdi, are not so fine as those of the Happy Valley. Lucknow wants the wool and water of Cashmere, and so cannot attain the softness and delicacy, for which the other is famous. For this reason, the local citizens prefer the embroidered garments, for which gold, silver, jewels, all kinds of threads and even common thread are brought into requisition, according to the means of the wearers. The ornamental designs employed in both classes of clothing, in the borders and sometimes in the centre are flowers, plants, and birds. Sometimes figures illustrating native life, are introduced; but then the effect is more gaudy than beautiful. On the whole, the ornamental designs are well and tastefully executed; and overcrowdiness is not generally attempted, which, when done as in the dresses of the dancing girls, looks too glary to be beautiful or picturesque.

The gold and silver work is also creditable, though in a city, where display of jewellery is of prime importance, these handicrafts occupy a secondary place. Hence this class of work was not brought to such perfection as the other arts.

The dyeing of cloth is deemed a high art of Lucknow. The clothes are colored not only in mass, but in beautiful lines of different hue after patterns of various designs, some of which are similar to those used by the embroiderers. The Lucknow *Chit* is in high repute, throughout Hindustan proper, and is in great demand, not only locally, but from Bengal and other remote provinces These pieces are printed from wooden blocks, in which are cut the designs.

The modeler's art and pottery of Lucknow is also esteemed in Upper India, especially by Europeans. The productions are pretty little things of clay burnt, illustrating native life in all its phases, in single figures or groups. Portraiture is also executed creditably. The principles of anatomy and proportions are fairly observed in the delicate carving and delineation of the limbs, physiognomical features and the intricate folds of drapery, Even expression is sometimes successfully represented in the busts and the gods of the Hindu mythology. In the imitation of fruits some of the modellers are very successful as to form and colouring. Taking a piece of sugar-cane, made of clay, in broad day-light, you cannot but be under the impression that it is a real thing, even feeling it by the specific gravity. Caricature and grotesque animals are also successfully executed, for which one by name, Hiralal gained a medal and first prize in the late Exibition. This modeler is well known for his beauty of execution and delicacy of details, if not softness of tone and exactness of expression, in all his productions. His *Nowraree* of Krishna and his wife seated on the howdah on an elephant made of nine beautiful girls, is an exceedingly good one. His protraiture is sometimes very happy; but in this some say he falls short of Gopal Das, who is dead, and Balkishen who is now blind.

The modelers labour under some disadvantages, for which reason they cannot aim at higher productions. The purchasers care for cheapness and the shortness of time they allow the art-potters to execute their orders. These orders consist of mere common place subjects, having no newness or merit in them. In the late exhibition, the modelers were ordered to make mere clay copies from the toy-books of children. Hence they cannot get time and means to perfect their works or to aim at originality. They have to conform to foreign vulgar and grotesque taste. There are few to appreciate their worth, much less to direct and assist them in a higher sphere of action. There is much room for improvement with a little encouragement and patience. But "be quick" is the order of the day; and the models are no better than bazár articles of children's toys and playthings. Theirs is now *cooly* work. If an industrial exhibition be held at least once a year, on principles broader than those of the last, there will be room for competition and improvement; and originality may be attained. Do not interfere with their taste but leave them to work out their own ideas. Fostering care and proper encouragement are all that they want. It is high time that the present rulers, who have put upon themselves the high responsibility of the people's progress, should do something of the kind, that the chastity of national æsthetic principles should be cultivated and advanced and not be moulded into a grotesque way and form.

Local sculpture is almost nil at present. Claude Martin, who brought many new industries with him, taught some of the local artificers of his day, how to carve out figures from stone. Not a few learnt the art and practised it in plaster, the want of the former material compelling them to have recourse to the latter. Innumerable statues, more grotesque than tasteful, were the production of his age, which adorned the palaces and gardens of the Kings and nobles, but chiefly in Constantia, where some of the old specimens may still be seen. But the introduction of the pedantic Greek models did not agree with the people's taste, and with the death of the so-called reformer, this denational tendency died out. Instead, the art was naturalized into that of the clay of a nature as we find them now, The plaster sculpture expired with the extinction of the kingdom.

Wood-carving was in a high state of cultivation, when Lucknow had its prosperous days. The furnitures and other articles of wood showed great workmanship in detail. Figures and animals, flowers and ornamental designs, were successfully cut out in relief or independently. The legs of their tables, coaches, &c. were tigers, peacocks, and *fairies*—standing or flying. These flying *Peries'* coaches remind us of the Prince of

China, in the Arabian tales, being carried away by the fairies, who indulged in the pleasure of love-making. The palanquins, *tamjans*, howdahs &c. were also carved out in beautiful designs, too numerous to be detailed. This art is now in a condition of utter decline. But Tazia making in talc is still a ligh art.

The local *painting* is in its last stage of existence. Neglected and forgotten, it is literally being starved out of the land. Here or there you may see a Bazaad Rakam in a dingy lane, still lingering in life, who boasts of his former achievements; but now with empty stomach, loss of sight, and premature old age, his very scanty productions are patent for their defects. There you would find a talented artist, named Hossein Buksh, who, finding no means of living, prostitutes his noble profession by cleverly forging stamps, and succeeds for years, till at last detected, he is sent to the Penal Settlements, there to labour and die miserably. The crime was not his; it was in the hard circumstances; and the innocent art dies unpitied. Dear reader, roses cannot grow when the garden is made a dreary sandy plain.

The history of native painting in general is too good and great a subject to be attempted in the category of notices of local arts I am here giving. I leave that matter to those, who are better circumstanced and informed. Suffice it to say, for the present purpose, that only the Hindus were the artist of the old age; the Mohamedans were forbidden by their Koran to give shape to their ideas. So under their rule the art declined, till the great Akbar restored it with other Hindu arts and worths. Now the Mahomedans began to practise painting, which was chiefly water-colour, on ivory, glass, and on paper; and book illustration and caligraply, which was an older art with them, flourished hand in hand. In his Augustan age, many artists rose to eminence for their historical or imaginative paintings. When Sir Thomas Row presented Jehangir with a picture, boasting that no other country could produce such a thing, the pride of the English ambassador was rudely broken the very next morning, by seeing four copies exectly resembling the original. The art however declined with the sun-set of Mogul greatness; and many Delhi painters came to the Court of Shuja-ud-dowlah. Many of their pictures may still be seen in the parlour of the old Nawabs. The Delhi school excel, in the laying of white and gold, on their paintings.

The Lucknow school, if I may so call the local art, smells strongly of European mannerism; for from an early time the painting of this place was influenced by the foreign artists, who came and temporarily settled here from time to time. Zoffani was the first artist of note, who was employed by Asuf-ud-dowlah. His principal paintings are the celebrated "cock-match," and "Hyder Beg's Embassy to Lord Cornwallis"; of these the originals are lost, but prints still remain. He also painted portraits of the Nawab, Claude Martin, and other nobles. Of Martin, there is still an original in the Calcutta Martinere.* After him came the

---

* The celebrated picture of the Cock-match, painted in oil, by Zoffani, in about 1785, fully illustrates the excitement and bustle of such a scene. Asuf-ud-dowlah, in his mad ardour for the fray, comes down from his *musnud*,—a most unroyal proceeding,—to bet, with out-spreading hands, large sums of money, for his bird, in opposition to Colonel Mordaunt, who, no less excited, comes forward and stands in an attitude of defiance. In the immediate foreground, their servants are respectively seen encouraging the winged combatants, who are hard at work to gain the victory. General Claude Martin, seated prominently on a corner of the Musnud, placidly contemplates the scene; while Golding, late Resident of Bettiah, and the prime cause of Captain Kinlochs expedition to Nepal and its failure, most familiarly caresses his bird for the next fight. In the back-ground, behind the *Musnud*, the painter, with pencil in hand, sketches the scene; the *Natch* girls regale the assembly with their songs; the *Bhisties* quench the thirst of the fatigued, within and without the tent, under the shade of a large tree and on the high platform; while Hossein Raza Khan, the minister, and Salaar Jung, the Nawab's brother, in the middle distance, heighten the whole effect, by counting the wager with their fingers crossed. This excellent picture of faithful portraits, if not fine grouping and composition, was long the ornament of Dowlut khana, the old palace of Lucknow. When Mrs. Parks saw it on 24th January, 1831, it was "fast falling into decay." This as well as other valuable pictures were ruthlessly destroyed by British soldiers in 1858. The Cock-fight, was printed in 1794, with a key. This picture, which was painted on Copper plate, was in the Jawahir Khana of the last king,—whence Ali Naqi Khan took its to his house at Gowghat.

The picture, representing Hyder Beg's Embassy to Calcutta, has some big elephants in the middle distance, of whom one holds a human being in his probœcis, whether to kill or to play does not appear clear. In front of the elephants are some men going ahead in an irregular way; while in the foregrounds are some seated figures, of whom one is a half naked woman. The scene is laid down somewhere near Patna. Altogether the picture is more an imaginary representation, than a faithful record of an historical event.

The other pictures of Zoffani are portraits; Lord Teigumouth took a portrait of Asuf-ud-dowlah, when he came here in 1797. The history of a comical likeness he drew of the Nawab, is thus recorded in Wilson's Wonderful Characters. "Zoffani, the celebrated painter, in a humorous moment, had painted the Nawab at full length, but in high caricature. The picture, being at Colonel Martin's, where old Zoffani resided, and the Colonel's house being frequented by vast numbers of natives, especially those, who, when the Nawab wanted money, took his jewels to the Colonel's to be pledged, it was not long before the prince was informed of the joke. In the first moments of irritation, he was disposed to make the painter a head shorter, and to dismiss the Colonel; ...... but as nothing could be done without his dear friend Mordaunt; a messenger was despatched, requiring his immediate attendance, on matters of the utmost importance. ...... "Mordaunt found the Nawab foaming with rage, and about to proceed with a host of rabble attendants, to the Colonel's; however he got the story out of the Nawab as well as he could, and argued him into a state of calmness, sufficient to let his purpose be suspended until next day. So soon as could be done with safety, Mordaunt retired, and as privately as possible sent a note to Zoffani, with intelligence of the intended visit.

A Meeting while Lightning flashes.

After an old native drawing

Homes, father and son. Saadat Ali Khan, invited the elder Home from Madras and entertained him in his service at Rs. 1,000 a month. Ghazi u l-din retained him; and the younger Home was aid-de-camp to His Majesty. The elder Home in his old age retired to Cawnpore, where be lived with hospitality, till he died.* His and his son's productions were chiefly portraits. Some group compositions were also painted, as Sleeman records, of one he saw, in which Rajah Bukhtiar Singh stood behind Nawab Saadat Ali Khan, as his aid-de-camp in a hunting excursion. After the Homes came Charles Mauntz, known as the German painter in "The Private Life of an Eastern King," and one of the five boon companions of the King, Nasir-ud-din, who entertained him at a handsome salary. He produced many excellent

---

"No time was lost; and the laughable caricature was in a few hours changed by the magic pencil of Zoffani, into a superb portrait, highly ornamented, so inimitably resemblant of the Vizier, that it has been preferred to all, which has been taken at sittings. The Vizier did not fail to come, his mind full of anxiety for the honor of his dignified person, attended by Mordaunt, whose feelings for his freind's fate were speedily dissipated, when on entering the portrait chamber, the picture in question shone forth so superbly, as to astonish the Vizier and to sully even the splendour, which his whole equipage displayed on the occasion.

"Asuf was delighted, hurried the picture home, gave Zoffani 10,000 Rs. for it, and ordered the person who had informed him of the *supposed* caricature, to have his nose and ears cut off. Mordaunt, however, was equally successful in obtaining the poor fellows' pardon, and as the Nawab would not detain him as a servant, very generously made him one of his pensioners."

* I sate for my portrait to Mr. Home four times. He has made several portraits of the King (Gazi-ud-din) redolent of youth, and radiant with diamonds, and one of Sir E. Paget. He is a very good artist indeed, quite gentlemanly old man, brother of the celebrated Surgeon in London;—who come out to practise as a portrait-painter at Madras during Lord Cornwallis, first administration, was invited from thence to Lucknow by Saadut Ali a little before his death, and has since been maintained by the king at a fixed salary, to which he adds a little by private practice. His son is a Captain in the Company's service, but is now attached to the king of Oudh as equery and European aid-de-camp. Mr. Home would have been a distinguished painter, had he remained in Europe; for he has a good deal of taste, and his drawing is very good and rapid; but it has been, of course, a great disadvantage to have his own works to study, and he probably finds it necessary to paint in glowing colours to satisfy his master. *Bishop Heber's Journals* 1824.

An artist of great respectability and very considerable talent, grew old in the service of Saadut Ali Khan and his successor, This gentleman retired at an advanced age, to spend the remainder of his days at Cawnpore, where he kept up a handsome establishment, and until the loss of his daughter and increasing infirmities rendered him averse to society, had been wont to exercise the most extensive hospitality to the residents of the station. The place of Mr. Home is supplied, at the Court of Lucknow, by Mr. George Beechy, who had distinguished himself by several masterly efforts of the pencil before he left England, and whose portrait of a native female, sent over and exhibited two years ago at Somerset House, attracted the attention of the best judges in the art. It is said, he had access to the royal Zenana for the purpose of taking the portrait of the favourite wife of the king. *Mrs. Roberts, Scenes and Characters of Hindustan*, 1837.

portraits of His Majesty in his English and native dress. His likeness of one of the queens of the King was greatly admired as one of the handsomest of eastern beauties. The next European artist of importance was Beechy, who was portrait painter to the last king. He got a name in the London Exhibition of 1851 for an admirable painting of a Begum.

During the time of Gazi-ud-din Hyder, a native artist rose to fame; his name was Lala Thakurdas, he was clever both in oil and water colour painting. His Rags and Raginis (airs of Hindu music) were a series of allegorical figures and landscape paintings that were then in high repute. There is an anecdote of him. A Resident, while on a talk with the King, spoke of native art in a tone of contempt. Thereupon the King ordered the Lala to produce an exact copy of a Government note, which the Resident had there given His Majesty. Thakurdas, though not knowing a letter of the English language, made a facsimile so successfully, that when next morning, the King asked him to select the original from the two notes His Majesty handed over to him bewildered Resident Saheb, after great comparing, turning and twisting, took the copy as the real. The King laughed to his heart's content, and after pointing out the original, consigned the copy to the fire of his *hookkah.*

In the reign of Mohamed Ali Shah the native artist who rose to fame was Mohamed Ali, titled Máni Rakam, whose works had great delicacy of touches, and placidness of expression. The grand Durbar scene, given in this book, is from a pencil sketch of his. His son Fuzl Ali titled Bazad Rakam was the private artist to the last King. He took the portraits of the Royal Begums and painted many a beautiful zenana scene. His grandfather was also a painter of old ; his oil sketches are very good and bold in conception. There were many other artists ; of whom the most noted were Saheb Rai and Bitchoo Beg.

The favourite subjects of the native painters are or rather were, besides portraits, zenana scenes, young ladies, sometimes with a Rajah or Nawab, sitting together reclining on musnad, chatting, bathing, or hearing the Domnies singing, or swinging in a wooden frame. Love-matters about Laila and Majnoo are also introduced. Sometimes religious subjects are depicted. In a bathing scene, the ladies are surprized at seeing a horseman suddenly coming in the foreground. In a love-matter, a prince is seen on his elephant, talking to a princess, who with her companions stands on the roof of a palace, in a bent posture to receive her gallant or to take a flower or present from his uplifted hand. At a night-scene, a lady is frightened at the lightning that flashes and claps the more for protection her laughing beloved, who had come in the stormy weather, to meet her, at the appointed out-door place. The lightning is represented by a serpentine line of gold; in fact gold is too much used in native paintings; even the sun is represented by gold. The background of all the pictures is shown by and invariably consist of a parapet wall, sometimes with a pavilion in the centre, relieved by shrubs and flowers, above which lies the sky with a little cloud in the distance, in the middle of which is a flight of birds. Beautiful young faces are always painted; old age and ugliness are seldom attempted, because none like them. Sometime children are introduced to enliven a mother's joy. Nude beauty in a reclining position is also painted, with a not too minute knowledge of anatomy. Occasionally a royal procession to a Musjid, or hunting in a jungle, is fairly done. A hermit's scene in a forest, consisting of long-bearded *fakirs* and high-bosomed *fakiranies* and a stream gliding by the sylvan cottage, is altogether beautiful. A battle-scene is though seldom represented with a multitude of figures, in an irregular array and fight with sword and shield. The mythological subjects, chiefly of Rama and Krishna. are mostly encouraged by the people. Young Krishna playing on a flute Orpheus-like attracts deer, and antelopes and young ladies across a river, one of whom in her eagerness to be near the musician swims on almost against the current which rises in ripples before her face and in serpentine little waves passes by her half-dipped ears. This scene is extremely beautiful.

To judge, from a critical point of view, of native painting, before the European influence was felt, we premise by saying that there was no oil painting in the olden period. The water-color painting on ivory, glass, or talc and paper was generally more of a miniature kind than well sized pictures. The colors were laid in mass after the manner of the Jeypore school. The gradation of colors as well as the principles of light and shade were subjects not much understood; while drawing and designing consisted of a few lines without contour and anatomical details. There was no knowledge of the difference between back-ground, foreground, and middle-distance; and perspective had no retiring lines or vanishing points. The architecture and garden background is shown by a few horizontal, vertical, and oblique lines. Grouping was not very creditable; for the composition is of mere detached figures, and foreshortening was beyond the ken of the native artists. The posing of the figures, either standing or sitting is not very artistic, like the general arrangement of their picture. The folds of drapery are conventional. In spite of mannerism and other defects, the native pictures are still generally beautiful to look at. With regard to landscape painting, which is not purely so, the mountains are shown by a mass of unmeaning purple or green. The water is not bad; and trees are better. The sky and clouds are heavily laid, showing no atmospheric space. The figures being subordinate to the whole picture, where no anatomical accuracy or expression is required, looks to advantage. As to animal painting, elephant drawing is generally superior to that of the Europeans. But horses and dogs are very inferior; while antelopes, camel and birds are passable. Flower painting is good.

These remarks apply to the native painting, when it was in its lowest state of decline, as it presumably was after the sunset of the Delhi dynasty. When it recovered and improved by the aid of European culture, the results were not so happy as could be expected. For firstly, the European artists, who came here, did not teach well those, who with great difficulty and expense, became their pupils. Secondly there were no exhibitions, galleries and good models, that they could compete and improve by comparing, copying and studying. They could not get any access to instruction or good pictures, that were in the palaces. Lala Thakurdas became a great painter by his own exertions than by any one's teaching; and there was a King to patronize him. It is said of him, that he u ed to engage himself day and night in his favourite calling; often he forgot to take his food; and in order that sleep might not interrupt him in his work, he used to bind a lock of his hair with a strong thread to a hook on the wall or ceiling, that whenever falling drowsy, it would remind him of what he was at. The present state of local painting is very pitiable, as already, stated. The principal requirement of it, the portraiture, has been usurped by photography, which has given it the last stroke of death.

Local photography began to flourish from about 1850, when an Englishman of the military line came here. *Chotay Miya*, designer of Hoseinabad and Kaisarbagh buildings, acquired the art from him and practised it to great profit and pleasure. His portrait taking was very creditable, and his architectural views were in high demand, one of which, of Kaisarbagh adorns the frontispiece of Gubbin's "Mutiny of Oudh." Joining the mutineers he lost his fortune and name and died a miserable man. The old views of Lucknow taken just after the Mutiny, and at the time of the demolitions engraved in this book, are presumably copies of his photographs. After him, Mushkoor-ud-dowlah was the famous photographer of Lucknow and Oudh. His figures and views are excellent. He had an evenness of tone which common photographers cannot attain. Many of his views are printed in this book. He died a rich man, and is known by the title, which the ex-king of Oudh gave him. After him comes Daroga Abbas Ali, who is a promising and enterpising photographer of no mean merit. He has published some books with photo-illustrations, *viz* :—"the Lucknow Album" of 50 buildings in English, the beauties of Lucknow, about 25 dancing girls of this city, in Urdu; and lately the "Taluqdar's Album" of about 400 barons of Oudh, in English and in Urdu. Though there are patent faults and defects in them, yet on the whole, they are creditable to one, who has no knowledge of English and the high art. Asgar Jan, the brother of Mushkoor-ud-dowlah is also a known photographer.

Of ornamental designs and caligraphy, I will not speak at length. There are innumerable beautiful patterns for these classes of works, as may be found in old manuscripts, and inner-plastering and painting of buildings, chiefly over arches and under cornices, in which great skill is shown. Much ingenuity is also shown in paper cut in beautiful flowery designs, or drawn by the thumb-nail only. In fireworks also some of the designs are exceedingly good; in this a Nawab of slender means excels and stands the first in Upper India.

To judge of local architecture from an æsthetic point of view, we should consider and contemplate the subject from two sides,—outwardly and inwardly—to see and to feel. To see pleasurably we expect that the building should have well-balanced and well-graduated outline and superficies, of which the highest will be the middle point, and the ends more elevated than the other lines. This rule holds good with regard to tombs and Hindu temples ; and the Lucknow *Makbaras* will satisfy you in every respect. But in ecclesiastical architecture (Mohamedan) the highest point is not kept in the middle, but at the ends, as you will find in the towers of Musjids and Durgahs. In the latter case, the effect is not so grand as in the former, though as elegant. With regard to palaces and domestic architecture, which, unlike European structures, are not single blocks, but ranges of buildings, with courtyards in the middle of many of them, requiring more area than height, these two lines of beauty are not generally observed. It is a complex subject. Hence the effect is not so imposing ; for here is too much repetition and continuation of the same heights and superficies. This defect is somewhat remedied by bastions, towers and pavilions being judicously placed at the corners and intermediate points. Still the effect is flat. Chutter Munzil and Kaisar Pasand, however, do not labour under this disadvantage. On the whole Lucknow architecture leaves a very favourable impression on the minds of the beholders, more so as it is relieved here and there, in the foreground and back-ground, with trees, gardens and open space ; and with regard to palaces singly, they make up their shortness of height by the extent of ground they occupy.

Now to see inwardly within a palace, tomb, or temple, you want the colonnades and arcades corresponding, relieved by a variety of designs. In short, variety should be wedded to uniformity, producing a harmony of the whole. Secondly you require space, that your eyes may not be offended, and your sight interrupted by too much crowding of minute parts. In this respect Lucknow makes a very bad impression on the European visitors.

Now we come to feel. To feel is to enjoy and live in it. In this the tastes of the Europeans and natives differ ; the latter love too much ornamentation, crowding and display of lanterns, mirrors and other furniture on the walls and ceilings ; the former hate crowding, but still leaving the dead walls of their rooms white-washed and naked, have their floors filled with too many chairs and sofas. So desiring little less crowding on the walls as in the Zenana halls, the rooms of Lucknow are more comfortable to the natives, than to the Europeans, whose tight dress forbids them to sit and lounge on the plane carpetted floor. There are also three points in which the Europeans must yield the palm to native architecture, I mean, courtyards, flatroofs and echoes. The courtyards are very enjoyable things. They have pretty little gardens, tanks fountains, and seats. The lines of flatroofs serve for sleeping, promenading and giving a fine outside view in summer nights and winter days. No windows or sky lights being allowed, the rooms especially in the tombs and *Musjids*, echo when one speaks, prays sings. This has a good effect. For particulars on architecture, see further on in the third part of this book.

Music has dealing with two senses, eyes and ears. The eyes see dancing (*natch*) and expressions (*battanā*); the ears catch music, vocal and instrumental. Lucknow dancing and giving expression to singing are celebrated throughout Hindostan. In dancing, the feet, thighs, waist breast, hand and arm, head and eye-brow, even muscles, are required to be moved, separately and conjointly, gently or quickly, according to the cadence and time, of which a unit is made up of four parts. Evidently this dancing is far more difficult and complex than that of the Europeans. The unit is a simple time; the compound time is generally made up of four units. The native dancing is regulated by these compound times, single, double or treble. Group dancing is now seldom exhibited.

Now suppose the concert is complete, the instruments are ready; and the dancing figure, male or female, stands, in a bent attitude, with one leg crossed over the other, one hand out-spread, and the other with open palm on the breast. The music is begun and the standing figure moves on her limbs, firstly slowly and then rapidly. The palms of the two hands are alternately closed and opened with evolution, vertical and horizontal, in cadence to the tinkling of the anklets of the feet. The step is now lowered, now raised; the feet now advance, and now recede—circling, bending, oblique, straight; while the whole body and muscular development go on in a sympathetic movement. The head is not idle, and the eyes and face show expression, that speaks to you without words. This way the dancing goes on in simple or compound time in a variety of motions and expressions of anger, placidity, pleasure or pain. The native audience, much delighted, looks on breathlessly. The cursory looking Europeans, not understanding local music, and familiar with quicker and wider motions of whirling and jumping, pronounce native dancing as monotonous and uninteresting. They should have patience and understand it before forming their opinion. Many also are prejudiced against it as being obscene; but in fact the Lucknow-natch is far more decent and decorous than many of the performances of the very slenderly clad European dancers, who generally do so in pairs, male and female. It is high time that we should disabuse the English of their idle prejudices. Some one should write a treatise on native dancing as well as music in general, illustrating and explaining their chief features.

Singing is a branch of music, which is very little understood by the Europeans. Naturally they have less perception of the delicate and minute, than of the sublime and great. Hence native music, which is rather in semi and middle tones and does not generally show a display of high notes and quick time, seems monotonous to the European ear. The native music is like a line, that makes its wave softly and delicately; whereas the European is like a line that goes angularly in quick steps. The latter is exciting and active, the former is sedate, passive and contemplative. So that those conversant with one, cannot be expected to esteem and understand the other; and consequently while the Europeans despise the local art as monotonous and uninteresting, the people hate the foreign music as vulgar and barberous, and boast of their own superiority over the other,—unlike the case in painting, where they easily yield the palm to the Europeans, and eagerly seek to be taught by them and to get some of their productions, even prints. Those Europeans, who are habituated to native music, prefer to hear it to any other.

The music of Hindustan is divided into different classes. *Thoongri* is the music of quick times, in which Lucknow-*Gazals* are sung and noted. These Gazals are made of very lively airs and sentiments, that easily please the audience. They are very simple; and many Europeans not unoften like them. *Kaharwa* or the music of the Kahars (bearers,) a low caste, is of quick oblique time, which is also pleasing; it resembles the *Khemta* of Bengal. It is however a *Dehatee* (country) music. *Tappah* and *Kheyal* are a series of airs, whose time of cadence is not so quick, as the other two; and which is made up of flourishes of notes, and the complex exercising of the voice and turning of the instrument. The natives are very fond of them; which the Europeans of course not understanding, do not like to hear them. In this also Lucknow has or rather had a

After a native Painting.

P.C.M. 29.12.82.

"Natch before a Nawab Saheb."

very good name. *Dhurpad* is the highest form of our music. Its voice is deep, its airs are grave, its singing is solemn, and time slow and complex. The beating of the drums *(Tabla)*, that always accompany the music, then resembles the rolling of distant thunder which is dying away. This class of singing is very difficult and Lucknow has no name in it.

These are some of the chief classes of native music, as adapted to cadence. There is another kind of classification as regards notes. These are of six sorts, called *Rágs*, which are adopted to the six seasons of the year, or sung according to the temperature of day and night. Each of these main airs has six wives, called *Rágnees*, who have produced a progeny too numerous to detail. All the airs are said to be typical of different sentiments, or rather giving the idea of divers imagery. *Bhairawa* is a Rag of Bramhan figure,—a bearded old holy man,—a hermit—who rises at dawn of day, to worship the Creator of the universe after holy bathing in a sacred river; while *Bhairawee* his first wife collects flowers for him in a garden close by. She is however, turned here into a licentions woman of various forms and artifices. *Basanta* is the god of spring—a beautiful sportive youth. who sitting under a tree, in a fine landscape and enjoying the cool breeze of the time, plays with his wives, one of whom *Holi* is all laughter with *Rang* and color. *Behag* is a young handsome girl, who in a moonlit midnight, walks and searches with plaintive notes, in a forest region, for her husband, who is gone to some other quarter. And so go on a series of fine imagery of airs and ideas.

With regard to the professors of the art, dancing is performed by the *Natchwalies*, called also *Taifas*, in the Mardana. They are public women of no morality, and hence they are not given admittance into the sanctity of the Zanana, where the *Domenies* sing. These *Domenies* seldom dance, but sing and play on instruments. They lead a chaste life. There are also male musicians, young and old. The boys dance and sing lighter airs and subjects, while the aged do the graver.

The *Bhanrhs* are capital commedians of this city. Their performances are short and to the point. They speak and act, generally, with a double meaning. While they seemingly praise you, they covertly attack you by hinting some of your weak points in a jocular style. Under the British rule, their freedom of speech and action has been considerably curtailed; and hence they are declining. Their satires are not now so open as they were before, which, having a moral basis, were very effective. It is said of Asuf-ud-dowlah, that upon one occasion, his body-guards were in arrears of pay; they had no way to represent their grievance to the Nawab. At last they induced the Bhánrbs to enact a scene that might lead to their redress. This they did capitally, and their aim was successful. On another occasion in a primier's house, they invoked blessings on the Begum and her prosperity to be fixed for ever (Kaim meaning firm as also the name of her paramour.) The indirect satire was enough for her, and she mended her conduct, and thus escaped public scandal. So you see the aim of these buffoons had a high moral tone, which benefitted society greatly. But now these good influences are gone. The fear of libel-action has closed the mouth of the satirists; and the people get less moral as a consequence. Still "the opportunity of ridiculing the governing class is too good to be lost, while the strange and in some points the abhorent features of English life furnish ample materials for witty mimics. The court of justice, the police officer, the Englishman at home, with all their defects, their ignorance of the language, their dependence upon the court officers, their lassitude and neglect of duty, their cheroots and brandy, are mercilessly exposed The practices of the thieves, the oppressions of the landlords, of native officials, are also favourite subjects of the Lucknow dramatists." *Oudh Gazetteer.*

Of theatrical representations and dramas, *Indra-Sabha* is an original production of Lucknow. It is a Hindu idea, worked and adopted to Mahomedan taste. A fairy, dancing girl to Indra, falls in love with a prince, whom she at once takes to heaven, in order to show him the court of the god, for which offence the mortal being is confined in a mountain cave. The dancing girl, however, at last effects his release by pleasing the god and appeasing his anger. The plot is simple, and the management s not complex. There is no scientific contrivance however. The conversation is carried on in songs and verses, of which the sentiments and acting are chaste and elegant.

The poems of Lucknow have no high merit in them. The themes for composition are generally about love, in which the sentiments, words, and rhyme are arranged, without deep pathos of feelings, or breadth of view, though on the whole, they are pretty to uuderstand, tasty to feel, and sonorous to hear. Love is usually a hackneyed subject, and consequently wants originality of thought and newness of design. Heroic themes are not favourites with the citizens of Lucknow; but in the country the ballads about Saadat Khan, the Rajahs of Gondah, Wazirnamah &c., are spirited compositions, bespeaking bold sentiments ana original though simple arrangements. These performances are superiord to those of the city, in all respects, except in elegance of expression and such lesser qualities of second class poets.

Let me now conclude with a piece of advice. Dear Englishmen, rulers of the land, you should leave off your prejudices as unworthy of your race and position, and let us meet in the midland of mutual concession in the field of compromise. Both of us will be benefitted as to fine arts, sentiments and feelings. And your and our enjoyments will be doubled by the reciprocal reflection. It is your double duty, both from principles of humanity and as sovereigns of the land, that you should not any longer discourage one arts by your contemptuous unsympathy. It is high time that you should soften your conduct and policy, which has hitherto been exclusive. You should arrest the rapid progress of ruin and decline; and be men in a higher phase and sense. Let us forget the past and conjointly aim at a happy future. The fruits will be golden.

PART III.—ARCHITECTURE.

CHAPTER I.—*Archœology of Oudh.*

The archœological remains in this province have not yet been properly investigated. The attention of the local Government and the public in general has not hitherto been drawn to the subject to the extent it requires; even though it is a well known fact, that Oudh, the ancient Koshal, was almost the cradle of Aryan colonization, and that the different types of the people, who, one after another, came here and rose to power and sovereign position, left vestiges of their civilization, layer after layer, which requires a thorough search and most penetrative exploration. But no comprehensive investigation has hitherto been conducted. This important chapter cannot therefore possibly be as exhaustive, as it ought to be.

The archœological area of Oudh, or the united Provinces of North-Western-Province and Oudh proper, is bounded by Nepal on the North, river Jumna on the West and South, and Behar on the East. The principal ancient cities are (1) Benares, said to be founded by Mahadeo of the Hindu Trinity, and Dibodas, one of its kings, long before the Buddhistic period, (2) Ajodhyá, or *never-to-be conquered* city, by Ikshaku of the Suryabanshi dynasty, of which Ramchundra of the *Rámáyana* was the best known; (3) Srávasti,* now Sahet Mahet, on the Rapti, (4) Hastinapore, on the Ganges in Rohilkund, and Indraprastha near Delhi founded by Judhisthir of *Mahabharat*, and Mathura of Krishna, and Birát, of Draupadi's father (5) Kanouj (6) Allahabad or Prayag, founded by Bharadwaj, one of the Vedic Munies or saints, (7) Jounpore, and (8) Lucknow. These towns are representatives of the eight chief historical epochs and stages of ancient civilization. Besides these there are many minor towns, such as Semraon near the Nepal frontier in the Gorukhpore

* Srávasti, built by Raja Srávasta, the son of Yuvanáswa of the Solar race and tenth in descent from Surya himself. Vikramaditya, its king, 500 years after Buddha, became a persecutor of the Buddhists. Here the famous Manoshita, the author of the *Vibhásha Shastra*, being worsted in argument by the Brahmans, put himself to death. The local dynasty flourished from about 100 B. C. to 400 A. D. The city was completely deserted in 632 A. D. The town fort is semi-circular, with the river on the North East and the great Jetavana monsatery-mound on South West, being 1000′×700′ by 15 feet high which has a Jain temple. A third mound near the north end of the central line of the enclosure has a colossal figure of Buddha, 7′ 4″ in height and a Buddhapad. *Orajhar* mound or basket-shakings a mile away from the Jetavana is identified with the Eastern Monastery. Nine other monasteries were also traced. Sahet Mahet, the remains of the ancient city as now called, was capital of Rajah Sohil Deo, whose ancestor were reiging in the time of the Pandus, when the city was called Chundricapuri.

district, the capital of the later Suryabunsies, when expelled by the Mohamedans from Oudh ; Kapilabastu, the birth-place of Goutama Buddha, near Ajodhya ; Ahichhatra in Rohilkund ; Sankasya in Doab, Manikpore, and Kousambhi near Allahabad, Nimkhar * near Seetapore, and Newal and Sonchonkote near Lucknow.

The styles of architecture, prevalent in the different periods are the buildings of earth and wood employed in the prehistoric times. In the days of Ramayana and Mahabharat, the building materials used were bricks and stones. In the description of cities, we find that the fortifications had high towers, ditches and forests around, one within the other ; and the royal palaces were situated within citadels, that were erected on elevated mounds in the middle of the city. The palaces had different courts, arranged according to designs, which we have no means now to determine accurately. The description of Pataliputra, given by Megasthenes, the Greek ambassador, in about 300 B. C., will serve as a type for all others. Palibothra was like a parallelagram in form. It was 9 miles in length and 2 miles in breadth, and was surrounded by ditch, 30 cubits deep ; and the walls were adorned with 570 towers and gates. The superstructure of the walls was of wood,—which was pierced with openings for the discharge of arrows. The ditch served both for defence and as a sewer for the city.

The principal sources, from which archœological information can be gathered, are of two classes, antiquarian (1) remains and (2) records. Antiquarian records are subdivided into local and foreign. The local records, that is to say, old books, are very ancient. In the *Vedas* there is a special book, called *Shilpashástra*, or art of building, giving general directions as to domestic and ecclesiastical architecture. Manu advances a little anJ advises the king to select a commanding position in a mountainous

* *Nimkhar.*—" A famous fort, with a great number of idolatrous temples and a reservoir." In Ain-Akbari the reservoir is called the *Chackratirtha*, where the disc of Vishnu fell ; it is hexagonal with a diameter of 120 feet ; clear water springs from below, and flows out by the south side into a swampy rill about 20′ broad, called Godaveri Nala. It is surrounded by temples and Dharmsalas. The fort is situated on a precipitous mound to the North of the pool, about 1100′×400′×50′ ; the west end is a high cliff, called the *Shahburj*, which overhangs the Goomtee, the gate on the east is arched ; and built of materials partly bricks and partly kunkur blocks, which betray by their carvings and the *swastica* symbol or mystic cross their Hindu origin. There is a well 8½′ broad and 51½ deep.

country for the seat of his capital, with ditches and forests surrounding the fort ; and the castle with his palace is to be on the highest and central point.* *Ramayan* goes further and gives an improved idea of a capital such as Ajodhya† and enumerates in detail all the sacred places of importance in Koshal. *Mahabharat* vividly describes Hastinapore and gives in detail how Judhisthir, the eldest Pandu, founded his new capital at Indraprastha, (vulgarised Indraput) near Modern Delhi, and describes the capital of Karna at Debipatan near Tulsipore, and Beiratkherha near where still an annual *mela* is yearly held, Mandhata ka Killah at Mannua, Raja Nala's Fort at Nagraon. *Kasikhanda* sings the glories of Benares and the innumerable holy places thereat ; while other *Poorans* keep the name of the prehistoric Hindu architecture and considerably helps to develop that of Buddhistic persuation. The Buddhistic architecture was perfected under Asoka the Great ; and inscription-pillars, *Dharmsalas* or Serais, *Bihars* or Monasteries and *Stupas* covered the land in every direction, at Sravasti, Ajodhya, Kanauj, Kosambi, and other cities.

At the revival of Hindu religion, Buddhistic architecture declined ; and that of the Hindu flourished in all its ancient glory ; though many of the Buddhistic improvements were retained and adopted ; as one can easily detect from the peculiar domes of Lodheswar near Byramghat and other temples. But the erection of columns, monasteries and topes were put a stop to; and many buildings especially Bihars were demolished ; those only escaped

---

* "Let the king fix his abode in a district containing open champaigns, abounding with grain, inhabited chiefly by the virtuous, not infected by any maladies, beautiful to the sight, surrounded by submissive mountaineers, foresters, or other neighbours, a country in which the subject may live at ease. There let him reside in a capital, having by way of fortress a desert rather more than 20 miles around it, or a fortress of earth, water, trees, armed men, or of mountains......A fortress of mountain has many transcendental properties. One bowman placed in a wall is a match for 100 enemies......Let that fort be supplied with weapons, money, grain, beasts, Brahmans, artificers, engines, grass, and with water. In the centre of it, let him raise his own palace, well finished in all its parts, completely defended, habitable in every season, brilliant with *white stucco*, surrounded with water and trees."

† Ajodhya is thus described in Ramayana. "The streets and alleys in the city were admirably arranged ; and the principal streets are well watered. It was beautified with gardens, fortified with gates, crowded with charioteers and messengers, furnished with arms, adorned with banners, filled with dancing girls and men, crowded with elephants, horses and chariots, merchants and ambassadors from various countries. It resembled a mine of jewels or the residence of *Sri*, (godess Lachmi). The walls were variagated with divers sorts of gems, like the divisions of a chess-board ; the houses formed one continued row of equal heights, resounding with the music of the tabor, the twang of the bow, and the sacred sound of the Vedas. It was perfumed with incense, chaplets of flowers and articles of sacrifice, by their odour cheering the heart." Carey's translation.

the vandalism of the age, which stood under the protection of jungles. At this time many temples were raised; some of large dimensions and very beautiful; and the Jains occupied the sacred places of their expelled brothers, the Buddhists, as at Sravasti and Ajodhya. In 400 A. D. Fa Hian, the Chinese pilgrim, records in his journals the decline of Buddhistic architecture and faith; while Hwen Thsang, in 630, says that Sravasti is already over-grown with jungles, and Ajodhya again a Hindu city, which Vikramaditya of Sravasti or Ujain, a great enemy of the Buddhists, restored at the beginning of the Christian era, and where he built 360 temples according to the number of days of the lunar year, detailing the every-day life of Rama and his party.

After this period, internal discords ensued; and the country was covered with jungle forts. The higher caste thus got weakened; and the low caste people, such as Bhars, Tharuhs, and Ahirs, rose to power.

The principal styles of architecture, employed in Oudh, may be thus conveniently divided into eight classes,—four Hindus and four Mohamedans. The Hindu epoch comprises (1) the Archaic from an unkown period to about 250 B. C, (2) Buddhistic, from 250 B. C., to about 500 A. D., (3) Mediœval Brahmanic, from 500 to 1,200; and (4) Modern Brahmanic from 1,200 to the present time. The Mosulmán epoch consists of (1) Pathan general (1,100–1,400), (2) Pathan Jownpuri (1,400—1,500), (3) Mogul (1,500–1,700), and (4) Naishapuri (1,750—1,850). Of the English period, no style has been hitherto developed; nor has it anything worth mentioning on this subject.

The Archaic period has some remains in Oudh which are however covered or lost to such a degree under later settlement of different races, that it is not easy to detect their pure Aryan architecture. So that it is very difficult to judge of its style. Suffice it to say that the famous Buddhistic architecture, which was perfected under Asoka the Great in about 250 B. C., is the outcome of the pure Aryan buildings. There could not have appeared the *Topes,* had no *Samadhi* or funeral mounds existed before; nor could *Bihar* (monasteries) have come into being, unless Thakurdwarah or temple-house preceded it. The celebrated pillars of Asoka were no new constructions; for columns of victory or of good deeds, *Jayastombha* or *Keertistambha,* are every where mentioned in the old books.

There are many cities of this period in existence. Ajodhya was the far-famed capital of Ram Chandra, and the *Ramkot* and its bastions can still be determined with tolerable accuracy. *Ramkot* and *Hargam*, in the Seetapore district, have mounds, in which the relics of a very old period can be easily traced. *Mannua*, or Manpore about 24 miles north of Lucknow, has a very high and extensive mound, called the killah of Mandhata, one of whose descendant, Babrubahan was the son of Arjun of *Mahabharat.* He is said to have married a daughter of the former, and the offspring killed the latter in a battle field, now known as *Runnua*, contrary to what the epic records. The mound is several miles in extent and about 50 feet in height at the highest point. There is a Nullah on the northern side ;—in fact, a ditch can be easily traced all around. Broken bricks and kunkur stones cover the whole ground ;—which are an inexhaustible supply to the neighbouring town, of which all the buildings are erected of these materials. The walls are said to have been about 10 feet in thickness, which is confirmed by the lines of excavation. The bricks, which are found at great depth, are said to crumble down, as soon as they are exposed to air ; no entire brick can be taken out, unless they are heated without exposure, and handled with the greatest care, thus attesting to their great antiquity. Innumerable statues, chiefly broken, are seen lying about exposed in different places, where the villagers have collected them. Many of these statues look exceedingly beautiful and so fresh, that they seem to have been carved out a few days ago. Great anatomical knowledge is displayed in the delineation of the limbs and even the muscular development of the different portion ; while the expression in the face, even comical, is very happily executed. These relics of a very old sculpture show great skill and artistic taste of the people of a bygone civilization. The statues are all representations of the Hindu mythology. The place requires careful exploration and preservation.

In the Kheri district, there are also many extensive remains of old cities, of which those at Bhetoa and Naurungabad are very important. One of them is identified with *Berat* of *Mahabharat.* The kingdom of Matsya is said to have flourished here ; and the five *Pandus* took refuge here with its king during their exile. An annual *mela* is still held here ; and the local tradition points to different places, held sacred in association with demi-deified brothers. On excavation, beautifully carved bricks, kunkur-blocks and potteries and statues are found. "The vast area of the city, the enormous thickness of the masonry walls, and the artistic specimens of pottery produced, point to a period of far greater wealth, and of not less intelligence than are possessed by the Hindus of Oudh in the present day."

The ruins of Nagraon in the Lucknow district are also very extensive. The city of Nala Rajah, which was here, was surrounded by twelve lakes, which were connected by drains or rather tunnels (*Nals*), through which the women of the king used, it is said, to bring water in mud pitchers. These tunnels, some of which are of tin, are still discovered all over the town on excavation. Coins and jewels were a few years ago found. It is said that the treasure of king Nala is buried in the mound. It is curious that *Nal* means pipe. There is a beautiful episode about this king in the *Mahabharat* ; he is widely known for his liberality ; and there is a celebrated proverb in connection with his misfortune, that once befell him.

Rajah Nal par bipat parhí : ... *On King Nal misfortune fell ;*
Bhuni machlí jal ko chalí. ... *Fried fish to water swam away.*

That these ruins belong to a pre-Buddhistic period, is proved by the very old bricks and kunkers, tradition of the people, the tenour of the *Mahabharat* and the nature of sculptured fragments, among which no statues of Goutama are ever found. These Hindu statues, which are exceptionally good, also disprove the favourite theory of the modern archœologists, that the sculpture began to flourish in India after it was taught here by the Greeks. For (1) the statues show preiminently Hindu faces ; (2) they are far superior to those, which are modern ; and (3) no Greek ethnological features can we detect in them. If the Hindu sculptors were taught by the Greeks, it is natural, that they should betray some features of their imitation of the purely foreign art.

Nor does it stand to reason, that the Buddhists at once grew to a great building and artizan race, without previous development—the result of very long training. The Chinese travellers mention Hindu statues in all the Brahman temples ; while the old Aryan scriptures mention by name or description many a specimen of artistic work. The theory that all archœological remains in India cannot date anterior to the Buddhistic period cannot hold good on fuller consideration. The natural conclusion therefore is, that antiquarian remains of the Aryan period must exist along with those of the Buddhists, which careful and unbiased investigation will bring out in time.

Another fact worth noting is that the kunkur blocks, which stood the natural decay of ages, and which capitally serve for architectural materials, have not been carved or used since the time when the Mohamedans began pulling down Hindu edifices and building their own with materials they got ready at hand. Accordingly the kunkur-stones ceased to be dug, carved out and built in structures of later times as soon as the supply of ready-made materials was exhausted. But why should not now, when the architectural regeneration, as of every thing else, of the people ought to begin, if not already begun, this inexhaustible mine be dug, and beautiful bricks carved out and used as more durable and artistic material, is a subject, which escapes the attention of every body, officers or private men. These kunkur blocks deserve better treatment and place than mere metalling of roads or protection embankments to bridges.

The Buddhistic style was naturally of pure native growth. The *stupa* construction was but the development of an old idea; so were pillars and monasteries. The palaces, fortification and domestic architecture did not appear, in the least degree, to depart from the old rules of the *Sutradhar* (mason) and *Shilpee* (architect). The difference between the two styles consists in this, (1) that the later one improved upon the other, and (2) that the whole architecture was employed to illustrate the life and doings of the founder of the religion, to an extent and system, which were not attempted before. So that Buddhistic architecture was more durable and more widely felt, as in Cabul, Tibet, China, Burmah, Ceylon and other countries. While it is very difficult to find the remains of Aryan architec ture, that of the Buddhistic religion are abundant and can be traced everywhere.

I beg to remark here again on the fashion of the modern archœologists to trace every thing to the Grecian influence; though there is no substantial ground to confirm their theory. If the bands of honey-suckle and beaded mouldings in Asoka's lion-pillars be imitations of Greek designs, and if Grecian gods on coins found in Cabul and Punjab show that Asoka perfected his buildings after those of Greece,—(hence called 'Indo-Grecian Period'), why is not Sanscrit the offspring of the Greek tongue? for here the similarity is greater. In the same way, the 'Indo-Scythian Period' can be dismissed; for there is no Scythian architecture in existence to attest that such an influence was once felt on the face of earth; nor is there any Grecian building on the soil of India to prove the foreign influence. The fact is, that the modern archæologists try to read the antiquarian remains according to the lights of Grecian or Chinese travellers only, who however were not correct in their records ; nor even do they consult the originals, but grope on according to the lights of defective translations, in which they force their own guess-work readings.

During the Buddhistic period, the principal centre of architecture in Oudh were Benares, Ajodhya, Sravasti, and Kapilabastu. Kapilabastu was the brithplace of Gautama Buddha, who spent his boyhood here ; it is now identified with Bhwila Tal mounds in the Basti District, about 15 miles North East of Ajodhya. Benares was the place, where he first began to preach or *to turn the wheel of Law* ;—the archæological remains here are (1) the great stone tower, called Dhamek, (2) a large brick tower, (3) traces of monastries, (4) a high mound of solid brickwork, crowned with an octagonal brick tower, called Choukandi ; and (5) three lakes. Ajodhya was the seat of a kingdom, where Buddha is said to have remained seven years ; and many buildings rose on all sides in association of his stay. Sravasti was the capital of another kingdom,—whose king and minister were almost the first to become the disciples of Buddha ; and so it was crowded with buildings, many of which have been identified by General Cunningham. Fa Hian describes with minuteness the fortress already ruined, abounding with monastic buildings, pillars, shrines. At Tandwa, near it, are also some ruins of importance, and the Hindus still worship a statue of Mayadevi as Seetamai.*

After the Buddhistic period comes the Mediæval Brahman style in the order of succession. Temples grew in the place of stupas and monasteries ; and sculpture took the figures of Vishnu, Mohadeva and Párbati in lieu of *Mayadevi*, and Goutama Buddha. Numismatics were chiefly devoted to the illustrations of the Hindu mythology. The coins of this period generally represent a humped bull and a four-armed goddess, presumably of *Durgadevi*, generally called *chaturbhujah.*

In this period, Kanouj* emerged into a seat of empire ; and Ajodhya was bereft of Budhistic influence. *Vikramaditya*, a noted king of Ujjain and the great enemy of the Buddhistic creed, restored Ajodhya from the

* *Tandwa* has a mound of brick ruins, 800×300×20 feet, near which is a jheel, called Seeta Devi Tal. At the South West corner is the remains of a large *stupa* ; diameter 70′. There is a statue of Seeta Mai or rather Maya Debi. Kasyapa Buddha here performed his meditations under a Banian tree.

jungles, which had overgrown it. "His main clue in tracing the ancient city was the holy river Sarju; and his next was the shrine, still known as *Nageshwarnath*, which is dedicated to *Mahadeo*, and which presumably escaped the devastations of the Buddhist and Atheist periods. With these clues, and aided by descriptions which he found recorded in ancient manuscripts, the different spots (360 in number), rendered sacred by association with the worldly acts of the deified *Rama*, were indentified,—to which pilgrims from afar still in thousands half-yearly flock."

In course of time low caste, such as Bhars, usurped the place of high caste dynasties and reigned in Asokpore, Manikpore, Dalmow† and other unimportant towns. They built forts of mud and bricks in their seats of power, which however could not successfully withstand the victorious arms of the Mohamedans, even though Sohildeo of Asokpore defeated and killed Syed Salar at the great battle of Bahraich. In fact, we have no means to determine the nature and extent of Bhar architecture, unless we assume, the that they resembled the purely utilitarian buildings of the Talukdars under late native Government. The Bhars and Tharuhs seldom aimed at ornamental edifices.

---

* *Kanouj*.—Mahmood Guzni in 1016 saw "a city which raised its heads to the skies, and which in strength and structure might justly boast to have no equal." It was originally called Kanya-Kubja or the hump-backed maiden" owing to the curse of Vayu on the 100 daughters of *Kusanabha* Harsha Vardhana was one of its noted king (607—648) A. D. The city had 84 Mohallas, of which 25 still remain. The killah is 4000′ in each face, 60 or 70′ high, being triangular in shape, the northern point having the shrine of Haji Harmayun. On the West is the temple of Ajay Pal, and on South East a large bastion, called *Kshem Kali Burj*. The city had 3 gates at the 3 points. The situation is very commanding; *Bala Pir* tomb is midway between Ajay Tal and the Burj. *Sita ki Rasoi* is in the centre of the highest mound, and *Rang Mahal* near Ajaypal's temple. At Kanouj very old coins are found; (1) Rang Mehal is the ruins of the old palace; (2) Hindu pillars of the Jumma Musjid, and of Musjid Makdum Johania; and (3) Hindu statues of Ram and Luchman and others in the village of *Singh Bhowani*. The other remains are mounds of all sizes, covered with broken bricks, walls and figures. Rang Mahal citadel cover an area of 240′×180′. Seeta ki Rasoi has Juma-Dina Musjid, 108′×26; all the Hindu cloisters have been re-ananged for the purposes of Mohamedan worship, (5) Suraj Kund has an annual fair in *Bhadam*. According to Fa Hian, the great stupa of Asoka, 200′ in height, was in the North east of the Ganges on the spot where Buddha had preached.

† Dalmow has an old fort, situated on a bluff point, about 100′ high, overhanging the Ganges. In the inside is a rained Musjid of Shah Jehan's time, and a *baradwari*, from which a bucket can be lowered down to the Ganges. Dalmow is founded by Rajah Dal, an Ahir, brother of Bal, who used to drink much, especially in the month of Phalgun. One of the *Shurki* kings of Jounpore attacked the fort and killed the brothers in that month. The two widows of the late chiefs prayed, and the fort overturning they killed the invader, whose tomb is at Makanpore. In the month of Phalgun an annual fair is held in honor of the brothers. In latter times there was a famous Hindu saint, whom a Nawab of Lucknow visited once, and who predicted, that "as you always stay in your palace, dancing and singing like women, so will your throne be ever as weak as a woman."

After the Mohamedan conquest, the hitherto pure Hindu style got mixed with that of the ruling race. Hence the dome of temples was after the foreign mould, principally of the Salzami kind ; though the pointed ones with steeples were not lost sight of, and the domestic architecture began to feel the foreign influence. In this period, the chief buildings erected were the temples, town and tank at or near Ajodhya by Man Singh and his father, Dursan Singh ; Hanuman Gurhi also was built under the Mohamedan rule, about 300 years ago. But in general it should be recorded, that no great edifices were allowed to be erected by the intolerant Mohamedans, with whom it was a favourite article of creed to destroy temples and statues.

Of the Mohamedan epoch, the Pathan style comes first in the order of succession. The first Moslem irruption in Oudh was effected by Syed Salar Masaud. He commenced his operation of prosletysing or rooting out idol-worship at Satrikh, which was his head-quarters for a time. From this place he sent out expeditions to Benares, Manikpore, and other places. Some obstinate battles ensued between the followers of the two faiths; and fields of fights were thickly strewn with martyrs' tombs. At Biswan about 20 miles north-east of Lucknow, are some very interesting remains of the transition period between the Hindus and Mohamedans. Of these, the most important is the Ekratia Rowzah Shahid, which is said to have been built in one night, whence the name ; but it appears, that it was not finished ; the dome was not built over it. The materials of it are large kunkur blocks and bricks, which were indiscriminately fixed one over the other, it seems, in great hurry; which evidently belonged to some Hindu buildings. In general, early Mohomedan structures were built of Hindu materials. There are four graves, evidently two of males and two of females. This building is rapidly going to ruin ; for many banian trees have grown over it, which add greatly to its picturesque though destructive effect. There is another tomb, called tbe Dirgah of Choupan Shahid. The Musjids at Bahraich, and Sundila and at Fatehpore, are also fair specimens of the early Pathan style. The tomb of Guran Ghori and shrine of Norehni Khurd-Mucca at Fyzabad are about 700 years old.

The architectural productions of the *Shirki* style are chiefly confined at Jownpore,* though specimens may be seen at Sultanpore, Rae Bareli and Makhanpore, near Dalmow. " The style of buildings adopted by the kings of Jownpore seems to be formed by a fusion of those of the Ghori and Khilzi Pathans of Delhi. In both of the fine mosques of Kotub-ud-din Aibeg at Delhi and Ajmere, the great central arch rises high in front of the main dome. All the musjids of the Shirki Pathan kings have the same peculiarity, with the addition of the fretted or cusped arches of the Khilzi Pathans." The gates and other parts of their buildings betray adaptation of Hindu influence; in fact, the architects, employed by them, were Hindus. The style should therefore be more properly called Hindo-Pathan, rather than any other. There are, at Rai Bareli, the remains of a very large and high fort with a well built by Ibrahim Sharki of Jownpore. The diamater of the well is more than 100 feet. The building materials are very large bricks, 2' × 1½' × 1'.

The specimens of Mogul architecture are the Musjid of Báber Shah at Ajodhya, bridge at Jownpore, Musjid at Biswan, Arungzebe's musjid at

---

* In Jounpore or *Jámadagnipore* or *Jamanpore* the objects of note are (1) fort, the walls of which were demolished by an Engineer after the mutiny, overhanging the river called *Kararkote*, named after a demon Karar, killed by Rama, (2) *Atala Debi's* temple, built by Jay Chandra in about 1180, (3) *Bijay-mandar* and *Tal*; (4) an old Musjid 130⅓×23', in the fort,—of the early Bengali type, that is, a single arcade supported on carved Hindu pillars with three low domes in the middle, (5) *Atala Musjid*, built by Ibrahim Shah on the site of the old Hindu temple, is the most ornate and beautiful; its size is 252'×248'; and the courtyard = 176×160'. The grand feature is the highly decorated propylon, or great central arch, with a smaller propylon on each side. The propylon is 75' high, with a base of 54½, and a top breadth of 45'. The musjid proper is devided into five compartments; the central room is covered by a dome of 30' diametre, one long room of a single storey 62' × 32' on each side, and two low room on each corner. It was designed by a Hindu architect, named Padumari, in 1407 A. D. Hence there is a mixture of the Mohamedan arch and Hindu architecture. (6) *Khalis Mukhlis* musjid erected on the site of Bijay Chand's temples in about 1417; very little of this mosque now remains, except the great propylon, which is 68' broad at the base, with a broken arch of 25' span; behind this is a great square, 65⅔' covered with a flat roof supported on ten rows of Hindu pillars, being 114 in number. (7) *Zanziri* Musjid at Chachakpore, owing to the chain like appearance of its ornamentation. (8) Jami musjid, 250'×58', is the largest mosque in Jownpore; the building was finished in 1438 by Mahmud Shah; its plan is like that of the Atala; but it has a high platform; and the cloisters are piled up to the height of 3 stories on each side of the gateway. (9) *Lal Durwaza musjid*, 212'×188', of Bibi Raji, built in 1444—59; the musjid proper is 177'×159 and the propylon is 47' broad and 59' high. There is an entrance hall, which is wanting in the other musjids, (10) *Stone Bridge*, double, was built by Akbar, in 1567, though known as Pul Mohamed Munin Khan. It consists of two separate portions with an island in the middle; one of which was on artificial channel, being diversion of river, when it was erected; subsequently that was also bridged. The bridge is one of the most pictursque in India. "Its long line of arches and piers, all of the same size, is relieved by the light pillared rooms, which crown the ends of the piers on both sides, and form a handsome street of detached shops." The roadway is 26' broad in clear width, with a solid stone parapet of 2'—3" on each side. The whole length of the Bridge is 654' - 3". The main bridge to the north consists of 10 pointed arches of 18'—3" span, resting on piers of 17' with abutments of half thickness. The smaller bridge to the south has only 5 arches..." *Cunningham.*

Lucknow. The mosque at Biswan is a very pretty one, with a *Mukbara* on one side and a *Mosafir-Khana* on the other. It was built by one Shaikh Borheh about 200 years ago. In this style also, the Hindu influence exercised still more appreciably, especially in domestic architecture. Its chief charateristic is the lavish use of ornament, both inside and outside.

But the lavish use of ornament was extensively employed, both inside and outside, of buildings of the *Naishapuri* style; which however prejudicialy interfered with the chaste design or main construction of architectural productions. The chief centres of this style were Fyzabad and Lucknow. Of the buildings of Lucknow, details are given in subsequent chapters. There is also a very pretty architectural group at Khyrabad, built during Nasir-ud-din's reign by one Mucca, who was the king's Darogah, and a tailor by profession. The group consists of a Kadam Rasul, on a high platform, tapering with earth, a pretty Emambarah, and an extemely beautiful Musjid, with gardens and houses and another Mukbarah, being that of his father, at the back and sides. The characteristics of this group are peculiar though pretty; the domes are all perforated according to fanciful designs; the Musjid has three serpentine Minars, and the cornices of the Kadam Rasul hangs down in the midle.

The chief buildings of this period at Fyzabad are (1) Calcutta Khurd fort near Miranghat, built after his defeat at Buxar by Shujah-ud-dowlah along with the city fortifications,—of which *Samanburj*, near his palace, was one of the principal bastions, from which at a considerable distance, the river flowed. But the Nawab is said to have induced it by offering up 1,25,000 cows and milk in proportion, to change its course and to flow under his castle. (2) *Golabbari*, which includes courts, gateways &c., is the mausoleum of Shujah-ud-dowlah, who prepared it as the final resting place of his remains; and here he was interred, being the first of the dynasty, whose corpse was not carried away to Delhi, (3) *Motimahal* and other buildings adjoining, which were royal palaces, situated near the *Dilkhosha*; (4) The *Tirpolia* or three-arched gateways on the three sides of the *Chouk*, which together with the Musjid make up a very good architectural view; (5) *Bahu Begum's* Mausoleum is a very beautiful tomb of the Begum of Shujah-ud-dowlah. She left all her property and money under the security of the British Government, which were transformed into a fund for pension to her different relatives and dependents, whose descendants still enjoy it Besides these chief buildings, there are many other edifices worth mentioning, such as those of Darab Ali Khan, Salar Jung, the royal gardens, public *Serais*, Emambarahs and tombs.

CHAPTER II.—*History of modern architecture.*

The oldest building of importance is the Musjid of Aurungzebe, (1656-1706,) who built it to root out the local idol-worship, on the sacred place of the Hindus, in Luchmontilah, now within the Mutchibhawan fort, overlooking the Asfi (stone) Bridge. There are also two old tombs still existing, erected by two Subadars before the time of Saádat Khan ; the one is in Aligunge ; the other is in Ahiagunge. There were many other buildings formerly, but they were destroyed in the general demolitions of 1858. The Durgah of Minah Shah, the leader of the first Mohamedan colony of Shaikhs, and the founder of modern Lucknow, in about 1450 A. D., is now no more ; that of Peer Jalil, a companion of his, is in a tottering state. Two fairs are respectively observed still, on the anniversary of their death, over their graves. They are now sainted, and so prayed to. The oldest Hindu quarter is Ranikuttra ; that of the Shaikhs was in Ismilegunge, the line of demarcation being probably the Nullah, a part of which serves as ditch.

Saádat Khan did not not build any place of importance. Being a man of warlike disposition, and constantly living in camp, he did not permanently fix his head-quarters anywhere. When he came to Lucknow, he simply rented the Punch Mahal and Mutchibhawan, at 535 Rs. from the local Shaikhs. Sufdar Jung constructed the Jelalabad fort, as a check to the turbulent Baises, also his father-in-law's tomb at Delhi, and left unfinished the building of his intended capital at Pánparh Ghat. He raised some sheds and a fort, for his temporary residence, at Fyzabad, whence the town is still locally called *Banglá*, (Anglicised Bungalow) which literally means thatched house, the name being derived from Bangla, (Bengal) where thatched houses prevailed in those days. Shujah-ud-dowlah erected his father's tomb at Delhi, and some palaces at Fyzabad, which was his fixed capital. These three sovereigns, however, did not much care about buildings and other apparently effeminate matters ; their attention was wholly engrossed with political and military affairs. The architecture of this period followed the latter Delhi style.

With the accession of Asuf-ud-dowlah, and the transfer of the seat of Government to Lucknow, the situation changed ; he was a servile ally of the British. Being personally relieved of all cares about state-affairs, owing to the constant foreign interference, he turned his undivided attention to architecture and other cognate arts, which, being free from

Delhi influence, had high local tone, of which the effect, though not sublime, is grand and beautiful to the extreme. The principal group is that of the great Emambarah, Musjid and Roomi Gate, which taken together, according to Bishop Heber, is the grandest view in the world.*

But shortly after, foreign taste began to prevail, and the new style, still in its infancy, visibly declined after the death of Asuf-ud-dowlah. Saádut Ali Khan was almost the creature, or was compelled to be so of the English; and he could not but follow the bad taste of his officious friends. General Claude Martin, a soldier of fortune, who had raised himself as an influential and favorite courtier to the former Nawab-Vizier, built Farhad-Buksh in a semi-Italian style. The Nawab took fancy to the novel edifice, and bought it at Rs. 50,00,000 He also encouraged the General to construct Constantia in a quite original and grander style, to be purchased after its completion at a *crore*. These two buildings exercised great influence on the latter architectural productions of the city. Henceforth the local architecture was not national and pure, nor adopted to popular needs; "because a double government and constant interference insensibly forced the architects into an awkward mimicry of the models then followed in England, tawdry in style and bald in design." An English Engineer by name Macleod was forced upon him. But as Kefait-ullah, the great builder of Asuf-ud-dowlah's Emambarah, was not yet dead, Saádut Ali Khan built some edifices in the chaste style of his predecessors, as the tomb of

* The country houses at Chinhat, also the garden pavilions at Aish Bàgh and Chàr Bàgh (the latter now occupied by the railway station), were built by Asif-ud-daula, as were also the Yahiàganj and stables annexed. The Wazìrganj that gives its name to the present police thàna, which he founded in the name of his adopted son Wazir Ali Khan; Amàniganj, Fatheganj, Rakàbganj, the Nakhkhàs, Daulatganj, Begamganj, and Nawàbganj,— these are all situated in the Wazirganj and Chauk thànas.

Other Ganjes founded in his time were.—

The A Hàta Khànsàmàn, built by the king's chamberlain, who on its completion invited the Nawab to an entertainment in it.

The Tikaitganj and the Bazàr Takait Ràe, which are both in the Chauk, built by the king's prime minister, Mahàràja Tikait Ràe.

The Tirmaniganj.

The Tikri.

The Chhàoni Hasan-ud-din Khan.

The Hasanganj Bàoli.

The Bhawàniganj.

The Bàlakganj and Kashmiri Mohalla, which are in the Saàdatganj thàna.

The A Háta Súrat Singh.

The Niwàzganj.

The Tahsinganj

The Khudàganj of Nagaria, which was founded by the mother of Asuf-ud-daula in the same day on which she laid the first stone of Aliganj, on the north side of the river.

The Ambarganj.

The Mahbubganj.

The Top Darwàza, in the Daulatganj thana.

The Khiyaliganj

The Bazár Jhaúlál, in Wazirganj, founded by Mahárája Jhaúlál, Kayath, finance minister.

Hasanganj was also founded by Hasan Raza Khan on the north side of the river.—*Oudh Gazetter.*

his mother in Golagunge, and the Lal Baradwari, (Throne-hall). Of the mixed foreign style, the buildings of his reign are Dilkhosha, the old Residency, latterly known as the Banqueting Hall, then as Hospital, &c.

Gazee and Nasir-ud-din Hyders followed the debased style. Though they built some good specimens of the old Saracenic style, in which the former erected the two tombs of his parents, and the Shah Najuff; the latter Báráh Imám and the Kerbula, which he left unfinished. During Nasir-ud-din's reign, the Anglomania was at its height; still the interior architecture was of the pure oriental style.* Society would not conform to the denational taste of the foreigners. It is easy to give a foreign turn to the ideas of a nation, in matters of luxury and the creations of fancy, not so as regards affairs of necessity and utility and religion. And so it happened in Lucknow, its luxury was anglicised; in other respects, it was as oriental as before. The ecclesiastical architecture was therefore not affected, but retained its old purity; while palaces and gardens took a foreign cast. The result was that Ghazi built the castle-like Khurshed Munzil (sun-palace) in the style of the English baronical age.

Mohomed Ali Shah attempted a renaissance or restoration of the older style, both in architecture and Government; he succeeded to a certain extent in his group-production at Hosseinabad. Umjud Ali Shah, however, had his taste falsified; and he took great pleasure in having his palaces painted in very gaudy colours.† And Wajid Ali Shah, who fell still deeper into the bad style, produced the Kaiserbagh, a range of palaces having a mixture of all possible kinds of style, without judgment shown as to its symmetry, or skill displayed as to the arrangement of its minor parts. The son was less happy in architecture as in all things else than even his father.

The buildings, erected under the English rule, are of no architecture at all. The Engineer's simple aim is to cover and enclose space for the habitation of men, and no further. Look for example, the Barracks in the Cantonment and Railway structures in Charbagh. Bulrampore hospital

---

* It is a curious circumstance, that many of the palaces in Lucknow have fronts in imitation of the palaces in Naples, Rome, &c., and the native palace is beyond in an enclosed space. Mrs. Park's *Wandering of a Pilgrim*, 1830.

† On the way (round the palace to the Goomtee), I had ample opportunity to observe one of the fancies of the king, which consists in having all the houses of the city painted white, or in colours, and covered with scenes of Indian life. Von Orlich'es *Travels in India*, February, 1843.

is undoubtedly beyond the æsthetic principles of architecture ; while Wingfield Munzil and Canning College are sad failures as attempts to orientalize English designs.

Of the two styles, the older one is superior to the latter, not only in boldness of execution, originality yet chasteness of design, and purity of details, but also in the solidity of its masonry and in its durability. In effect also, it has advantage over the other. The latter cannot bear a near inspection. When viewed from a distance, the former looks solemn and grand; and the latter, airy and fairy-looking. These two styles may otherwise be noted as the country and the town styles, for the architectural principles of Asuf-ud-dowlah were generally adopted beyond the direct influence of Lucknow, as in Tikiatgunge, Miangunge, and other places, where massive and castle-like buildings were necessary for use rather than the airy and unsubstantial mansions, which were required for luxurious citizens only.

Comparatively speaking, old Lucknow stood as one of the finest cities in the world, in the splendid views it gave to sight-seers. Even Delhi loses its ground of importance, when the gorgeous display of architectural grouping is considered ; for the specialty of Lucknow consists or rather consisted in the beautiful massing of its palaces, well relieved of one another, when viewed from a distance.*

---

* Although Dehli possesses larger and finer edifices than Lucknow, yet its appearance is not nearly so imposing as that of the capital of Oudh. There are not so many tall *minars*, which always form a chief beauty of a Mahomedan city. The domes are few in number, and not guilt, while the material of the chief buildings is red sombre stones, instead of the white *pucca* (brickwork) which has so fine an effect at a distance. In Lucknow too, all the principal objects are finely grouped ; whereas at Delhi they are much scattered, and many of them are distant several miles from the city. Mintern's *New York to Delhi.*

The view of the city is beyond exception one of the most picturesque in the East, only rivalled by Benares of all I have seen east of Cairo. It is a view so purely oriental, it is impossible for one, who has not been in the East to realize it, the number of palaces, public buildings, domes, minar ets of temples and mosques, with that dream-like halo encirclig it—an oriental sky and atmosphere ! Ireland's *From Wall Street to Cashmere.* November 1853.

A vision indeed ! A vision of palaces, minars, domes, azure and golden, cupolas, colonnades, long facades of fair perspective in pillar and column, terraced roofs,—all rising up amidst a calm still ocean of the brightest verdure. Look for miles and miles away, and still the ocean spreads, and the towers of the fair city gleam in its midst. Spires of gold glitter in the sun. Turrets and gilded spheres shine like constellation. There is nothing mean or squalid to be seen. There is a city more vast than Paris, as it seems and more brilliant lying before us......Wilderness of architecture, which renders the place a marvel to us...... In a blaze of gilding spires, cupolas, domes, stretches the vast Kaiserbagh. Not Rome, not Athens, not Constantinople, not any city, that I have ever seen, appears to me so striking and beautiful as this ; and the more I gaze, the more its beauties grow upon me. *Russell's Diary* 1858.

Chapter III.

Domestic Architecture.

To go deeply into the subject, we must, first of all, enquire into the wants and then the luxuries of the people. So that our first business is to judge domestic architecture from the utilitarian point of view. The middle and low classes live on the joint-family-system ; so that their house requirements are of the most economical description ; the smallest space to accomodate the greatest number. Hence the domestic architecture, especially of the Hindus, has no airiness. All is close and compact, being composed of dark cells, whose ventilation even is not regarded ; because it will take a little extra space, that may be used for some tangible utility. Windows are never allowed, but superabundance of recesses and niches everywhere is fondly indulged in. No open ground is kept in the front, back, or side of the house, but is turned into a very woody garden, that prevents the entrance of air as well as light.

Take for example a common Bunniah-house. He is a shopkeeper; and he sits in the front-room of his house attending to his business. Behind his shop is the Zenanah, of which the courtyard, where are the indespensable well and stone-god, is not more than 5 feet in either way. Now he requires at least eight rooms to accommodate his whole family ; (note, family in India means not only wife and children but all other dependent relatives of the master of the house). The family of the Bunniah consists of say an old mother, or aunt, a brother's wife and children, his own wife and children. His eldest son is married ; so is his eldest daughter, whose husband permanently or occasionally lives in the house : each of the two pairs require separate rooms. The old woman has another, with whom the unmarried girls sleep. The wife too requires a separate compartment ; and she takes charge of the younger children ; while the Bunniah himself spends the day and sleeps during the night in the shop-room, with his sons, who are grown up, but not yet married. Besides these, more rooms are required, one for dining, one for stores, and one for bathroom. The family also needs a kitchen, and some flat roofs on the first story, to lie and sleep upon in the sultry nights of summer, and to bask in the sun in winter days. The flat roof of the second story, especially in Mohamedan houses is not generally exposed ; but it has always very high parapet walls, that the females may walk or take air unseen by the public. The ever-present monkeys make unceremonious depredations every hour of the day, whenever they find the inmates of the house engaged or unwary. Hence a bamboo framework is also required to cover the Courtyard as a protection from them.

The plan of such a simple house, about 15′ × 20′, is shown. The double shaded portion is the upper story, having three large rooms and four corner-rooms—one for stairs, one for store, &c., two of which the wife and brother occupy opposite each other, and the married son and son-in-law in the side-rooms. The required flat-roof is also given on two sides and in the little jutting out of the verandahs all around. In the lower story, there are four comparatively large rooms with the four corner-cells, of which one is for stores, one for latrine, one for stairs, and one for entrance, if it is made separate from the open shop, which is in front of the house. In the room opposite the shop, lives his old mother or aunt. This room has a verandah (*varamdah* literally means transept—some portion of the main plan going beyond), which has *chicks* (bamboo screens) in the three openings and serves as the dining hall. It has a wooden framework of pillars and planks for its front wall, like that of the shop. One of the side rooms is for kitchen, the other for contingent purposes, say for a relative, who may come on a ceremonial visit. In a corner of the courtyard is the well, by the side of which is a little raised platform or pillar, on which is placed a polished stone, representing Siva, or the plant Tulsi, over-shadowed by an extra jutting out of the verandah roof. The roofs are projected inside over the courtyard for beauty as well as convenience, that the upper rooms may communicate independently of one another. On the little parapets, raised on the edge of the projecting roofs, is placed the bamboo framework as a protection from the depredations of the monkeys. In front of the shop, is a platform, over which the roof projects, forming a little verandah outside the wife's room, also covered with bamboo *chicks* to serve as screen for the women, when looking at a procession or any other *Tamasha*, that may pass that way. This screen also keeps away the troublesome monkeys on the three other sides, except one or two little holes or skylights to let in light. The *purdah*-system, that is of exclusion and veiling, will not allow any windows on any side but the front or that facing the road.

Now when the house belongs to other than a Bunniah, then instead of a shop, there will be in front a sitting room for the men and their friends. This room is the *Mardana* of men of small means. Here the style differs a little, though the economic principle is. not yet lost sight of. The wooden front wall is displaced for one of substantial material. Two plans and views, of a Hindu and Mohamedan house are given ; (Uniform letter are employed to explain the diagrams, as G for entrance or gate, K for kitchen, S for store, St for stairs, V for verandah, L for Latrine, W for Well, Cy, for courtyard, M. for Mardana, Z for Zenana.)

Now let us advance a little higher, and suppose that the house, now to be considered, is that of a rich man. The Hindu building will now materially and widely differ from that of the Mohomedan. In both cases, the dimensions of the house will be greater, and the court-yards will be at least two, one for the Mardaná and the other for the Zenáná. In entering a Hindu house, (see plan,) you first find the Mardana, the abode of the males. The front part of the court is double-storied, and has imposing rooms. In the middle of the courtyard is a little temple, where the members of the family pray and worship. In a corner is the well ; a little flower-garden is attached to it and the temple. On the two sides there are cells or thatched sheds for quarters for servants, cattle, &c. The fourth side has no rooms, but is simply enclosed by a wall. Then entering the Zenana through almost dark rooms or tortuous passages, you find another courtyard, well paved with tiles, stones, or *khoa.* On the four sides as usual are four ranges of rooms, flanked with verandahs and platforms with flights of steps. The three sides are two-storied ; and that range, which is between the Mardana and Zenana, has a third story. The kitchen is in the Zenana and is on that side, where there is no second story.

With regard to a Mohamedan gentleman's house, first you find a grand-looking gate with guard-room and servant-quarters adjoining it. Then the Mardana is entered. The courtyard is large and is more airy than that of the Hindu. It is surrounded by cells or commodious rooms. On the prominent side is the Emambarah or the house of the saints, if the owner be a Shiah ; or else a little Musjid is added in a corner, that the inmates might pray conveniently. The sitting room of the master of the house is a large commodious room, adjoining the Emambarah. In the other rooms are accommodations for the Dewan (manager) and his Office, and the Moulvi to teach the boys of the house. In the upper story—in a corner of the open flat roofs,—is a wooden pavilion, where the Nawab Sahib sits with his freinds in the cool of the evenings of summer. There is also a Tykháná or under-ground room in one of the ranges, where he retires during the day-heat of the hot season. Then raising the curtain, you enter the Zenana, which has a separate courtyard. In the middle is a wooden frame work for swinging. There is a back-door or two, that any one dying, his corpse may be taken out thence ; so that the usual passage may not be polluted by its exhalation.*

---

* Zenana :—Imagine to yourself a tolerably sized quadrangle, three sides of which is occupied by habitable buildings, and the fourth by kitchens, offices, lumber-rooms, &c., leaving in the centre an open courtyard. The habitable buildings are raised a few steps from the court ; a line of pillars form the front of the buildings, which has no upper room ; the roof is flat, and the sides and back without windows, or any aperture through which air can be received. The sides and back are merely high walls forming an enclosure, and the only air is admitted from the front of the dwelling-place facing the courtyard. The apartments are divided into long walls, the extreme corners having small rooms or dark closets purposely built for the repository of valuables or stores ; doors are fixed to these closets, which are the only places I have seen with them in a Zenana or Mahal (house or palace occupied by females), the floor is either of beaten earth, bricks, or stones ; boarded floors are not yet introduced.

As they have neither doors nor windows to the halls, warmth or privacy is served by means of thick wadded curtains, made to fit each opening between the pillars. Some Zenanas have two rooms of pillars in the halls with wadded curtains to each, thus forming two distinct halls, as occasion may serve, or greater warmth be required. This is a convenient arrangement where the establishment of servants, slaves &c., is extensive.

Besides the *purdahs*, the openings between the pillars have blinds neatly made of bamboo strips, together with coloured cords ; these are called *Jhilmills or Chiks.* Many of them are painted green ; others are more gaudy both in colour and variety of patterns. These blinds constitute a real comfort to every one in India, as they admit air when let down, and at the same time shut out flies, and other annoying insect, a desirable object to foreigners in particular.

The floors of the halls are first matted with the coarse date, leaf matting of the country, over which is spread *shutrangies*, a white colico carpet covers the *shutrangie*, on which the females take their rest.

The bedsteads of the family are placed, during the day, in lines at the back of the halls, to be moved at pleasure to any chosen spot for the night's repose, often into the open courtyard, for the benefit of the pure air. They are all formed on one principle, differing only in size and quality ; they stand about half a yard from the floor. The *musnud* is spread on the floor if possible near to a pillar about the centre of the hall. Looking-glasses or ornamental furniture are very rarely to be seen in the Zenana even of the very richest females.

On the several occasions of assembling in large parties, as at births and marriages, the halls, although extensive, would be inadequate to accommodate the whole party. They then have awnings of white calico, neatly flounced with muslin, supported on poles fixed in the courtyard, and connecting the open space with the great hall, by wooden platforms which are brought to a line with the building, and covered with *shutrangi*, and white carpets to correspond with the floor, furniture of the hall, and here the ladies sit by day and sleep by night very comfortably.

The kitchen and offices to the Zenana occupy one side of the quadrangle ; they face the great or centre hall appropriated to the assembly. The fire-places are all on the ground, something resembling stores, each admitting one sauce-pan, the Asiatic style of cooking requiring no other contrivance.

Now let us ascend further, and consider the palaces of kings and nobles. A palace is composed of many courts and blocks of buildings ;—one for elephants, another for camels, a third for cavalry, and so on according to the nature of the guards. Beyond these are the quarters for royal servants and offices. Passing all these courts, you enter, through a large gate, with double curtains, the palace proper. The courtyard of this palace is a very pretty flower garden and crossed by a long masonry-tank, that extends from the inner gate to the Baradwari in the centre. This tank has many fountains, which, when playing, have a beautiful effect. There are also conduits of water, that go along the paths and little alleys of the garden. Marble kiosks are interspersed at equal distances. The rooms, that surround the four sides of the rectangle, are large and spacious. In the middle of each side is a Baradwari, as in Moti Mahal, north west part. This is but the Mardana or Khás Mokám of the King. On one or both sides of this Mardáná are the royal seraglios of castle-looking appearance, as in Mulka Jahán's and Chhoti Shahzadi's. These seraglios are of many stories in height. So that the palaces of Lucknow are vast in extent and complex in design. See general plan of Moti-Mahal for an example.

CHAPTER IV.

The general characteristics of local Architecture.

The architecture of Lucknow has been so often condemned by superficial European visitors, who, without understanding its nature, design and utility, pass their immature opinion, that it is high time, that we should disabuse them of their prejudices. It is very unfair to judge of a foreign country by the standard of one's own ; and to criticise Lucknow architecture by the rules of Palladian Art, shows the partial and defective knowledge of the critic. It betrays narrow-mindedness, nothing else. And when the critic belongs to a ruling race and is of official position, he does great mischief to the subject-nation, which cannot but abide and conform to his false taste and whimsical dictates. The ruled thus lose their originality and peculiarity of style, not only in architecture, but in every thing else ; and are reduced to such a strait, as to be capable of doing nothing but to ape and exaggerate the vices of the ruler. This has exactly happened in Hindustan, and Lucknow especially.

Yes, I admit, that the European critic can condemn Lucknow architecture, to the extent, that Italian art is adopted to oriental purposes; this, however, has never been a success in India. But to think that, because the Italian style has been a failure here, therefore all other branches are no better, is a fallacy of argument of the same class, as to conclude that because one member of a family steals, therefore the whole family is of bad character; or rather, because one fails in imitation, he has no originality or any other qualification. The truth is, Lucknow architecture has better and inner parts, which no superficial observer can discover.

Hitherto the local architecture has been judged from two points of view only,—*viz.* (1) when seen at a distance, (2), when seen at a near view. In both cases, external features only are considered. But interior features, decorations, &c., are altogether lost sight of. None has seen them from an analytical point of view, so as to detect and discover what is intrinsically bad or good.

According to Ruskin, architecture has three virtues:

(I.) "That it act well and do the thing it was intended to do in the best way"—that is as regard the convenience of the dwellers, and not the pleasures of foreign tourists. So the English visitors have no business to enforce their opinions, when they do not tally with those of the residents. And native modes of living are quite at variance with those of the Europeans,—as has been already explained. No European can with certainty say that a Church would excite devotional feelings more than a Mohamedan *Musjid* or Hindu *Mandir* (temple) can do; nor can a house, closely built like *Bungalows*, and without having any inner opening for courtyard, as those of the wintry climate of England, suit the really torrid zone of Oudh.

(2). "That it speak well and say the thing it was intended to say in the best words." Thus a tomb should look of a solemn character, a Musjid grave and pure; a palace airy and elegant; and the ornaments and decorative construction should be appropriate to the nature of the work. Now Lucknow architecture is not so condemnable as the Englishmen in general think. Whether seen from a distance or from a near point, the local edifices will not disappoint you, if you judge them by the pure principles of the Indo-Saracenic Art, and not by that of the Renaissance School of Italy, now antiquated, and always misunderstood and ill-applied.

(3.) " That it look well and please us by its presence, whatever it has to do or say." When seen prospectively and at a distance, Lucknow architecture has, at least had a most favorable impression on the mind of the visitors. This has been noted and recorded by all the travellers, who came here in the time of its glory. But when taken from a near point of view, the buildings do not look so well. Some even hold that they cannot bear near inspection ; they cannot be dissected and be seen separately in parts. This is a most sweeping remark, without having any foundation. The natives, and those who understand the art, do not so denounce them ; nay they look on with satisfaction and approbation.

Now before we proceed with details, it is well to consider and test Lucknow architecture by Fergusson's principles. If architecture consists of ornamented and ornamental construction, surely Lucknow buildings should have more respect, than the pedantic edifices erected, here and there, now and then, by English Engineers, with a vulgar taste of Europeanism and orientalism abominably mixed together, such as those at Baroda, Hyderabad, Gwalior, and even here among us,—for example Balrámpore Hospital, Canning College, Wingfield Munzil The fact is, that the English architects, not understanding native necessities and luxuries produce buildings, quite at variance with the requirements of men and climate. A student of the Roorki College designed and planned the Bulrampore Hospital. Ghassi, a Rájput draughtsman of Ajmere, tutored by an Engineer, had his defective drawings of the Canning College, executed with great modifications and alterations; and the production is no better than " white-washed ugliness," as Fergusson would have it. Is it that the local architects (Mehmars), the descendants of those, who built the great Emambarah and other beautiful edifices, are dead, that you plead for your European ugliness at an extravagant cost and worthless taste? Is it that they cannot meet and design according to the requirements of the present age, that you import vulgar and abominable productions ? Have you ever sent for and consulted them, whether they can build original and elegant designs cheaply and economically ? Alas, want of sympathy has been at the root of the subject-nation's deterioration; and the vanity of the rulers treads us down to utter helplessness and dependance, unoriginality and imitation!

But to my point. Let us continue to apply Fergusson's maxims. (1)—The greater the mass of a building, the more grand and effective is the purpose. Now the local buildings have each many courts with commodious rooms and stately pavilions; the extent and area, covered by them, are vast; and the out-offices enhance the beauty of the main blocks. So Lucknow shows to great advantage, even above Dehli and Agra, though it has no castle or fortress.*

(2.) In stability, the Lucknow palaces considerably fall below that of other cities where stone architecture prevails. But in brick-masonry, the local architecture does not yield to any. When the better half of the city was ruthlessly demolished, the sappers and miners had arduous tasks and great difficulty; for many of the blocks of buildings withstood several of their attempts to explode them. They were as hard as stone. The great Emambarah of Asuf-ud-dowlah, erected a century ago, looks as if it was built a few years back; though it was never repaired, and is made an arsenal for guns and other heavy military stores. The stone-bridge, tottering in its ruin, still stands undamaged by the high flood-current of the Goomtee; while the New Bridge, constructed by Bruce a few years ago, yields and is fractured and repaired almost every alternate year.

The celebrated Bailie Guard garrison remained beseiged almost securely within the walls of common houses, without any proper rampart. These common brick-walls were thoroughly pierced by cannon balls of the enemy. And yet they withstood their severest battering. Many of them even now, after so many years stand solemnly without repairs, defying storm, rain and time, thus attesting the strength of their masonry. The walls of Shah Najuf did not yield to the severe bombardment of three hours, by numerous very heavy cannons, resorted to by Sir Colin Campbell, in his Relief of Lucknow.

* The great extent of the buildings, called the king's palace, surprized me. It is not properly a palace, but a contiuuation of palaces, stretching all along the banks of the Goomtee, the river on which Lucknow is built. In this, however, the royal residence in Oudh but resembles what one reads of the Seraglios at Constantinople, the Khan's residence at Teheran, and the imperial buildings at Pekin. In all oriental states, the palaces are not so much the abode of the sovereign only, as the centre of the Government: little towns, in fact, containing extensive lines of buildings occupied by the Harem and its vast number of attendants; containing courts, gardens, tanks, fountains, and squares, as well as the Offices of the chief ministers of state. Such is the case in Lucknow. One side of the narrow Goomtee ...... is lined with the royal palace; the other is occupied by the *rumna* or park, in which the menagerie is (or was) maintained Its extent is the only imposing feature about it, and this struck me more forcibly than any magnificence or loftiness of structure would have done. *Private Life of an Eastern King.*

(3.) If largeness and expensiveness of materials enhance architectural effect, then certainly Lucknow loses its ground of importance ; for here materials are cheap. Besides the bricks are very small, which, however, set admirably and take to the cement, prepared in the country, producing great stability of masonry. There are very large bricks also, by the name of Ilmasi, from Ilmas Ali Khan, the great eunuch and Nazim of Asuf-ud-dowlah's time, who made and used them in all his buildings.

(4.) The Lucknow architects always gave great depths and took extra space for their works, so as to have ample field for ornamental construction and play of imaginative mouldings. They never aimed at mere engineering, but to leave a margin for the production of the softness of architectural effect.

(5.) With regard to forms, "the square and angular are characteristics of strength and power ; curves of softness and elegance ; and beauty is produced by the effective combination of the right-lined with the curvilear." In this principle also, you will find that Lucknow does not fall by comparison, if you scrutinise minutely and without bias. The city, however, labors under two disadvantages, or defects if you like to call them ; (1) want of height proportionate to length ; and (2) the length is too great for the breadth of a building ; I mean a range of rooms in one side of a court. Take for example one side of Kaiser Bagh ; it is about 1000 ft. in length, 40 in breadth, and 50 in height. It is only two stories in height, which is the same throughout the extent ; and though, inside, the monotony of elevation or facade is broken and relieved by bastioned verandahs and the gate, that towers all, yet the flat effect of the whole form is not much improved.

(6.) Proportions of parts to one another and to the whole building are points, very difficult to determine. They differ according to taste, circumstances, conveniences and purposes. We will however roughly find out some ratios. Given a unit-court of square or rectangular plan, the open yard should be equal to the area, covered by the rooms in the four sides ; that is, half of the whole. Now supposing a side of a square court, of which the range of rooms is flanked by a *verandah* (corridors), the length should be ten times the width of the rooms or verandah separately, or five times the breadth of both collectively. But the breadth of the rooms must be greater than that of the verandah. Now we will calculate and find out the results. Beginning with 30 ft., as the average breadth of the rooms and verandah together (width of room = 14′, and of verandah = 10′, total = 24′, leaving 6′ for the three walls), the side of the courtyard will be 150 ft. and that of the whole = 210 ft. In the middle of each range, the rooms will be larger and more imposing than those of its sides, with regard to elevation; the whole range being of two stories, the central portion should have three stories; and the four corners four kiosks, or turrets. The side, opposite to the gate, is the most prominent and ornamental. This principle is best illustrated in the inner court of Moti Mahal and the Emambarah buildings, the river facade of Chhutter Munzil. and the Kaiserpasand. As regards the inner proportions of a room, the height should be less by $\frac{1}{4}$ of breadth, which is also less by at least $\frac{1}{4}$ of length, or $h : w : l :: 1 : \frac{5}{4} : \frac{25}{16}$ Thus given the height of a room as 20′ from ceiling to floor, the breadth should be 25′, and length 31¼′. According to Fergusson, however, given 30′ as length, the breadth will be 15′, and height $= 7\frac{1}{2} + \sqrt{30} =$ say 13′; this ratio also is sometimes observed here. Occasionally these two ratios as to internal dimensions of a room, are deviated from; and a third proportion is resorted to; *viz.*, height is one-fourth in excess of width, thus $w = 20$; $h = 25'$; $l = 31\frac{1}{4}$.

This one-fourth (or one-third sometimes) being more or less than one another is almost a universal rule with the native architects. Take for example, the facade of a Musjid. It is divided into three rectangles, of which the middle one is greater than the side ones by one-fourth. The height of each of the rectangular pieces is $\frac{1}{4}$ greater than its base. The same proportion is observed with regard to the three domes, of which the chief pinnacle measures from the floor $\frac{1}{4}$ less than the total length of the facade, while the height of the two minarets is $\frac{1}{4}$ greater, whose highest point, when joined to the opposite end of the base, touches the side of the middle dome; or when the minaret is less by $\frac{1}{4}$ of the total base, the line joining the end of the roof, touches the two domes other than the near one by the outer sides.

These rules, which also apply to tombs, Emambarahs, Baradwaries, &c., are subject to modifications. Generally speaking, the proportions of native architecture are more complex than those of European art; and in comparison, Lucknow does not lose its importance as a principal seat of oriental architecture. It is very unjust to pass an unfavourable opinion on the local architecture, simply because in some columns or such some minute parts, they do not observe the so-called classical principles.

(7.) Regarding ornament, constructive aud decorative, Lucknow will not disappoint you, if you have the patience to make closer inspection of the local buildings. Musjid, being the house of God, is an edifice of chaste design, where ornament is very little allowed; yet it is grand looking in its simplicity. But in an Emambarah, the house of the saints, Mokurbah, that of the departed, Baradwari and others for the luxurious, the ornament used, is both constructive and decorative.

The ornaments, that adorn the local buildings, are of various patterns and designs. The constructive ornaments are made in the body of the masonry and in the arrangement of the plan; while the decorative consist of mere plaster work on the superfices of walls. Thus taking an arch, for example, the constructive ornaments will be the five little arches along its semi-circular edge line, recesses, string courses, and little columns; while the decorative, the flowery designs on the plaster. Generally speaking, these ornaments look beautiful, whether in single bands or in group; but when carried to extravgance, as is sometimes done, covering a large space, the effect is confused.

(8) If colour brightens architectural effect, then Lucknow must make a very high impression on the minds of the beholders. And certainly the red-ochre of the Lal Baradwari (Throne-pavilion) has a very grand and at the sametime sombre effect; and the yellow of Kaiser Bagh, when seen from a distance, gives the idea of a golden fairy look. The white washing, when employed with a mixture of talc powder, lends a peculiar silvery appearance. The talc-powder is generally used along with plastering and colouring on the external faces of walls; it thus heightens the effect. The colouring shows to great advantage, when employed internally and in ornamental painting.

Thus on the whole, the building art of Lucknow, as of Indo-Saracenic in general, has some principles of its own to guide the Hindustani architects. They aim to produce not only useful, but ornamental and tastefully regulated buildings, which, while filling all the wants of native life, have such a margin left, as to allow the means of luxury, and to supply a beautiful sight. They never entertain the ambition to erect simply engineering warehouses, railway-sheds, or military barracks, at a so-called economical expense, which, well managed, and left to native architects, can suffice for better-looking buildings. The *Mehmars* understand rules, and can design quite originally, if wanted of them, or according to the requirements and directions of the owner of a building to be erected. Yet Government and Railway Companies are throwing out money on a false taste, false economy, and false productions, and recognise not the qualifications of the native architects.

It is the prime duty of Government to foster native art, not to destroy it. So whenever building works are ordered to be constructed, there should be some stamp of local architecture. Thus a barrack built at Benares Cantonment should have ornaments, decorative and constructive, of the neighbouring city. The Engineers should only look to the plan and the general arrangement of the main work, leaving the superstructure and superfices to the Mehmars, who would give them a local character by the adjustment of the minor parts and the ornamental pieces. The golden fruits of this step will be that not only native art will be sustained and improved, but Government and the building companies will learn real taste and economy by better procedure and results. Government should orientalize itself in its internal policy. For this purpose it should entertain a native consulting architect, of course sub-ordinate to the European one. He should be conversant with all oriental styles, provincial, and continental, Hindu and Mosulman It should be his business to see, that all important buildings that are henceforth to be constructed, have a local character in them, discover and record all local styles not yet brought to light, and to superintend schools for Mehmars, to be educated especially for the purpose.

CHAPTER V.

The classification and different kinds of local buildings.

The local masonry is generally composed of brickwork. Iron is never used. Stone is employed only in cornices and little columns. Timber is required for beams, domes, &c., for domestic architecture of the common people, in eaveboards and verandah-front-walls, which are got ready prepared with beautiful carving at the shops of the city.

The local brick-masonry is one of the best of its kind. The cement, called *Kámp*, joins and attaches to the bricks admirably and lasts long.

The bricks, being very small, are well adapted to any delicate ornamental design, which the fancy of the architect may direct. In erecting a column or arch, even the naked brickwork shows exquisitely the decorative arrangement of its sides or body.

The external facade of a house is generally a dead wall, except in the front side. That portion of dead wall, which is too much exposed, is relieved by a little painting of a crescent moon, animals, flowers or birds, and cornices. But the internal arrangement is quite ornamental, though windows are seldom allowed. Here the wall of a room is broken by shelves, recesses, flowery bands, skylights and cornices. In palaces, which are of large dimensions, and surrounded by gardens, high walls, or outer courts, the external facades are relieved by decorative designs of windows, verandahs, balconies, and other ornamental features.

The columns and pillars of Lucknow, like many other things, have no great peculiarity in them. They generally resemble one another in the Indo-Saracenic art, no matter how local and distant they are. So that Delhi, Agra and Lucknow, the three principal seats of Mohamedan power and architecture, have each very little individuality of style, but a sameness pervading all. The Emambarah, however, is a peculiar production of this city, the builder being of the Shiah dynasty. We have also Baradwaries, instead of Dewan-i-Khas and Am, the plan and facade of which do not resemble those of the other.

In the body of a pillar, there are ornamental string-courses, with slender columns, on the two sides ; while the other two have each their faces, beautifully recessed up to the arch. The columns have, ornamental bands, straight or serpentine, bases and capitals, which have no resemblance to those of Greece and Rome. Some of these architectural pieces are very happy productions. The dead space of the spandrils is filled up with ornamental patterns, while string-courses run up to the lower cornices.*

* Among many original idea to be recommended for the imitation of British architects is one of a pillar composed of three fishes twisted together, standing on their tails, their heads forming the capital, which would have been admirable and appropriate, if adopted in the new market of Billingsgate. By the way, the fish is the badge of the King of Oudh; and one in silver, about six inches long, is fastened in front of the turbans of certain of his attendants. The first Mohamedan King, who used it, was Khoosro Purwez, King of Persia, and grand-son of the celebrated Nowsherwan, who ascended the throne when the moon was in the constellation of the Fish. From him the custom has descended to the Delhi emperors, who accord the use of it, the *Mohrchal* or fan of peacock's feathers, and the Nalki—a peculiar sort of palanquin,— to highly favoured servants or relatives.

Many of the cupolas of the Royal palaces are crowned with plumes of ostrich feathers of metal guilt, set in a circle—a sort of Prince of Wales' coronets. This again is surmounted by an umberella, which has in many instances succumbed to the influence of the weather and the weakness of the stick, and descend crushing the aforesaid plume, and looking altogether forlorn and miserable. W. Carpenter, June 1856.

In the openings of walls, such as doors, windows, skylights, and arches, the arrangement in the edge-lines is ornamental. It is the principle of the Indo-Saracenic architecture, never to allow dead spaces and dead lines to make a building look flat, naked and uninteresting. Hence you will never find in the most common and poorest building, even the graves, something, that will not arrest your attention. In fact, the native architects are partial to the curvilear lines more than those of any other nation. Similarity of ornaments, if not of form and design, you will never see in any two buildings. Native architects always aimed to produce something new and beautiful, even in the most orthodox and unchangeable design, such as Musjids.

The roofing of local buidings is done with concrete over planks of wood, (but not tiles), spread over beams. Underneath is hung tightly a painted thick cloth ; and the ceiling looks beautiful with scenes from fairyland and ornamental borders.

The parapet-walls over roofs are composed of little arches, domes, and turrets, that are symmetrical with the lower portion. The cornices, double or single, generally boldly project out, and not badly relieve the higher wall. The supports to the cornices are ornamental flowers or figures of elephants and angels, as you will find in Kaiser-Bagh gate.

Some of the Lucknow-domes, though less prominent and known, are more beautiful than even those of Delhi and Agra. There is a class of domes, which are of eight kinds, called *Saljámi* (turnip-like), which have great gracefulness in their contour. They are made to swell in the lower part, even beyond the edge-line of their pedestals ; and so have a bold yet good effect upon the superstructures of buildings. There are many other forms of domes in Lucknow ; but none approaches to the softness and gracefulness of the *Saljámi*. Compare the dome of the Golagunj Mokburrah to that of the little Chhutter Munzil, which is of Italian type. How ugly and uninteresting the latter looks ! In fact, in dome-architecture, European art falls considerally below that of the Indo-Saracenic.

The vaulting of the interior architecture is generally not less tasteful than the *Saljami*. The vaults are edged with ornamental borders ; while flowery bands and recesses travel up and meet at the zenith, which is cut in a beautiful square or circular recess. In vaults of larger dimensions, such as of Mokburahs, (Mausoleums), there are also circular skylights, with ornamental surroundings. In the vaults of the Great Emambarah of Asuf-ud-dowlah, there are beautiful balconies, detached and continuous.

The woodwork for architectural pieces, such as verandahs, front walls, balconies, pavilions, eaveboards, columns &c., is executed from many tasteful designs. The employment of these wooden pieces shows, how cheap and yet not inartistic is the arrangement of the domestic architecture of the people. It also proves that in the first colonization of the Gangetic valley, the architecture employed was that of wood, not bricks; as timber was easily procurable from the neighbouring forests. From wooden houses originated the architecture of the more durable materials.

Musjid is a Church, where the Mohamedans assemble, and facing Mecca, pray generally on Friday, that being their Sabbath day. Hence the most important Musjid of a city is called Juma Musjid; Juma meaning Friday. Mecca being almost due west of Lucknow, the back of every Musjid is turned towards the capital of Arabia. An extensive platform fronts the Musjid; there generally, and not in the interior, the faithful are seen, every morning and evening, to stand, bow, and pray in lines. The primary object of the two *minars* (towers), which stand on the two corners, was, that the chief priest could conveniently, from the highest point, call the faithful to prayer, at the five stated times. That practice has now dropped into disuse; and the Mulla reminds his flock of the time from the platform only. The building proper has a verandah corresponding to the inner halls, having three, five, or seven arched openings, of which the middle one is the largest. The sanctum sanctorum is in the recess of the back wall, just opposite the largest middle arch. The domes, generally three in number, top the building; and the parapets go around in quite an ornamental way, and thus heighten the whole effect.

Emámbaráh, or house of the 12 saints, *Bárá-Emám*, is a rectangular-planned building like a Musjid. Its back is turned towards the south, in imitation of the original, at Kerbulá, which, being almost north, faces Mecca south-way. Its plan is divided lengthwise into three larger rooms, and six smaller ones at the sides. In the third inner room, of which the floor is higher than those of the other two, the *taziahs*, or representation of tombs of

Ali and his two sons at Kerbula, and other sacred relics, are placed during the Mohurrum. In the middle room, the graves of the builder and his family lie enclosed within a wooden railing. The outer large room is a verandah or ornamental adjunct, where chandeliers, lustres, &c., are displayed. In Emambarahs generally, the roofs are flat except that of Asuf-ud-dowlah, which has vaults, and that of Hosseinabad, which has a dome. There is, like a Musjid, a large platform in front of Emambarahs, which is covered with conopy during the Mohurrum. An extra part juts out from the main platform, with railing, having a little reservoir for water, the original purpose of which was, that the faithful might wash their hands and feet before engaging in the religious services of the Mohurrum. It is now however a repository of coloured fish. There is also a lengthy masonry tank, which extends from near the platform to the gate opposite the Emambarah proper; while two lines of rooms, on the two sides, complete the court. There is also an outer court, surrounding the inner one, as in Chhota Emambarah in Huzrutganj, or adjoining the side, as in Hossainabad. There are little gardens and detached buildings in the two courtyards.

The Emambarah proper is a well-furnished building, with lustres, coloured lanterns, mirrors, &c. too innumerable to be detailed ; while the Musjid, being the house of God, is never ornamented with such paltry things of human creations ; but the naked though decorative architecture is left alone to tell its effect *

* The Emambarah is a sacred place, erected for the express purpose of commemorating Mohurum ; the founder not unfrequently intends this also as the mausoleum for himself and family. But we generally find Mukburrahs (mausoleums) built in conspicuous situations, for the remains of kings, princes, nobles, and sainted persons. Of the latter, many are visited, at stated periods, by the multitude, with religous veneration, the illiterate attaching considerable importance to the annual pilgrimage to them ; and when,—to secure the influence of the particular saint's spirit, in furthering their vows,—mothers present their children, in numbers beyond all calculation ; and each having something to hope for who visits the shrine, presents offerings of money and sweetmeats, which become the property of the person in charge of the tomb, thus yields him a profitable sinecure, in proportion as the saint is popular amongst the ignorant.

An Emambarah is a square building, generally erected with a cupola top, the dimensions guided by the circumstances of the founder. The floor is matted with the date-leaf-mats, in common use in India, on which is spread a Shutrungi, (cotton carpet) and over this a clear white calico-covering, on which the assembled party are seated, during the rehearsal periods of collecting together to remember their leaders (*mudglis*). A reading desk, or pulpit (*membur*) is placed in a convenient situation for the reader to face Mecca, and his voice to be heard by the whole assembly of people: it is constructed of silver ivory, ebony &c., to correspond with the Taziah, if possible : the steps are covered sometimes with gold cloth or a cloth of black or green, if a Syed's property, being the colour worn by that race for mourning. The shape of a *membur* is a flight of steps with a flat top, without any railing or enclosed place; the reader, in his recitings, occasionally sitting on the steps, or standing as may be most convenient to himself.

On the walls of the Emam-barah, mirrors and looking glasses are fixed in suitable situations to give effect to the brilliant display of light, from the magnificent chandeliers suspended from the cupola and cornices. The nobles and the wealthy are excited with a desire to emulate each other in the splendour of their display on these occasions; all the mirrors, glass lustres, chandeliers, &c., are brought together to this place, from their several stations in the mansion ; and it is due to them to admit the effect to be often imposingly grand, and the blaze of light splendid. I have frequently been reminded in these scenes of the visionary castles conjured to the imagination, whilst reading the "Arabian Night's entertainments."

Mukbarah or mausoleum properly is of a square or octagonal plan, of which the superstructure is surmounted by a grand-looking dome, with four or eight little ones or kiosks around it. There is a large central vault under the dome, having on the four or eight sides verandahs or rooms, some of which are reserved for graves of relatives. In the central hall is the tomb, or rather its copy, of the sovereign, for whom the mausoleum is erected. The tomb is surrounded by wooden screens. The real grave is below the floor, in the *tykhana* and in the ground. Around the vault, in the upper story, are passages or arched rooms, one over the other. There is the usual court, single or double, on the four sides of the Mukbarah. *Durgah*, is another class of tombs, built especially for saints to be burried in.

Baradwari is a pavilion, having literally 12 doors or arched openings. It is a building, having for its purpose, airing, while it shelters the inmates from the sun and rain. To get the greatest amount of breeze in this close and sultry climate, is a matter of prime consideration with the local builders of palaces; and so when they design mansions, and lay out gardens, they add these luxurious adjuncts, in the most elevated, open or central positions. When attached to the body of a building, they are halls; when detached, they are pavilions properly. They are erected on raised plat forms, and are generally of one story. The central hall of a Baradwari is surrounded on four sides by verandahs and corner rooms or bastions. Doors are not often attached to any of its openings, interior or exterior, but the Kaiserbagh Baradwari has glazed doors in the outer openings, and Lal-Baradwari has wooden doors in the inner. Gardens generally surround these pavilions; and a long masonry tank or two extend at right angles.

On each side of the Tazias,—the whole length of the wall—banners are ranged, in great variety of colour and fiabric; some of them are costly & splendid. I have seen many constructed of the richest embroidery, on silk ground, of gold and silver, with massy gold fringes, cords and tassels; the staff is cased with gold or silver, worked into figures of birds and other animals in every variety; the top of which has a crest, in some a spread hand, in others a sort of plume, and not unfrequently a crest resembling a grenade, formed of the prececious metals and set with stones of great value.

On the base of the Tazia, the several articles are placed, conceived likely to have been used by Hossein at Kerbulla; a turban of gold, a silver tissue, a splendid sword and hilt, the handle and hilt set with precious stones, a shield, the Arabian bow and arrow, wax-lights red and green, are also placed in great numbers about its base, in silver or glass candlesticks; and censers of gold and silver, burning incense perpetually during Mohurrum. Many other minor tributes to the Emams are discovered near the Taziah, as choice fruits and garlands of sweet-scented flowers, the offerings of ladies of the family to their relatives' Tauzia,

The remarkable plainness of the mosque, contrasted with the superb decortions of an Emambarah. excited my surprise. (The one is devoted to God, the other to the Emams).

In Asiatic buildings niches and recesses prevail in all convenient situations, and here they are appropriated for the reception of the relics of antiquity and curiosities; such as models of Mecca, the tent of Hossein, the gate of Kerbula, &c., these three are made of pure silver, and rest on tables of the metal. Many curious sabres, of all ages, shield, chain-armour of the ancients, lances &c, arranged with much taste, adorn the interior. *Mrs, Meer Hossein Ali's Observations on the Mosulmans in India.*

f

In fact, these tanks, gardens, pavilions, conduits, fountains and statues of cast iron and plaster, are the indispensable requirements of the palaces of Lucknow. Even the Emambarahs have these tanks and gardens.

The *Verandah* (Persian várámdah-transept the part of a room or building going beyond its main plan of body) is a colonnade or arcade, which, attached to the main blocks, has the effect of subduing and toning down the glary and heaty effect on the interior in summer, and keeps a little even temperature within in all the seasons. The verandah also covers the nakedness of single-lined rooms, to which they serve as ornamental additions, affording convenience to the inmates. In the court of a house, whether Mardana or Zenana, these *venandahs* serve as covered passages to the rooms around.

Tykhana is an under-ground room, where, during summer-days, the inmates retire to avoid the *loo* and the heat. It is generally built under the floor of the house. Its plan differs with the requirement or taste of the house-holder; but it generally coincides with that above it. The sketch-plan and section of the Tykhana of the Residency, Baillie Guard, are given to illustrate its arrangement.

The *Hammam* is the bathroom, planned according to oriental purpose and taste. Its requirements are that there should be reservoirs for waters of different temperature. It is a vaulted building with central and side-rooms. A well is attached to a corner, from which water is lifted up on the roof and is distributed by pipes to the different reservoirs, under one of which is a fire-place for heating the water above it. There are also many fountains, so adjusted as to be of different temperature, that play on the almost nude bathers from ornamental situations. A plan and interior view of a bath-room, attached to the old Residency, latterly Banquetting Hall and since the mutiny, the Hospital, in Ballie Guard, are given for better elucidation.

Darwázá or gate is a prominent feature of a Lucknow building. It has generally three arched openings, of which the middle is large enough to allow elephants with howdahs to pass in or out, as those of Hosseinabad, and Chota Emambarah. On the two sides of some gates, which have but one opening, there are bastions, that, at the top, are crowned with towers, as those of the Kaiserbagh, Saadut Ali Khan's tomb, Malka Jamani's Emambarah. The portions between the openings are composed of ornamented pilasters and niches ; sometimes female statues, made of plaster, are added, interior or exterior, to hold candle-sticks or lanterns. The contour of the arch-line is beautifully broken and relieved by being divided into five, and by ornamental plaster work, added to the upper part. Sometimes a balcony juts out from above the arch, with two more at the sides, over which the bigger arch spreads. The parapets of some gates run gable-like in the middle, showing bad taste and false adaptation of foreign ornaments, as that of Malka Jamani's Emambarah in Golagunge. The gates have generally flat roofs ; but the Luckhi-Darwaza of Kaiserbagh is crowned with cupolas, quadruple staircase arched in the form of a dome ; and the Roumi Darwaza is semi-vaulted and looks quite grand.

Bagh, or garden, is a harmonious distribution of trees and plants, shrubs and creepers, pavilions and kiosks, tanks and conduits, fountains and statues, over an extensive area, enclosed by high, if for Zenana, or low walls, if for Mardana purposes. They are so arranged, as to give the best prospective view, the freest ventilation and the coolest of shade in the bushes and vistahs to those, who are seated or might be promenading *

Howz (reservoir) is made after designs by no means of bad taste. It is embedded in the floor of a bathroom, or in the middle of a platform, that fronts a Musjid or Emambarah, in the transparent water of which coloured fish play most beautifully. There is another kind of masonry-tank, called *Nahar ;* it is of great length, that traverses a garden, square or courtyard, in the middle of which is sometimes a pretty little bridge. *Talao* are properly tanks of larger dimensions, that is dug into earth, and covered with brickwork for flights of steps, kiosks, Zenana bathing place, that is screened from public gaze by ornamental walls ; as in Hosseinabad, and Dursunnaggur, near Aujodhya. *Baoli* is a well of ornamental construction, surrounded by pillared or arched verandah, in a square or octagonal size, of one or more stories, to the water of which a flight of step goes down from one side, as in that of the Great Emambarah, east of its inner courtyard.

---

* King's garden. Such a place ! the only residence I have covetted in India. Don't you remember here in the 'Arabian Nights,' Zebeide lets her garden of delights, amidst the Caliph's palace of pictures. I am sure this was the garden of delights.' There are four small palaces in it, litted up in the eastern way, with velvet, gold, and marble, with arabesque ceilings, orange trees, and roses in all directions, with quantities of wild parroquets of bright colours glancing about. And in one place there was an immense bathroom of white marble, the arches intersecting each other in all directions, and the marble inlaid with cornelion and bloodstone ; and in every corner of the palace there were little fountains ; even during the hot winds, they say, it is cool from the quantity of water playing. Hon'ble Miss Eden's *Up the country*, 1837.

Pool (Bridge) is a series of arches over streams or rivers, over which roadway passes. The arches, employed in bridge or culvert-construction, in purely local architecture, seem to be borrowed from the Gothic pattern, though they are not really so. The difference between the Gothic and Indo-Saracenic arches of similar construction consists in their breadth, the ratio between the height and breadth being greater in the European than in the Asiatic ; that is to say, generally speaking, the local arches are broader than the foreign, and so look bolder and more elegant.

The roadway over native bridges is not often even ; it slowly rises in the middle from one side, and then goes down to its normal level on the other. This upheaving, which is quite uncomfortable, will be found in the Stone Bridge, built by Asuf-ud-dowlah in about 1780. But in the Jownpore and Tikaitganj bridges, this uneveness does not occur. On the bridges, on both sides of the roadway, there used to be shops and little houses.

The local bridges were built of different materials, of stones, bricks, iron, and boats. The Stone bridge of Asuf-ud-dowlah, however, is called so, not because it is thoroughly built of stone, but because it had stone-coping all over its body. The Iron Bridge, which was indented from England by Sadut Ali Khan, was built by Mohamed Ali Shah in 1840. Nasir-ud-din wanted to build it near Chhutter Munzil ; but his premature death left his plans unexecuted ; and the bridge was finally built where

---

One portion, however, struck me as being singularly picturesque. It was a lake, a small artificial lake, that occupied about the whole of a garden ; and in the centre of it, entirely unconnected with the shores or any side, rose a neat pavilion brilliantly painted externally, but of a picturesque form, with its pointed minarets and miniature domes. The water in the lake was perfectly clear and transparent, and numbers of large gold and silver fish darted about in it with wonderful rapidity. The pavilion, in the centre of this sheet of water, was reached by a boat, which was moored opposite the side of the palace, whence we had issued. It was entirely the most elegant structure in Lucknow. It contained but two appartments of moderate size, both luxuriously fitted up with divans running round the walls In the centre of the larger appartment, on a table, stood a perfect model of the entire palace, wrought with all that elaborate minuteness of details and perfection of colouring, so characteristics of the Indian artists. The pavilion, in which we stood, was represented in this piece of covering, by a miniature model, not larger than a walnut, and yet containing every spire, every little external ornament, and even the two rooms. Looking out upon the water, from the little island-palace, was enough to make you fancy, you had got into fairy land. The brilliant fish playing about incessantly, the richly decorated boat, the flowers that bordered the lake, lost in bushes, which almost hid the surrounding buildings, were features so novel and captivating, that I thought, were I the king, I should almost desert the palace for the pavilion. *The Private Life of an Eastern King* About 1830.

Zenana-garden. The house, dedicated to the ladies, was a good one, situated in a large garden, surrounded by a high stone wall. The orthodox height for the four walls of a Zenana-garden is, that no man, standing on an elephant, can see them. The building is surrounded with fine trees, and a fountain played before it, in which gold and silver fish were swiming, Near it was an avenue, in which was a swing, the invariable accompaniment of a Zenana garden. The season in which the ladies more particularly delight to swing in the open air, is during the rains. Mr. Fane Park's *Wanderings of a Pilgrim in search of the Picturesque*, 1830.

it now stands, being first of its kind that was constructed in India. There was a boat-bridge here, near where the modern *Pucca* (brick) Bridge now is, just in direct line with the road from Neil's gate. It was all boarded with thick planks, over which a layer of earth was spread, that travellers and animals could go conveniently. The *Pucca Pool* was built of bricks in 1864 by Bruce ; but it has no pretentions either as ornamental work or as an engineering achievement. In fact, while admitting that the art of bridging was not perfected in India, and though less waterway was allowed in local than in European building, yet from what little was done, we might safely conclude that in this branch of architecture, India will not yield to the European either in point of stability or convenience. The story of Shahjehan's intention of building another Taj on the other side of the river, connecting this with the other by a beautiful Saracenic bridge over Jumna shows that the art was once well understood here. The Jounpore bridge, built many centuries ago, is still of service to the inhabitants, though it was very seldom repaired and was many times drowned in flood. The bridge at Rai Bareli, over the Sai, built by Ilmas Ali Khan about 100 years ago, is also a very pretty specimen of Mohamedan bridge-construction. It is about 250 feet in length with a clear pathway of 39 feet. There are two ornamental pillars on each side, which enhance the beauty of the whole.

The construction of *Killah* (fort) was long an indespensable art with the inhabitants of Oudh. Ram had his far-famed *Kote* at Aujodhya ;—Mandhata had one at Manua, Rajah Nal had another at Nagraon ; and many others can be pointed, that belong to the ancient Aryan period. The Bhars and other low caste dynasties were not without their bastioned city-walls. The fort of Rajah Manikchand was a grand one, being built on an ancient mound, about 200 feet in height ; the gate was protected by additional bastions. His brother, Jey Chand of Kanouge had another on an equally high mound at Kurrah. Dalmow also had a formidable high fort, of which the gate with the great bastion still remains.

The Mahomedans also were not behind hand at fort building. The Killahs of Rai Bareli, and Jounpore, were celebrated in their days. They were of a system of 52 forts built by Sultan Ibrahim Shirki of Jounpore. The Shaikhs of Lucknow built the Mutchibhawan fort ; Sufder Jung constructed the Jelalabad. After his defeat at Buxar, Shujah-ud-dowlah too erected the Calcutta Khurd at Fyzabad. Talukdars too had each their citadels, from which they used to set at defiance the commands of Government officials. At the time of the mutiny, the rebels strongly fortified all available positions; and a British General was severely thrashed while attacking a mud fort on the Sultanpore road. The fortifications of Lucknow were formidable to the extreme. Three lines of defence were constructed with enormous labour; and the canal ramparts looked like high railway-embankments. The second line was run from Begum Kothi *via* Chounera Stables to the Khurshed Munzil; and the third was that of Kaiserbagh, which together with the Emambarah was a citadel in fact. The streets were also dug and turned into ditches, and *moorchas* (batteries) and *burjes* (bastions) were erected at every turn; while the parapet walls were all loop-holed for musketry.

The formation of forts in ancient times consisted of deep ditches, high walls and higher square towers; height was then considered synonimous with defence. Latterly instead of towers, bastions were introduced, which bulged out from the walls in a semicircular form. The Vauban's system and the triangular formation with glacis and walls, not higher than the incline was not much understood in India, still less in Oudh. Notwithstanding, the native forts several times successfully repulsed the attacking army of the British, as at Shahnujuf, Moosabagh and other places.

Serais or Dharmshalas are another class of buildings; they are constructed along high roads in towns for the staying and convenience of travellers, who walk from long distances. They are quadrangular in form, consisting of one gate with lines of rooms and verandahs on all sides. In the middle of the courtyard is a pucca well, a little Musjid for the Mohamedans to pray and a temple for the Hindus to worship. In the four corners are four bastions; while the parapet walls are loop-holed all around to fire securely on occasion of any attempts of Dacoits. The establishment consists of Bhatiaras and Bhatiarins, who prepare bread and see the convenience of the Mohamedans, a Chowkidar to watch, and a Bunia or two to sell grains and other edibles. These serais, which are indispensable to native travellers, are however not encouraged or built under the British rule; and it is strange to note, that while staging (Dak) bungalows are raised on roads, and refreshment rooms are opened at Railway stations, the native passengers and travellers generally feel great difficulty in not finding resting place in great Railway centres, and serais by the side of the high roads, which Government are constructing from time to time.

The construction of villages *(Gunge)* and towns is also a subject worth investigating. They were constructed on the same principle, as that of the serais; only here the main road crosses, and consequently the town has two gates with two other smaller ones at the two sides, that connect a second street, which crosses the main one. Lanes cross each other; and the bazaar shops are arranged in two lines of rooms with verandahs on the main road; and the private houses are at the back. On all four sides are the loop-holed walls, with four bastions at the four corners. Near the Gunj is sometimes a temple (a Musjid) with masonry tank. On this principle, Dursungunge was built by Rajah Durshun Singh, father of Maharajah Man Singh, and Mohanlalgunge, by the late Rajah of Sirsendi.

The construction of masonry tank (Talao) is also to be noted. In fact towns had no importance, where was no large tank. These tanks, quadrangular or hexagonal, are covered with flights of steps, of which one side is a covered one for ladies, to bathe, second for men, a third, merely incline for cattle to drink water; and the fourth merely ornamental. Kiosks and little temples are added here and there for adorning or adoring purposes; while a flower and fruit garden extends around, and enhances the beauty of the whole construction. On this principle the Reoti Ram ká Talao at Rai Bareli, Bukshi Talao and Hosienabad Talaos in Lucknow were built and are well-known.

The digging of canals for diverting the course of rivers, for ditches to fortification walls or for carrying water for irrigating fields, was a branch of engineering, not unknown to the native architects of old. Ali Murdan was a famous Engineer in Shah Jehan's time, who constructed the Jumna and Ganges canals. Nasir-ud-din Hyder, following the same incentive, designed a canal from the Ganges to Goomtee, surrounding the city of Lucknow for the threefold purposes of defence, irrigation and sewage. But the design was not carried into its fullest extent; for there was not sufficient will and supervision to complete it. Two other canals were cut in the mediœval times by one of the Rajahs in the Khyrigurh district, called Katni Nullahs.

CHAPTER VI.—THE CHIEF BUILDINGS OF LUCKNOW

May be classified into three sections; (1) palaces, (2) tombs and mosques, and (3) gardens.

SECTION I.—*Palaces.*

The principal palaces at Lucknow are the *Punch Mahalah* in Mutchibhawan Fort, *Dowlutkhana* of Asuf-ud-dowlah in Hosseinabad, *Farhat Buksh* of Saadut Ali Khan, *Chhutter Munzil* of Nasir-ud-din, *Moti Mahal* of Gazi-ud-din, and *Kaisarbagh* of Wajid Ali Shah.

Punch Mahal had five courtyards, from which the name is derived. It was built by the old Shaikhs of Lucknow, from whom Saadut rented it on Rs. 535. It was enclosed with fortifications all around, with bastions at short distances, of which a portion together with the old *Mutchibhawan* Kothi still exists on the North-East side. A plan of the site is given from Tieffenthaler's Travels, published about 100 years ago. On the west side of it are built the great Emambarah and Musjid with courtyard of Asuf-ud-dowlah.

Mutchibhawan.—The palace, which faces the Goomtee, comprises six principal courts or quadrangles surrounded by pavilion-like buildings. In first of these are two lofty gateways. On the outer, there is a handsome chamber, called the *Noubut-khana,* or music-room, forming an orchestra upon a splendid scale. The second court, encompassed by state apartments, is laid out as a garden, having a well or *bouli,* (in the centre,) round which are pavilions, opening to the water, and intended to afford a cool retreat during the hot-weather; the air is refreshed by the constant dripping of the fountains; and the piazzas and arcaded chambers beyond, within the influence of its luxurious atmosphere, are well calculated for sleeping chambers in the sultry nights, so constantly occurring throughout the periods of hot winds. Parallel to the second court, and at the eastward of it, stands a splendid edifice, raised upon an arched terrace, entirely of stone. This fabric, called *Sungee-Dalan,* contains a grand hall, surrounded with a double arcade, crowned with a capital at each angle, and one over the principal point, all of copper doubly gilt. At the extremities of the terrace, there are wings, and flower gardens stretch along each front, divided into parterres by walks and fountains. A corridor extends round this court, planted with vines, and out of these entrances, one with a covered passage is appropriated to the ladies. These gateways are decked with gilded domes; and the mosque, Zenana, and other buildings attached to the palace, give to the whole edifice the air of a city raised by some enchanter....And the palaces of the Hyderbagh, Hosseinbagh, and Seesh Mahal have nearly equal claims to admiration.—*Mrs. Roberts*, 1839

Dowlutkhana was the palace of Asuf-ud-dowlah, who built it for his residence, when he transferred his seat of government from Fyzabad to here. It had the usual courtyards and accompaniments of a royal palace, *Shish Mahal* or glass-house was one of its chief ornamental feature. The celebrated *Cock-Match* picture of Zoffanie long adorned one of its halls, as late as 1830. The throne Baradwari was near it, on the other side of Hosseinabad Tank.

Farhat Buksh was originally the residence of Claude Martin, who built it. Nawab Asuf-ud-dowlah, who took a great fancy to it, bought it from the General at, it is said, 50 lakhs. Saadut Ali Khan, who fixed it as his residence, made great additions, and built the *Lal Baradwari*, in front, with a *Nahar* (Masonry-tank) between them. The *Painbagh* was a very beautiful garden just opposite to the throne-hall.

Furhat Buksh.—The house is built on the bank of the river Goomtee, and boats passed under the room, in which we dined. He (General Martin) has underground aparments, even with the edge of the river, the most comfortable in the world in the hot weather, and most elegantly decorated. As the water rises, he ascends; the lower story is always filled by the river in the rains, and the second generally; when the river subsides, they are repaired and decorated. The two rooms, containing the company consisting of somewhat more than 40 ladies and gentlemen, were covered with glasses, pictures, prints, in short you could see no walls three feet from the floor. He had a pair of glasses ten feet in length and proportionately wide, and estimated his glasses and lustres only, in the said rooms, at Rs. 40,000 or 4,500£. It would require a week at least to examine the contents of his house. *Sir John Shore.*

This curious edifice is constructed entirely of stone, except the doors and window frames. The ceilings of the different apartments are formed of elliptic arches; and the floor made of stucco. The basement story comprises two caves or recesses, within the bank of the river and level with its surface, when at its lowest degrees. In these caves, he generally lived in the hot season, and continued in them until the commencement of the rainy season, when the increase of the river obliged him to remove. He then ascended another story, to apartments fitted up in the manner of a grotto; and when the further rise of the river brought its surface on a level with these, he proceeded up to the third story, or ground floor, which overlooked the river at its greatest height. On the next story above that a handsome saloon, raised on arcades projecting over the river, formed his habitation in the spring and winter seasons. By this ingenious contrivance, he preserved a moderate and equal temperature in his house at all seasons. On the attic story he had a museum well supplied with various curiosities; and over the whole he erected an observatory, which he furnished with the best astronomical instruments." *Higginbotham.*

Moti Mahal is a series of palaces, of which the courtyards are three, as will be seen from the plan. In front of the outer gate were two big towers, that were demolished after the mutiny. The gate had also two pillars on the top, which added greatly to its picturesque effect. In the outer courtyard the celebrated beast-fights of Lucknow were held; wooden or bamboo frames were erected and stages prepared all around; and the fighting animals were let in from trapdoors. Entering the inner gate on the west side, you would find a courtyard, which had *Tykhanas* and canals on the four sides; while pavilions and the central Baradwari stood on the three middle positions. In the middle was a *Nahar* or Masonry-tank; it extended from the gate to near the footsteps of the Baradwari which was very beautiful. The eastern pavilion was known as *Darsanbilash,* which means ecstacy from sight. In the other courtyard is the *Chouburji Khothi,* a quaint Bungalow-looking building. On the east side of this courtyard extended the royal seraglio,—where some of the zenana architectural pieces are said to be so beautiful, as not to be imitable. A ground-plan, that is attached, explains the general arrangement of the palace. The house of *Moti Mahal,* Khas and favourite Begum of the king, was in the North-east corner; whence the name is applied to the whole range of palaces.

Chhutter Munzil is a vast assemblage of palaces from near Baillie Guard to Khas bazaar and the Tiger Gate. This architectural group, of which the courtyards and side-buildings are destroyed, consisted of the *Sikchawali* Baradwari, where is now the local museum, the Clock Tower or *Latkan Darwaza* gate with *Jelokhana* just in front of Baillie Guard, the *Tehri* kothi, *General Sahib ki Kothie*, Farhat Buksh, Lal Baradwari, and the two Chutter Munzils proper. The greater Chhutter Munzil is a seven storied building, of which two storied Tykhanas are underground, and five stories above. The topmost is surmounted by a gilt umbrella-shaded dome,—whence is the name,—Chhutter Munzil literally meaning Umbrella-palace. The lesser Chhutter Munzil has a two storied Emambarah, surmounted by a dome with a big *Chattah*. On its two sides are two buildings—respectvely called Darshanbilas and Choulukhi or Chowguddiwali Kothie.

On the east side was the royal Saraglio—with *Bara-imam* and *Shish Mahal*. Between the two Chutter Munzils was a very pretty garden with a beautiful tank and an island, covered with a little pavilion,—which Hon'ble Miss Eden describes thus :—

"Such a place! The only residence I have coveted in India. Don't you remember here in the 'Arabian Nights' Zobeide bets her 'Garden of Delights' amidst the Caliph's palace of pictures! I am sure this was the garden of delights.

There are four small palaces in it, fitted up in the eastern way, with velvet and gold and marble, with arabesque ceilings, orange trees and roses in all direction, with quantities of wild paroquets of bright colours glancing about. And in one palace there was an immense bathroom of white marble, the arches intersecting each other in all directions, and the marble inlaid with cornelian and blood-stone; and in every corner of the palace there were little fountains; even during the hot winds they say, it is cool from the quantity of water playing; and in the Verandah, there were fifty trays of fruits and flowers laid out for us......It was really a very pretty sight." *Eden.*

Chhatter Munzil " has six principal courts. A large portal with iron gates, leads to the Futteh Mohullah, in which is the spacious hall, *Nowbutkhana*, where a military band usually performs every morning and evening. From this first court we entered the *Bowlee*, an oblongap rallelogram, ornamented with flower-beds, in the centre of which is a large marble basin, where little boats were plying for the amusement of the ladies, and many beautiful fountains jetted the cool waters into the air. The Furhat Buksh lies towards the river; it consists of open arcades and many apartments, which may be closed with the most costly curtains; and in the hot season are cooled by purfumed matted reeds, which the attendants maintain in a constant state of moisture. Opposite to the Furhat Buksh, flights of marble steps lead to the greatthrone-hall,—a splendid saloon, supported by pillars, where stands the golden throne, inlaid with diamonds, pearls and rubies.

Towards the east, parallel with the Bowlee, is the *Sungi Dalan*; it is built of hewn stone, and rises from a vaulted terrace. It is surrounded with double arcades, behind which are the apartments of the inmates. The four corners and the principal facade are crowned with cupolas, whose richly silver-roofs glistened splendidly. The inner space is covered with a most beautiful bed of flowers, interspersed with fountains and fine shady avenues and in the middle rises a small mosque with gilded minarets and pavilions for the ladies. There are four distinct entrances to the apartments; a covered one on the north side is for the ladies; one to the south for the king, and two portals on the east and west for strangers. The rooms are crowded with silk divans, works of arts, paintings and engravings. In almost every room there is a portrait of Nasir-ud-din Hyder, who was sometimes taken in Indian and sometimes in the European dress.

Adjoining this edifice on the east, is the Zenana, which contains a mass of irregular buildings, without external windows; they are the palaces, termed *Shish Mahal, Khurd Mahal,* and *Rang Mahal*, each of which is environed with small flower-gardens and fountains. Towards the north lies another garden, hemmed in by buildings, which contains the public offices; on the opposite side of the road, on the bank of the river, there are three bastions with cupolas covered with roofs richly gilt. In the centre is an octagonal palace, in which the king's mother resides. Von Orlich's *Travels in India* 1843.

Kaisarbagh (King's garden) is a range of palaces, of which the Zenana portion is a very large parallelogram. On the East side are the *Choulakhi* and *Huzrutbagh* with two Baradwaries, *Chandiwali* (silver) and *Naginawali*, the latter of which has been removed to *Baranasibagh*, otherwise called the Wingfield Park. Beyond the Huzratbagh extended another large courtyard, which is known as *Jelokhana*, where royal processions and tamashas used to form. Beyond still was the quarter of Nawab Ali Naki Khan, prime minister to the king. On the north side of the Kaisarbagh proper, are the two tombs of Saadut Ali and his wife, the *Chinabazar* and *Rahes Munzil*, which have been demolished lately, along with a wing of the main building to make room for the *Canning College*, lately built on the ground thus cleared. On the west side are Maharajah Balkishen's palace, and *Kaisarpasand*, built by Roushan-ud-dowlah, the prince of Nasir-ud-din Hyder, from whose name the building is popularly known. The Kaiserbagh proper has *Lunka*, a picturesque-looking double pavilion on the south, the stone Baradwari in the centre, and two tanks, at right angle to each other, with beautiful marble kiosks in the north; while an extensive garden spread out on all sides. The range of buildings on the four sides is composed of two storied handsome rooms and halls with verandahs of different designs to match and heighten their inner beauty, the ceilngs of which were covered with cloths, painted with different fairy scenes. The two handsome gates on the east and west sides are called *Luckhi Darwaza*, because they cost *lakh* of Rupees each. In the same way the *Chouluckhi* or four Lakh's palace was so called, because it cost the king 4 lakhs to buy it from the royal barber, who built it. It was the head-quarters of the rebel queen.

In the garden are two buildings, one the stone Baradwari, and the other called *Lunka*. The Lunka has a raised platform and a beautiful kiosk in the middle; on the two sides of which are two small Baradwaries. The roofs of the verandah of these Baradwaries slope innerwards, while that of the central hall is lower than that of the verandahs,—an arrangement quite at variance with the common practice of other buildings, where the verandah-roofs gable lower than that of the central room. Notwithstanding this peculiarity, the *Lunka* is a beautiful edifice, of which the slender pillars enhance the whole effect. Under the rooms are pretty *tykhanas*. There were also two wings of double pillars but with no roof; in the corners were octagonal bastions, on which were two high bamboo staffs for the royal pegions to rest after their daily exercise of flight.

There were three marble kiosks on the north side; two on the tank, and the larger one at the head of the little bridge, where the king, "Soubeh Oudh ká Kanhaiá" used to rest after dalliance with his bathing Begums. There are also four large wells in the four corners, which had pillared kiosks to cover them. Besides there were two conical-shaped pavilions on the two sides of the central stone Baradwri. In fact the pavilions and kiosks were located at every available quarters to enhance the beauty of the whole group of palaces. The two gates, called *Luckhi Darwaza*, are grand; their plan is round in the centre with two verandahs on the sides; and two or three arched rooms are in the two other sides; while plaster-statues stood one upon another, in order to hold candle-sticks for lighting purposes. There were four gilded cupolas on the four corners; and the grand middle portion domed into a quadruple stair-case, crowned by a kiosk, long since distroyed. The two inner balconies on the sides of the three-arched gate prettily project out from oval doors, and have domes crowned by the royal insignia of Oudh, namely, the crown held by two fairies. The cornices have elephant and other animal supports, which look not less elegant by their subordinate positions.

Kaiserbágh:—Imagine court as large as the Temple gardens, surrounded with range of places, or at least of buildings well stuccoed and gilded, with fresco-paintings here and there on the blind windows, and with green jalousies and venetian blinds closing the apertures, which pierce the walls in double rows.—In the body of the court are statues, lines of lamp-posts fountains, orange-groves, acqueducts and kiosks with burnished domes of metal.—The buildings, which surround the court, are irregular in form: for here and there the lines of the quadrangle are broken by columned fronts and lofty porticoes before the mansions of the household, which are resplendant with richly gilt-roofs and domes. Here and there the invaders have forced their way into the long corridors. From the broken portals issue soldiers laden with loot or plunder. Shawls, rich tapestry, gold and silver brocade, caskets of jewels, arms, splendid dresses. Court after court the (plundering) scenes still the same. These courts open one to the other by lofty gateways, ornamented with the double fish of the royal family of Oudh, or by arched passages, in which lie the dead sepoys, their clothes smouldering on their flesh.

The court we have now reached was exceedingly narrow, a *cul de soe;* one side was occupied by open sheds, in which were broughams, carriages and harnesses and native palkies with velvet hangings richly gilt, and a lot of trumpery, such as might be seen in a coach-maker's shed, wheels, axles and such like. The other side was formed by a line of store houses with rooms above them, and a series of doors, leading out on the Court, strongly barricaded. Just where we turned into the Court, there was a stone topped well somewhat in the shade.

If the Tuileries, the Louvre, Versailles, Scutari, the Winter-palace, were all to be blended together with hovels worthy of Gallipoli, and an interior garden worthy of Kew, they would represent the size, at all events, of the palaces of the Kaiserbágh and the gardens inside. The work is evidently Italian, but most hedious, ludicrous, and preposterous are the Hindu (?) statues in plaster imitation of the Italian subjects, which here and there deck the pedestals in the gardens. There are a very really grand marble statue, a charming Venus and a dove, a very fine nymph with hounds, and a severe Appollo.—*Russell's Diary. 1858.*

Seen from a distance, the Kaiserbágh "looked itself again, truly regal and beautiful, a worthy palace for so fair a city; the plastered buildings became marble halls and gaudy tinsel showed in the dim distance like gold; while a hundred gilded domes beneath glanced and glittered in the sun, and the tapering minarets and massive mosques again established their claim to be considered as the work of spirit-hands; and the beauty of the whole was so dazzling, that one felt at a loss how to give expression to those feelings of admiration and delight, which were kindled at the sight.

So should Lucknow be viewed by those, who would form an idea of its extreme beauty; not to be dissected nor criticised bit by bit; for it will not bear it; not as a miniature, but as a large picture, or rather as a piece of exquisite tapestry. There is then a gayness of colouring about them, and they have such ever-changing prismatic tints like shot silk, as they lie beneath the blue unclowded eastern sky, basking in the sunlight, ever flashing and sparkling like champaign, or continually dyeing the warm sunny rays, as they receive them, many lustrous hews, and then like a polished mirror, reflecting them back more resplendant than before. *Megendie's "Up among the Pandies."*

The principal buildings in the Baillie-guard were the Residency, the Banqueting Hall, the Begum kothie, Dr. Fairer's, and Mr. Gubbin's houses. The Banqueting Hall was the old Residency, built by Saádat Alí Khan for Colonel Baillie; it was a two-storied building, with verandahs on the four sides. It was used as a hospital during the mutiny. On the east is a deep masonry-tank; a little beyond were the out-houses below which the ground level being low, another story, as a *Tykhana* to the main building was constructed. Its square pillars are coverd with beautiful plaster work. In a corner is a small pretty bathroom. Close by is another building, where was the Treasury. The gate is near it; and the guard-rooms were in a wing on the left side; whence is the far-famed name of *Baillie-guard.* Gazee-ud-din Hyder built another building for the same Resident. It is now known as the *Residency.* It was also a two-storied building, having two verandahs on the two sides. There were two towers on the two other sides, of which a broken one still remains. On the south side the building is connected by an incline, to a *Tykana*, a square building, of which one story is up and one below the ground. There is a central hall with verandahs all around. In this building, the women of the 32nd Regiment were located during the terrible siege the garrison was subjected to. In a corner room of the Residency, Sir Henry Lawrence was mortally wounded by a cannon ball from the Padshahbágh *Moorchah* (battery) of the enemy.

These buildings were thus described by a traveller in Amjad Ali Shah's reign:—

Residency :—This villa is a strong building, two stories high with verandahs attached to both sides. The lower apartments open into small but very elegant fruit and flower garden, on the side of which there is a walled basin for swimming : the usual bathing apartments are at the four corners of the house, adjoining the bed-chambers. This charming residence, like most of the houses occupied by the English in this city, was built by Europeans, who were in the service of the Viziers and kings of Oudh, whose aide-de-camps they were : the king keeps them in repair and has left them to the English free of expense.

In the immediate vicinity of this house, separated from it only by a wall and. garden, is the palace of the British ambassador at this court. It is erected on a small eminence, and consists of two large handsome buildings, which are opposite to each other, and have a colonnade in front. In one of them, which contains three stores, the apartments under ground (Tykhana) are for the hot season : all the apartments are spacious and handsome, and are fitted up in the most costly and tasteful manner.

From the platform of this house there is a magnificent view of the whole city, which appears like a panorama, and which with its many minarets, gilded cupolas palaces, sepulchral monuments, and gardens, traversed by the navigable Goomtee, has a very grand effect.

In the second edifice are the apartments, spacious saloons, furnished with costly chandeliers, mirrors, and silk divans. It is the custom of the ambassador to return the invitation to breakfasts and dinners, which he has received ; the king therefore is present at these feasts two or three times in a year, with his sons and the officers of his household, amounting to more than twenty persons ; the king however always brings his cook with him, and takes nothing but tea. As soon as, dancing begins, His Majesty invariably retires. Von Orlich's *Travels in India* 1843.

The other buildings are not important from an architectural point of view, though historically they are. In Fayrer's house, Sir H. Lawrence died ; and here Outram, Havelock and other chiefs met after their heroic relief or rather re-inforcement of the closely beseized garrison. Gubbin's bastion was a chief post of the garrison, where the Financial Commissioner maintained his position with great tenacity.

The Begum Kothie, in Huzrutgunj, is a range of buildings, lining the road. The central building, which was enclosed by innumerable courts is a three-storied building. The central hall is large and commodious ; and its view from a distance looks pictursque.

Malka Jahán is also a vast assemblage of edifices, built by Agá Meer, prime minister of Gazee-ud-din Hyder. It is composed of many courts, of which the principal one is the Emambarah. It is a grand hall, three rooms deep; and on the two sides are smaller rooms. The mansion of the Zenána is opposite to the Emambarah, and has a court of rooms and halls on four sides, and a wooden pavilion on a raised platform in the centre. High walls surround the roof all around. The *Mahal Serai* is a separate court on the east side of the Emámbarah. There are two other courts on the west side, with gates and all the appendages of a royal palace. There are also two large halls on the second story, one on the Emambarah and the other just in front on the largest room of the Zanána, which look pictursque from distance.

Section 2.—*Tombs and Mosques.*

There are two beautiful noted mosques in Lucknow, the Juma Musjid of Hosseinabád and the Musjid of Asuf-ud-dowlah, attached to the Emambarah in the Muchibhawan fort. Both of them have three domes; and their minarets are so high, that they can be seen from miles around. The fort Musjid has been appropriated for the requirements of a military garrison, being used as a magazine. The Hosseinabad or rather Muftigunge Musjid is used for Friday prayers of the faithful; and here the Eedgah festival is held with all the show of a *Mela* (fair). There is another Musjid on the Lachman-tilah, built by Aurangzebe of Delhi about 300 years ago.

The principal Emambaras of Lucknow are the great Emambarah in the fort, another in the Hosseinabád, and a third in Huzrutgunge.

The great Emambarah was built by Asuf-ud-dowlah in about 1780, during the time of a severe famine, in order to open works for the relief of his suffering subjects. For this purpose a very hollow piece of ground was filled up, and foundations were run deep. The walls were repeatedly pulled down and rebuilt in order to prolong completion of the work and to give ample relief to all. During the night time, the work was pushed on; so that the veiled women of the Zenána of the higher and middle classes, ashamed to come out during the day, might get relief of few silver pieces under the cover of darkness.

This chaste building was the result of a competitive design, which was required to be thoroughly original, not copy of any structures, and which was to surpass in beauty and magnificence anything of the kind ever constructed. Moheb-ullah and Kefait-ullah, father and son, were the name of the successful architects; and the edifice they conceived has filled the hearts of the sight-seers from distant countries with delight and admiration.

The Emambarah in extreme measurements is 303′ long, 160′ wide, and 63′ high; it is sub-divided into a central and six side rooms, and a verandah and a corresponding sanctuary on a raised level. The dimension of the central room is 163′ long, 53′ broad, and 49½′ high, and the intrados, or inner line of arches, is 68′. The thickness of the walls all around is 16 feet. The vaults on the above are of ornamental designs relieved by balconies, communicated with the roofs, stair-cases and outer bastions by dark and tortuous passages. The hall is the largest in the world, where no wood-work has been used. The chaste proportion of the several parts, the richness and variety of details, and the general good taste pervading the whole edifice, denote conception of a superior kind. It is a redeeming feature of the otherwise weak reign of Asuf-ud dowlah.

The Emambarah has a court, on the east side of which is a *bowlee* or a large octagonal well, approached to its water by a long flight of steps, and surrounded by arched rooms of five stories. The west side of the court is occupied by the Musjid, and the front by a three-storied gate. There is another courtyard and gate on the outside, beyond which, right and left, is the street, flanked by rooms and a gate in front, and two other gates on the east and west. The west gate is the grand looking *Roumi Darwáza*, a semi-circular vault of great height, having three small openings. It is faced on both sides with some imitation of leaves which rise one above the other from the base, and radiate above the spring line forming a pointed arch. Between the leaves is a series of ornamental balusters projecting, which were said to have been intended for fountains. A tower crowns the archway. The *Roumi Darwáza* is so called, not because it was a copy of one at Constantinople, but because it is in the direction of the Turkish capital, called Roum by the natives of India, in the same way as other cities have gates.

The Hosseinabád Emambarah was built by Mohamed Ali Shah, the third king of Oudh. The outer courtyard is of a parallelogram form, which has two gates on the east and west. The eastern gate is grand and extremely ornate, having three arches; it is corresponding just in front of the great *Roumi* gate. From the outer gate, you enter another on the left side, which has a *jowab*—corresponding one in front. Within the inner gate is the courtyard of the Emambarah proper, where you will see three small buildings, of which one is a mosque, and the second a small copy of the far-famed Taj of Agra. In the middle is a lengthy masonry tank with a miniature iron bridge in the centre, and a junk with a wooden horse on it.

Beyond these and occupying the most prominent view, stands the Emambarah, a rectangular building, divided lengthwise into three rooms with smaller compartments in the sides, after the manner of the great Emambarah of Asuf-ud-doulah. The partition-walls are arched and profusely ornamented in arabesque. In the centre are the graves of the king and his mother.

This building, which is surmounted by a graceful gilded dome, stands on an elevated platform, part of which projects frontway. It is, during the Mohurrum, covered with cuttings of tapestry, borne on poles encased with ornamental silver plates.

On the north-east of the outer compound lies a large octagonal tank, covered with flights of steps, and having a *Zenána* ghat on one side. On the north of it is the *Baradwari* of Asuf-ud-doulah. On the west is the *sátkhandá*, or the seven-storied tower, which was built up to the fourth story, and left unfinished, when Mohamed Ali Shah died.

The Chhota Emambarah or *Makbarah* of Umjad Ali Shah is also built on the same plan, with two courts, one within the other, surrounding it. The two gates, three arches each, are good specimens of their class. The outer gate is by the side of the Huzrutgunge road. The Emambarah itself is a rectangular building of the same plan as that in Hosseinabad; but it has no dome over it like the other. There are two smaller courts adjoining the Emambarah. On the whole it has no architectural pretension beyond its extent. But it has great historical association; all the outer buildings were strongly fortified; and a severe and sanguinary hand-to-hand battle would have been fought, but for the very skilful sapping Sir Colin resorted to in the final capture of the city. Russell thus describes it just after its occupation by the English.

Chhota Emambarah.—We passed from Court to garden and from garden to court, through the wall of mosques and Zennanas, and long range of low houses, through archways, doors, working hither and thither, along the sap, by which our men had advanced through all these obstacles from the Begum Kothie. It is no exaggeration to say that the marble pavement is covered, 2 or 3 inches deep, with fragments of broken mirrors and of the chandeliers, which once hung from the ceiling; and the men are busy smashing them still. This mischief is rude, senseless and brutal; but no one cares to stop it.

All the casements of the Emambarah, every parapeted house-top to it, every portico, every colonnade in the court, was blocked up with brickwork, and pierced in every direction for musketry. And now when we are out in the streets, we saw what murderous work it would have been to have forced a passage through what was in fact nothing less than a double line of crenellated parapets and walls, inaccessible to scaling ladders, swept by grape and case from the defences at right angles to the line of the street and raked by the fire of the projecting palaces and gables, which would cross their musketry with that from the walls; the whole lines of the advance being dominated by lofty mosques, minars, the flat-roofed houses of the streets, and such citadel as the Emambarah itself would be when the gates were closed; and the Mess and the Coachmen's houses.—*Russell's Diary.*

Constantia or *La Martiniere* is the mausoleum of General Martin. He commenced building it at the request of Asuf-ud-dowlah, who wanted to buy a grand original edifice of his construction worth one crore. Before its completion the Nawab Vizier died; and his brother, Saádut Ali Khan, did not like to spend so much money for such an useless building. Accordingly the old General directed it to be his final resting place for his mortal remains; and he died before the building was finished. The two wings were added afterwards.

The plan of the edifice is square with the two semi-circular wings on the two sides; the column, which is about 130′ feet in height, stands in front on the east side, in the middle of a tank. A little further, the Gumti, after a bend, flows close by and enhances the beauty of the whole.

The main building is five stories in height; it has a *tykhána*, where the General is interred. The elevation looks picturesque by its arches and verandahs, and parapet-walls with plaster-lions and statues. The whole is surmounted by a quadruple stair-case. The ceilings of the inside rooms are composed of elliptic arches,—which are ornamented with flower-work and little plaster-statues. Altogether the impression produced on the spectators, is flat and not of the chaste kind. There is a want of naturalness which we see in pure native buildings; there is too much elaboration and pedanticness in the building to be extremely beautiful or faultless. One of its ultimate though hidden purpose was to make it a fortified house.

Constantia.—The idea of it was probably taken from those castles of pastry, which used to adorn deserts in former days. The mansion consists of three stories, gradually diminishing in the size of the square; so as to leave to the upper stories a broad span between the apartments and the parapet which covered the walls of the story below it. This was for the purpose of defence, with a view to which the building was constructed. The doors of the principal floor were plated with iron, and each window was protected by an iron-gate. Loopholes from passages above gave the means of firing in perfect security, upon any persons, who should force their way into these lower apartments. The spiral stone-staircases were blocked at intervals with windows; in short the whole was framed for protracted and desperate resistance. The parapets and pinnacles were decorated with a profusion of plaster lions, Grecian gods and Chinese figures, forming the most whimsical assemblage imaginable. Still the magnitude of the building, with its cupolas and spires, gave it a certain magnificence. In vault beneath it is the tomb, wherein General Martin is buried. The figures of four European soldiers, resting on their forelocks, surround it; and there are lights constantly burning in the room. *Marquis of Hastings.*

The General was apparently his own architect, and has produced a design somewhat fantastic in arrangement, which sins against most of the rules of pure Palladian Art to an extent, that would not be pardonable except in such a climate and under the peculiar circumstances in which it was erected. Notwithstanding this, there is something very striking in the great central tower, rising from a succession of terraced roofs one over the other, and under which are a series of halls, grouped internally so as to produce the most pleasing effect; while their arrangement was at the same time that most suitable to the climate. The sky-line is everywhere broken by little kiosks, not perhaps in the best taste, but pleasing from their situation, and appropriate in the vicinity of a town so full of such ornaments. Taken altogether, it is far more reasonable edifice than the contemporary capricio of Beckford at Fonthill; and if its details had been purer and some of those solicisms avoided, which an amateur architect is sure to fall into, it really does contain the germ of a very beautiful design.

The founder of the mansion lies beneath in a dimly lighted, vaulted chamber, in the basement of the great tower. His tomb is a simple plain sarcophagus, standing on the floor, and at each angle a grenadier in full uniform stands with arms, reversed in an attitude of grief, as if mourning over the fall of his master. The execution of the monument like everything about the place is bad; but the conception is the finest, that has yet been hit upon for a soldier's grave,—*Fergusson.*

Saádut Ali Khan's tomb, built by Gazee-ud-din, is a graceful building; its outward courtyard has been destroyed. It has under-ground cells, where the Nawab-Vizier is buried. Above is a large vaulted room with an imitation grave in the middle; four verandahs are on the four sides. The corner rooms are intended for stairs; small towers crown the stair-case; while a third dome overtops the second.

On accession to the musnud of Oudh, Gazee-ud-din observed that as he occupied the place of his father, his father should occupy his. So demolishing his mud house, he erected a temporary wooden tomb, before a grand mausoleum was to be built. This wooden tomb is thus described.

Saádut Ali Khan's tomb.—A superb monument is about to be erected over his remains; but in the meantime, they are distinguished with the utmost magnificence. The body was interred in the middle of a garden; a temporary building of wood, elegant in form and richly japanned and gilt, is raised over the grave. Within the edifice a canopy of cloth of gold overhangs the sodded receptacle of the corpse. A large tiger of green glass (made in England) stood on each side of the frame, that supported the canopy; and at the head were two large fishes of the same material. The fish in India is an emblem of sovereignty; attendants with chouries kept off the flies from the wreaths of fragrant flowers, which decorated the pillars of canopy; and several religious persons were employed in chanting verses of the Koran. *Marquis of Hastings.*

Close by is the tomb of Khurshedzadi, wife of Saádut Ali, which also the filial son Gazee-ud-din built. Though it is smaller in comparison to the former, yet it is more beautiful; for the main dome with its side ornamentations is graceful to the extreme ; while the second story with its four towers is happily constructed.

Shah Najuf is the mausoleum of Gazee-ud-din Hyder; it was built by him after a plan, which was said to be a copy of a shrine at Kerbula; and it was for this reason called Najuf Ashraf. It is a single-domed building, with two courts, one within the other, and a gate, which is not prepossessing; during the nine nights of Moharrum, it is profusely illuminated. During the lifetime of the king, the splendour of this edifice was very great, especially during Mohurrum.

Shah Najuf.—The entrance to the outer court or quadrangle is by a handsome gateway of bricks, plastered, and polished resembling marble. On each side of the gateway and carried up the two sides, in a line with the building, are distinct apartments, designed for the abode of the distressed and houseless poor; the back of these apartments form a substantial wall or enclosure. The Shah Najuf faces the gateway, and appears to be a square building, on a broad base of flight of steps with a cupola roof; the interior is paved with black and white marble tessellated; the walls and domes neatly ornamented with plaster and gold in relief, the bedding, cornices &c. of gold, to correspond on a stone-colour ground. The cupola and cornices on the outside are richly ornamented with plaster-designs, relieved with gold; on the summit of the dome is placed a crown of pure silver-gilt of an immense size.

The decorations of the interior, for the season of Mohurrum, were on a scale of grandeur not easily to be conveyed by description. The walls were all covered with handsome glasses and mirrors; the splendid chandeliers,—one containing a hundred wax-lights, in every variety, and relieved with coloured lamps—amber, blue, and green, mellowing the light, and giving a fairy-like effect to the brilliant scene. In the centre of the building stood the green glass Tazia surrounded by wax-lights; on the right of which was placed an immense lion, and on the left a fish, both formed of the same bright emerald green glass as the Tazia. The richness and elegance of the banners, which were numerous and well arranged, could be equalled only by the costliness of their several mountings.

The pulpit *(Mehmbers)* is of silver and of very handsome workmanship; the whole of the fitting up and arrangements had been made under the eye of His Majesty (Gazee-ud-din Hyder), and to his good taste may be ascribed all the merit of the well-ordered display on these occasions. He delighted in visiting this place,—this good and amiable king. On the evening of the Mehndi, the crowds of admiring people were admitted to view their Padshah's exhibition; until the distant sound of musketry announced the approach of the spectacle, when the multitude were desired to quit the Emambarah—*Mrs. Hossein Ali's Observations on the Mohamedans of India.*

The Kerbula of Nasir-ud-din Hyder is an unfinished square edifice, intended for a grand mausoleum for himself. It is a mixture of mosque, Emambarah and Mukbarah. There are two minars with gate facing the west. The complex vaulting is composed of Gothic arches; there is a double central room with cloisters in the four sides; in the central room is the grave of the king. There are two peculiar domes, one large, the other small, over the double central room. Two courts, one within the other in the usual manner, were intended to surround the main building; of this the inner one was built to a good height, but now destroyed. The premature death of the king left this grand edifice incomplete.

Huzrut Abbas ki Durgah is a holy shrine, wherein the banner of Abbás, a relative of Ali, who was killed in the battles of Kerbula, is deposited. It is an edifice, having peculiar towers and domes, like the Kerbula of Nasir-ud-din Hyder. Its origin is thus related:

Huzrat Abbas ki Durgah.—A native of India (Oudh) on his visit to Kerbula, had a dream, and as directed by the spirit, dug and found out the banner and staff of Abbás Ali, the standard bearer and relation of Hossein. He then returned to Lucknow and told Nawab Asuf-ud-dowlah about the precious prize he has brouht; who, rewarding the Hajee handsomely, immediately ordered a small building, in which the crest was safely deposited with due honors, and the fortunate pilgrim was appointed guardian with a liberal salary. The Durgah grew into general respect when a certain reigning Nawab built a new one, on the site of the old, on recovery from a serious and tedious illness, which baffled the skill of his physicians. Here the banners and Taziahs of the people, during the beginning of Mohurrum, are consicrated. The Durgáh is a square building, entered by flights of steps, from the court yard. The banner of each person is conveyed through the right entrance, opposite the platform, where it is immediately presented to touch the revered crest; this is only the work of a few seconds; that party walks on and moves out to the left again into the courtyard; the next follows in rapid succession, and so on till all have performed this duty. *Mrs. Hossein Ali.*

There are other pretty Emambarahs, Mukbarahs, and Musjids, in the city, which are too many to be detailed. The Musjid of Aurungzebe on the Luchmantillah is a prominent one ; that in Chouk is not less so. The Kerbula in Talkatora is a shrine, where all the Tazias of the city are buried after the Mohurrum. The Emambarahs in Chouk, in the palace of Malka Jahán, and the one known as Malka Zamaní in Golaganj are also beautiful pieces of local architecture. The Durgáh of Mina Sháh is now destroyed ; but that of Peerjalil is very old, still existing.

The Mokburah at Golagunge, built by Saádut Ali Khan for his mother, is a grand mausoleum. Its plan is octagonal; it has a main dome, around which are eight smaller ones. The basement story contains the real grave of Janab Alia, the Nawab-Vizier's mother ; the second story has a wooden frame with screen work surrounding an imitation grave. There are beautiful screen work in stone in all the windows and the door.

SECTION III.—GARDENS.

The principal gardens of Lucknow are Charbagh, Musabagh and Chinhut of Asuf-ud-dowlah ; Dilkosha of Saadut Ali Khan, Padshabagh and Walaitibagh of Nasir-ud-din Hyder, and Seconderbagh and Alumbagh of Wajid Ali Shah. Charbagh is a congregation of four gardens, as its name implies. It was a pretty extensive garden in the time of Asuf-ud-dowlah ; there were many large wells, whose water was conducted every where by conduits and fountains. Innumerable paths communicated with every part, recess and pavilion of the garden. It is now in ruins ; for the Railway Station and buildings have occupied its site.

Chinhut garden has a pretty building in the middle with outhouses and high walls around. It was intended for a summer-retreat, and deer were kept in large stock for the Nawab Vezier's sport. It is now in a neglected state.

Musabágh (mouse-garden) was built by the Nawab-Vizier, because he once accidentally killed a mouse. It also had a central edifice with a good gate and surrounding walls. During the mutiny, Huzrat Mahal fortified it and occupied it for a time, —until, being beseized by the English, she retreated towards the north. It is now thoroughly in ruins.

Dilkhosha was an extensive park with an Italian-looking building in the centre; here deer, nilgais and other animals of games were kept in large stock. The chateau in the centre had two stories with verandahs on the two sides, and towers on the four corners. The view of Lucknow from the roof of this structure was beautiful to the extreme, of which Russell gave a graphic description, quoted elsewhere. In the siege of Lucknow, in March, 1858, Dilkhosha was made the head-quarter of Sir Colin Campbell; and here before that event the mutineers manufactured their bullets &c.

Close by are the Bibiapore kothie and Wilaitibágh. At Bibiapore, Sir John Shore deposed Vizier Ali in 1798. It was a country seat of Asuf-ud-dowlah. Wilaitibágh is thus described by Russell in 1858.

Welaitibágh.—It must have been a very pretty spot, opening on the river by a flight of steps, with alcoves, covered walks, orange-trees, kiosks, abundant statuary in plaster, a platform for dancing, an orchestra, the ornamented roofs covered with gilded bosses and spires, tall cypresses and tamarinds bordered the orange plantations, and a wilderness of flower sprang up in their neglected beds. Every thing was fast going to decay;—the irrigation canals were choked up, the fountains were dry, the statues falling to pieces, the lattices in the kiosks broken.—*Russell's Diary.*

Seconderbágh was a royal garden, east of Shah Najuf, where during the mutiny a severe battle was fought between the English and the rebels; of the latter about 2,000 were slain. The garden had a bungalow-looking building in the centre with a court around. A pretty gate was attached to the court. But the garden together with the buildings is now in complete ruins.

Padshahbágh is a grand royal garden with a magnificent bath and palace in it. Groves and plants were well arranged; while a long masonry-tank is in the centre, just in front of the bath. Here was a *Moorcha* of the sepoys, and here the English established a large battery in the final siege of the city. It is thus described by Mrs. Park, when it was being constructed in 1831.

Padshahbágh is the most luxurious palace I have seen in India. A large space has been enclosed as a garden within a high-wall; it contains three houses and two gateways ; the first house is a most delightful one, all you can wish for in such a climate as this ; beautiful rooms, with six fountains playing in them, and everything in fairyland style ; then such a *hammám* ! or steam-baths containing rooms heated to different temperature, the heat of each increasing until you arrive at the steam-bath itself.

The apartments are built of white varingated marble ; and the roofs arched ; the rooms were so delightful that we felt every inclination to remain in the *Hammám* ;—the temperature was so luscious.

Crossing from this to the centre of the gardens, we entered another elegant building, supported on white marble pillars, beautifully finished, and adorned and furnished with crimson and gold.

On the left of the garden is a third palace, sacred to the ladies of the Zenana ; this house is built of marble, and covered with flower-work of pounded talc, which has exactly the appearance of silver, giving an eastern style to the palace. There are two handsome gateways, a steam-engine to supply the fountains, and a superb tiger in a cage. Every luxury of life may be contained within the walls of this garden ; it is at present scarcely finished, but displays great taste and beauty.—*Mrs. Park's Wanderings of a Pilgrim, 22nd January 1831.*

Alumbágh is also an extensive garden, having four bastions on the four corners of the walls. It has a high gate ; and a square edifice in the centre of the garden. It belonged to one of the Begums of Wajid Ali Shah. In 1857, Sir James Outram occupied it as a fortified position, and in front of it some severe actions or rather battles were fought between him and the mutineers.

Besides those mentioned above, there are many other buildings worth noticing. *Dilarám* is a picturesque Kothie in front of Chhutter Munzil on the other side of the Gumti. *Khurshed Munzil*, or the Sun-Palace, is a grand two-storied castle-like edifice with four towers on the four corners. The important event of the relief of Lucknow took place just in front of this building. *Tarawali Kothie* was the observatory built by Nasir-ud-din Hyder. Here were very good astronomical instruments, which were lost in the mutiny. There was also a beautiful balancing column in the *Tykhana*. The rebel-leaders held their councils here for a few months. Hyat Buksh, Noorbuksh and Zahurbuksh are also picturesque-looking mansions. Hyat Buksh, which was built by Saádut Ali Khan, has now been added and otherwise improved, and is now turned into a pretty Government-House.

Of provincial buildings, I need not for the present add a particular account; for this book treats chiefly on the capital. The two Musjids, fort and bridge at Jounpore have already been noticed; they were originally Hindu buildings, turned into Mohamedan ones. The stone pavilion, named Chehel Setoon (forty pillars) and other stone edifices at Manikpore, Newada and Kanouti are pretty ones of their class; they are now in ruins. The old shrine and houses at Suffipore, Bangarmow, Moradabad, Bilgram and Shahabád require a passing notice. The buildings at Shahabád are grand constructions. The Mokbarah, Musjid and fortified palace of Nawab Diler Khan, though now in ruins, still attract visitors from long distances for their massive strength, beautiful carving on stones, and original design.

In conclusion, I beg to draw attention of Government officers and general public to the neglected state of native architecture. Here at Lucknow, buildings are now and then destroyed. All the surrounding gates, and plaster and iron statues of Kaiserbágh have lately been pulled down, for what purpose is not known to the people. All the gilded domes have been sold, and in their place most unsightly ones have been constructed. China bazaar and the adjoining gates have long disappeared; they were sold at auction at almost nominal price. In short, vandalism here is in full swing; and gradually Lucknow is being deprived of its architectural ornaments. Is it that the municipality cannot afford a trifling sum for their repair? Does not the local officers feel, when buildings are broken-down, to see which every citizen heaves a sigh or sheds a drop of tear? If native arts are not to be extinguished, if the cultivation of æsthetic sentiments is to be effected, if local ornamental productions are to be revived and regenerated, vandalism is not the way to do it. In arts as in every thing else, improvement cannot be effected, if there is no guide to show, no pattern to serve, no example and old achievements to instruct and improve. Besides it is not well to destroy old and existing ornaments, when you cannot build new and better ones.

Architecture finis.

———:o:———